MUSIC AT RIPON CAT

The People
The Building
The Instruments
The Music

657 to 2008

Let the people praise thee O God
Let all the people praise thee

by

Malcolm S. Beer and Howard M. Crawshaw

MUSIC AT RIPON CATHEDRAL

First published 2008

British Library Cataloging-in-Publication Data
A catalogue record of this book is available from the British Library

ISBN 978-0-9531979-3-4

GHSmith
DESIGN PRINTING PUBLISHING

Printed and bound by G.H. Smith & Son, Design Printing Publishing,
The Advertiser Office, Market Place, Easingwold, York, YO61 3AB
01347 821329
email: info@ghsmith.com   web: www.ghsmith.com

MUSIC AT RIPON CATHEDRAL

CONTENTS

List of Illustrations

Preface

Foreword

Cathedral Choir Concerts	Cathedral Concert Society
Wakeman Singers	Lunchtime Concerts
Moody Choir	Ripon Choral Society
Ripon International Music Festival	St Cecilia Orchestra

A P P E N D I X

I N D E X

T I M E L I N E

List of Illustrations

PREFACE

This book grew out of an idea that it would be appropriate to mount an exhibition on 'The History of Music at Ripon Cathedral' to coincide with the National Festival of the Federation of Cathedral Old Choristers' Associations at Ripon in July 2008. Malcolm Beer, the Chairman of the Ripon Cathedral Old Choristers charged with planning the festival, commenced his researches in the late summer of 2006. So much information was forthcoming that it soon became clear an exhibition was not enough, and a book on the music at Ripon Minster-Cathedral over its thirteen hundred year history was called for. Realising that researching and writing such a book would be a major undertaking, Malcolm enlisted the help of his old friend and former fellow lay clerk, Howard Crawshaw. Thus began the joint project that was to dominate their lives for nearly two years.

Funding the publication was happily a short-lived problem. Thanks to Andrew Kitchingman and the Ripon Cathedral Music Custodians and a small group of Major Sponsors, the finance was kick-started, and there then followed an overwhelming response from a large number of people who readily agreed to support the book by becoming Patrons or Subscribers.

We, the authors, cannot adequately express our immense gratitude to all those who have made the production of this book possible, whose names are printed in the list of Major Sponsors, Patrons, Subscribers and Music Custodians. As a result of their generosity the entire publication costs have been met, and therefore all the income from the sales of this book will go to the Music Foundation, thus helping to ensure that the great heritage of music at Ripon Cathedral continues for many years to come.

We are conscious of the enormous debt owed to a multitude of people who have encouraged us and been extremely helpful in providing personal recollections, photographs, old documents, music and service sheets and in directing us to other sources of information. We have also benefited from advice from specialists in various fields (historical, liturgical, linguistic, musical and technical) and we are most grateful to them. We have endeavoured to include all of these persons in the 'Table of Acknowledgements' but apologise to any who have been inadvertently omitted.

There are some people we would like to mention by name; Kerry Beaumont, Andrew Bryden, Paul Burbridge, Joy Calvert, Alan Dance, Martin Davies,

Simon Deller, Mike Deeming, Bill Forster, Susan Goldsborough, Alasdair Jamieson, Brian Kealy, Xenophon Kelsey, Tom Leech, Richard Moore, David McKay, Oliver Pickering, Eric Record, Tony Russell, John Sayer, David Suddards, Maurice Taylor, Stephana Thomson, Mark and Katherine Venning and Eric Witts.

We are particularly indebted to Alan Duffield (a former Ripon Cathedral lay clerk and now member of the Royal Opera House, Covent Garden) who has undertaken an immense amount of research at The British Library into the music of Ripon Cathedral, and acted as our music advisor. He has also, virtually single-handedly, compiled the list of radio broadcasts from Ripon Cathedral by spending long hours at the BBC sound archives library at Caversham. We likewise wish to give special thanks to Graham Hermon (also a former Ripon Cathedral lay clerk) for acting as our photographer and graphics advisor, scanning and digitally editing the numerous old photographs and images used in the many illustrations in the book. Last but not least, our grateful thanks to Sylvia Pinkney who carried out invaluable editing and improvements to our often less than flowing prose, and to Janet Pickering who undertook the final meticulous proof reading and compiled the index.

To our wives, Joan and Susan, we wish to pay special tribute. Their constant encouragement, guidance and patient counselling of their often book-obsessed husbands has been little short of saintly, and we cannot thank them enough. Without their unfailing support this book would not have been possible.

Finally we would stress that neither of us are literary scholars and our only qualification for undertaking the writing of this book is a love of Ripon Cathedral and its music.

We hope you enjoy reading the book and dipping into it from time to time.

Malcolm S. Beer
Howard M. Crawshaw

FOREWORD

At the heart of any Church is worship, and at the heart of worship is music. It is with this statement in mind that I gladly write this foreword and commend this new and substantial book on 'Music at Ripon Cathedral' to you. In doing so, I want to thank all those who have made this publication possible. The authors and researchers, the sponsors and supporters and, not least, those who down the years have sung and played to the glory of God, thereby contributing to a story that is still unfolding. Their particular skill and dedication has undoubtedly led many people to God, and for that amongst all things we give thanks.

Music in liturgy goes back thousands of years. Long before the birth of Christ, for example, the first prophet Isaiah records his own calling which happens within the context of Temple worship. In that episode he attests to the glory and majesty of God and writes down Holy, holy, holy is the Lord of hosts. These words, used then in the Temple and now the substance of our Sanctus with the Eucharistic tradition of the Christian Church, have inspired many a musician, thus reinforcing the fact that the worship of God is often supported by the art of music.

At Ripon Cathedral this integrity of music accompanying worship has been evident from the beginning. One thinks of the time when Cuthbert and Wilfrid were here and undoubtedly used their voices to praise their Lord. After them have come many others; singers and instrumentalists, organists and composers, lay clerks and choristers, clergy and teachers. As you will read, it has not always been easy, but then the best things in life and faith are worth all the commitment we can give to them. It is as a testimony to that commitment that the music goes on and continues to flourish here.

In reading the chapters of this book myself, I have been particularly engaged by the sheer amount of music composed at or for Ripon Cathedral. What is clear is that those responsible have not only developed music at Ripon, but have also contributed to the wider cause and tradition of cathedral music throughout Great Britain.

As I remarked at the beginning, this book would never have happened without the time and energy given to it by many people. However, I end by offering thanks to four people in particular, those being Malcolm Beer, Howard Crawshaw and their wives. The publication of the book may now mean that the two wives can claim their husbands back!

Now read on, and thank you for supporting our music through the purchase of this memorable book.

Keith Jukes
Dean of Ripon
Lady Day 2008

Chapter 1

BEGINNINGS
657 – 1065

In the year 657 AD Alchfrid (Alhfrith, Alcfrith), son of King Oswiu (Oswy) of Northumbria, granted land to Eata, a Celtic monk from Melrose, to establish a new monastery at the heathen village of Rhypum, with Cuthbert as guestmaster. In 661, however, Alchfrid decided to grant the land to another monk, Wilfrid (born 634), who had spent some time in Rome and become enamoured with the Benedictine (Latin) rule which Alchfrid also favoured. As a result Eata and Cuthbert returned to Scotland along with most of the other founding Celtic monks, and Wilfrid was installed as abbot of the new Benedictine monastery.

Music was already becoming an important part of the liturgy in England. Augustine had introduced Gregorian chant when he came to England in 597, and his church at Canterbury rapidly became a centre for the study of plainsong. During the 690s Wilfrid spent ten years in Mercia and Kent, probably visiting Canterbury, and when he returned to Ripon in 703 he brought with him two singing masters from Canterbury, Aeona (Eowan) and Aedde (Eddi), to teach the monks antiphonal singing and instruct them in Gregorian chants. Aedde was probably Eddius Stephanus, who later became Wilfrid's chaplain and biographer. Thus voices have been raised to the glory of God in this place for over 1,350 years.

Wilfrid had been impressed by the stone churches he had seen on his visits to Rome and was determined to replace the timber structures at Ripon monastery. By 672 a fine new stone church had been built, and the chronicles of the day state that this was dedicated at a service *with a great concourse of priests, nobles and with much feasting.* Ripon's monastery and its splendid church rapidly acquired an enviable reputation thanks to Wilfrid, who died in 709 whilst on a visit to Oundle.

English monasteries, including that at Ripon, were well established by the year 750, as was the system of accepting young boys, known as oblates, into monastic life. These children were handed over by their families to the monastery, where they lived under a vow of poverty, chastity and obedience. On admission, the boys were tonsured, clothed in a habit, and expected to remain part of the monastic community for the rest of their lives. The usual age of oblation or entry into the monastery was seven, although sometimes younger boys were accepted; it is recorded that Willibrord, the eighth century missionary, later to convert the Friesians, was oblated to the monastery at Ripon as soon as he had been weaned.

These young oblates, including those at Ripon, were the early choristers of England, and the school at the Ripon monastery, which catered solely for its own oblates, could be considered one of the earliest choir schools. The boys were taught Latin, chant and liturgy, and they joined with the monks to sing in the choir as soon as they were able. The earliest written musical notation in England is believed to date from the tenth century, and presumably the chant was taught by rote and committed to memory. Initially the boys learned the psalms (words and melody) by heart, and then the liturgy set for the various days of the church calendar.

The boys and monks sang together every day of the year at mass and the seven Offices of the day; namely matins (later called lauds), prime, terce, sext, none, vespers and compline. Occasionally, vigils was also sung at some time during the night. The children generally sang with the adults in unison, although organum (the parallel doubling of the plainsong at an interval of a fourth or a fifth) was known by the mid eleventh century. Evidently, however, the boys sang parts of the service on their own.

Life for the boys at the Ripon monastery was demanding and discipline was strict; punishment for misdemeanours usually involved *severe fasts or sharp stripes in order that they may be cured.* However, they were generally well looked after. The children lived with the adult monks, but were specifically under the charge of a senior monk, who took great care of their physical and moral welfare and their spiritual development. They ate well, drinking beer rather than wine. The provision of care, regular food, education, and a level of protection from the perils of life at that time was an incentive for many poor families to present their boys to the monastery for oblation.

The first Vikings came to England in about 789 and their raids gradually escalated. This resulted in severe disruption to monastic life, which had virtually been destroyed across the whole country by the year 900. Ripon was sacked in 860 (and again in 950), and for a time the monks were dispersed and the choir ceased to sing. The situation reversed during the reign of King Edgar (959-975) when monasteries were re-built and monastic life, including the admission of oblates and the singing of the Offices, was restored.

Chapter 2

THE MEDIEVAL MINSTER
1066 – 1547

Around the time of the Norman conquest Ripon was converted from a monastery into a college of secular canons. The exact date and the reasons for this are not clear, but from this time there were no more monks nor oblates. It became a collegiate church, governed by a group of clergy called prebendaries, collectively known as the chapter of secular canons. There was no dean, but gradually over the years different prebends, or portions of land, were established to provide income for the canons. Eventually the chapter consisted of seven prebendaries, each being provided with a prebendal house near to the church.

The collegiate church itself was technically a minster until 1836 when it became a cathedral with the creation of the new Ripon diocese. However, because the old medieval diocese of York was so large, Ripon Minster, together with Beverley and Southwell, fulfilled the role of mother churches in their parts of the diocese – that is, they acted as cathedrals. Indeed these three minsters, together with the true diocesan church at York, were referred to as *quattuor matrices ecclesiae* (four mother churches). Ripon Minster was even called a cathedral in some medieval texts.

The seven prebendary canons at Ripon each took their turn in residence and fulfilled their duties, both within the parish and within the minster, particularly in the choir. In truth, however, absenteeism was rife throughout the thirteenth, fourteenth and fifteenth centuries. Canons were lazy, some had appointments at a number of other churches, and some were totally unsuited to the job. In 1290 the Archbishop of York, John Romanus, wrote to Ripon, admonishing them as canons *who take care to have their stipends paid whilst they seldom perform their duties, who exact the reward but do not labour in the vineyard.*

As the canons were often absent, six vicars were employed to carry out their duties, including the daily singing of the services in the minster. These persons were referred to as the vicars choral because they represented the absent prebendaries vicariously (as deputies) in the choir, and thus they were the early singing men of the choir. To assist them, the vicars choral had three deacons, three sub-deacons, six choristers, six thuribars (incense bearers) and one sub-thuribler, collectively called *ministri inferiores*. They fulfilled their own duties in the choir and, because the canons were frequently absent, the day-to-day singing was carried out by the vicars choral and the *ministri inferiores*.

The employment of the six vicars choral was initially a haphazard affair; they were engaged from year to year and had no statutory position nor fixed income. Accordingly Archbishop Corbridge of York, despairing of ever being able to control the canons, particularly their absenteeism, assembled the chapter at the minster on 13th September 1303 to regularise the position of the vicars choral. He decreed that each canon was to maintain a perpetual (permanent) vicar at a stipend of 6 marks (£4) a year paid quarterly by the canon whose work he performed. He also ordered that the vicars choral should *live together in due seclusion* in a house near the church.

From this time each vicar choral was appointed by the canon whom he served, but he had to have the support of the majority of chapter first. He also had to be a fit person with regard to chanting and be proficient in both plainsong and pricksong (music pricked or written down). He was also expected to administer the sacraments in church. As well as being a vicar choral, he was a vicar parochial with duties in the parishes, and when visiting the sick he was to *wear surplice and cope and carry a bell and lantern*.

Each canon was expected to pay his own vicar's salary, but this did not always happen. When the canons refused to pay, Archbishop Melton of York decreed, in 1331, that the vicars choral salaries should be paid out of church funds. The chamberlain's rolls of the minster show that this salary remained at £4 a year until 1546 when it was increased to £6 a year comprising £4 from church funds and £2 from the canons. This increase was short-lived however, for the collegiate church was dissolved two years later by Edward VI.

Nicholas of Bondgate provided the vicars choral with a house in 1304, where they lived together. This became known as the bedern, or home of prayer, and although we do not know its exact location, Bedern Bank survives today. This bedern was destroyed in 1318 by the Scots during one of their frequent incursions into northern England following their victory at the battle of Bannockburn in 1314. It was a hundred years later before, in 1415, Archbishop Bowet of York provided a site for a new bedern where the Old Deanery now stands. What happened between 1318 and 1415 is not clear. Probably for much of this period the vicars choral reverted to living in separate houses around the town, although there is evidence of some of them living together in 1408, when three of the vicars, John Ely, Richard Morton and John Quinton were summoned to appear before chapter and labelled *inobedientes, contumaces et rebelles* for refusing to live in the bedern. They were admonished, threatened with suspension if they did not move into the bedern, and with excommunication if they continued to rebel.

In the same year that the new bedern was built (1415, the year of the battle of Agincourt) Henry V granted a charter to the vicars choral of Ripon making them a corporate body, the College of the Bedern. The deed of incorporation referred to the vicars choral as *bearing the burden and heat of the day in the church*, and from this time they were able to elect from their number a provost, and were granted a common seal for the transaction of their business (see illustration next page).

Unfortunately the chapter failed to maintain the new bedern properly and by 1515 it was in a very bad state of repair. Rain water poured in *upon them at table and in bed and extinguished their fire*. Consequently the vicars choral all moved out again to live around the town. The provision of a bedern for communal living was not always appreciated by the vicars choral. Many preferred to live in the town and take wives and mistresses, even though they were supposed to be celibate. Indeed it appears that these men of the choir, who were men of the cloth, were also very much men of the world and frequently behaved very badly. Chapter records are full of reports of their misdemeanours and even criminal activity.

In 1293 John Romanus, Archbishop of York from 1286-1298, was highly critical of the musical abilities of the vicars choral. He stated that the singing in Ripon was *universally considered disgraceful* and he directed the canons to *remove their inefficient chanters and supply their place with properly qualified singers.*

Two years later Archbishop Romanus pronounced the sentence of degradation *from the order of chaunters* upon Walter of Levington and four of his fellow vicars for burglary, horse stealing and other thefts. Degradation in this context meant removal from the priesthood and was performed in a ritualistic and public manner. The archbishop sat in the nave of the minster and the accused vicars came before him and confessed their crimes. All then went to the west door of the church where, in full view, the vicars' robes were removed while the archbishop said *by the authority of God the Omnipotent, Father, Son and Holy Ghost, and by our authority, we take from you the clerical habit, we put you away, we degrade you, we deprive you and strip you of whatever rank, benefice or clerical privilege you possess.* To conclude this demeaning process the vicars' heads were completely shaved, thus removing their tonsures.

There is evidence of even more serious criminal activity by vicars choral; in 1302 Adam de Fenton was found responsible for the death of William Pollard at Heselton and suffered degradation. It is not clear whether this was actually murder, and there is no record of what happened to Fenton afterwards. In 1337 Archbishop Melton found that persons unknown, (whom he described as *sons of Belial)* had broken into his prison in Ripon and sacrilegiously released imprisoned vicars choral charged with murder and other crimes.

In 1312 Archbishop Greenfield of York found that the vicars choral attended dances and public shows, not the done thing for a priest of the time. They were out in the town at night, broke into houses, and *sought favours of women of doubtful reputation.* One of the vicars choral, William Pistor, was found guilty of inventing a game of chance called dyngethriftes (to ding is to drive or to throw with violence, and thrifts are savings). The odds were apparently stacked so heavily in Pistor's favour that his game was tantamount to theft, but he fled the town before he could be punished.

Various archbishops tried to control the behaviour of the vicars choral, usually in vain. On 21st May 1439 Archbishop Kemp of York held a visitation at Ripon Minster because matters there were so unsatisfactory. It seems fair to presume that the subsequent injunctions presented to Ripon reflected the behaviour at the time. With regard to the singing, he found that *the books are*

Seal of the vicars choral, 1415

not all noted alike and he instructed that *this be corrected by the precentor.* He also decreed that *care should be taken to ensure that the choir is properly divided so that a due balance may be maintained in the singing. Only those of good character and well instructed in singing and reading should be appointed to the choir, and if any vicar choral is absent without leave from any service he is to be fined one penny.*

On more general matters Archbishop Kemp instructs that *all walking about during service and carrying on conversations with one another and other ill behaviour is no longer to be practised. All ministers and others of the lower grades shall not carry swords or daggers under their clothes or habits. Fishings, hawkings and huntings are prohibited as unclerical.*

In 1537 Edward Lee, Archbishop of York, issued the following injunctions to the vicars choral because of their poor behaviour. It must be said that the third item, *vicars shall forbeare going to the ale-housses … and suspect company of women,* appears with remarkable regularity during these years. The vicars choral evidently enjoyed not only song, but wine and women also.

Injunctions geven by the most reverend fader in God Lorde Edwarde, Archbisshope of Yorke, Primate of England and metropolitane, unto the vicars chorall of the church in Riponn.

In primis that the saed vicars shall, on this side and before the feast of All Sainctes next ensuying the date hereof, beginne to kepe commens at their housse all to gedder at their Colledg, and it so begonne to continue according to the statutes of the same Colledg, unto the observation whereof they be boundon by their corporall othe, and as they woll awoide the payne of violacon of the same.

Item that the saed vicars shall have a lection rede at dynner and sooper every day of holy scripture, or of the booke lately compiled by the reverend fathers busshopes of Englande, or some oder booke contegnying good and holsome doctrine.

Item that the same vicars shall forbeare going to the ale-housses and playing at cardes, tables, and dice, and suspect company of women.

All which injunctions we commande you the vicars aforesaed to observe and keep under paynes of the lawe.

Dat at the monasterie of Fountaunce, the second day of Octobre, in the yere of our Lorde God a thousande fyve hundreth thurty and sevyn.

Just as vicars came to replace monks in the choir when Ripon ceased to be a monastery and became a collegiate church, so boy choristers replaced the young oblates. It is not clear when the first choristers were employed in Ripon Minster, but they were certainly singing regularly in the choir by 1230. In that year Archbishop Gray of York appointed one of the seven prebendary canons at the minster, the then Prebendary of Stanwick, Laurence de Toppeclive, as the first precentor and *rector chori*. His duty was to organise and conduct the music, keep order in the choir, and instruct the boys in music and grammar. The incumbent Prebendary of Stanwick continued to hold this position until the dissolution of the collegiate church by Edward VI in 1548, and chamberlain's rolls of the period indicate that the minster had six choristers up until this date.

In the early days the choristers lived with the canons in their prebendal houses, a situation which held in many English cathedrals as well as Ripon. This was unsatisfactory however; the canons were frequently absent, the boys were not always cared for very well, and they were expected to act as servants in the household. Consequently in many cities specific boarding houses were created for the choristers and some historians consider these to be the first choir schools in England. The situation with regard to a school for the choristers at Ripon at this time is not, however, entirely clear.

Some historians believe that collegiate churches had an associated grammar school as a matter of course, and it may be that Ripon had such a school. Hard evidence of a grammar school in Ripon comes in 1348, when the sheriff was ordered to arrest Richard master of the *scole hous* on a charge of felony. The sheriff could not find Richard and he was outlawed. After this date the fabric rolls of the minster regularly refer to a schoolmaster; *magister scolarum* (1354), *Thomas the skulemayster* (1379), *Richard scolarum gramaticalis* (1396), and in 1546 the *scolemaster* who was paid an annual salary of 40 shillings (£2).

The grammar school at this time is thought to have stood on the site of the present cathedral hall in High St Agnesgate, and the masters were all employed and paid by the canons of the minster. Indeed on Sundays and festivals they were required to be present at the processions and at high mass. Whether a separate choir school existed in these early days is not clear. It would have been perfectly reasonable for the master of the grammar school to teach the choristers since he was employed by the chapter, and this was certainly happening in other parts of England by 1300. We first have evidence of two separate schools in 1439 when Archbishop Kemp decreed that *deacons, sub-deacons and choristers should attend the schools* (plural) *and if found to have inadequate knowledge shall be refused admission to the choir until they prove themselves fit as regards character and learning.* Stronger evidence appears in 1504 when it was decreed that *all ministri inferiores are to attend the grammar school and the song school or be dismissed.* It is, however, possible that the song school was merely a room within the grammar school where the minster choristers were trained.

The education given to the choristers in the medieval Ripon schools gradually developed over the centuries. In the thirteenth century the *rector chori* (precentor) was solely responsible for teaching the boys music and grammar, which meant Latin. Later the choristers' education improved, and by 1348 a dedicated teacher was employed to teach grammar, although the *rector chori* continued to teach music. The first text books appeared in the early thirteenth century, but there was no such thing as a formal school curriculum until the early sixteenth century; the teacher merely taught what he thought was appropriate. In these earlier times everything at school, whether sung, said or read, was in Latin, but by the late fourteenth century English was asserting itself.

Time spent by the boys at school had to be fitted in with singing in the minster choir. Eight services were sung every day; at mass the choristers, together with the vicars choral, sang the Kyries, Gloria, Sanctus, Benedictus and Agnus Dei, and also the propers for the day, antiphons, graduals and responsories. In course of the full round of the seven services of the daily Office they sang the appointed psalms, and the canticles, such as the magnificat at vespers and the nunc dimittis at compline. Vigils might additionally have been sung through the night. So much time spent singing would have severely limited the boys' education, but the cathedrals and collegiate churches, including Ripon, developed a system that became widespread in England. Only two choristers were on duty each week, except on Sundays and feast days when all six sang together; even then it is doubtful whether the two boys on duty attended all seven Offices every day. This created a three-week rota, one week on and two weeks off, leaving ample time for school.

In the later middle ages the choristers had a uniform which was provided by the chapter. In 1447 the minster paid 14s. 6d. for cloth for the liveries of the six choristers and by 1540 the cost had increased to 24 shillings. We do not know the design of these uniforms but the colour is recorded, although for some reason this changed over the years. In 1475 the uniform was *coloris blodii* (coloured blue) but in 1478 it was *coloris blodii melly* (coloured blue medley or mixture). In 1502 it was *coloris tawne*, in 1513 *rusceti coloris*, in 1520 *coloris marble,* and in 1540 *coloris russett.*

The choristers were also paid an annual salary by the chapter, and the chamberlain's rolls of 1447 show that a total of 60s. 8d. was paid to the boys that year. This may mean that they each received just over 10s. 1d. (50 pence), but the older boys may have been paid more. Exactly the same sum was paid out in 1546. The choristers' income, however, was sometimes boosted by money left in the wills of canons. In 1371 Canon William de Dalton died, leaving 20s. to each vicar choral and 3s. 4d. to each chorister. The boys were not always so fortunate, however, for in 1433 Precentor John Dean left 20s. to each vicar choral but only 4d. to each chorister.

During the early middle ages monodic plainchant, later possibly with some organum, was the only music sung in church. In the late thirteenth and early fourteenth centuries, however, polyphonic music emerged, and it is thought that by the beginning of the sixteenth century the singing of polyphony by a choir of men and boys was widespread. This change was not to everybody's taste; John of Salisbury thought that this *defiled the service of religion* by its *womanish affectations in the mincing of notes and sentences,* and Ailred of Rievaulx complained both of the polyphony and of the organ accompaniment *to what purpose is that terrible blowing of bellows, expressing rather the cracks of thunder than the sweetness of a voice?*

The development of the four-part chorus of treble, alto, tenor and bass was a major step in the evolution of church music over the centuries. Polyphonic music required a greater degree of skill than plainchant, which led to the adult members of choirs being professional singers, known as lay clerks, rather than clergy who happened to be able to sing. This transfer of singing responsibilities to professional lay singers became widespread in England during the 1400s, but Ripon appears to have been rather slow in this respect. Salary lists right up to 1546, two years before the dissolution, show six vicars choral and six choristers but no mention of lay clerks. It is not until 1605, after the reconstitution of the collegiate church by James I in 1604, that *syngingmen* (lay clerks) are referred to in Ripon Minster records.

The advent of polyphonic music also led to the appointment of professional organists to teach and direct the choirs. The first organist of Ripon, Thomas Litster, was appointed in 1447. He was responsible for the teaching of polyphonic music to the singers as well as for playing the organ. He had an annual salary of 10s. (50 pence), just a little less than each of the choristers and much less than the vicars choral. Litster's successor, Lawrence Lancaster, appointed in 1478, had his salary augmented by an annual supplement of 3s. 4d. for playing at the daily Lady Mass. The organist's salary remained fixed at 13s. 4d. per year until the dissolution of Ripon Minster by Edward VI in 1548.

Chapter 3

THE REFORMATION
1548 – 1603

Edward VI's Act of 1547 ordered the wholesale abolition of the Chantries and with this came the dissolution of the collegiate church in Ripon. On Easter Day 1548 the chapter was disbanded, the chantry priests and vicars choral dispersed, and the choristers disendowed of their annual salaries and clothing allowances. The choral foundation ceased to exist. Chapter revenues were appropriated by the Crown and added to the possessions of the Duchy of Lancaster. Ripon was reduced to the status of an ordinary parish church, and a small stipend provided to pay for one or two ministers to look after the parish. This sorry state continued until 1604, when James I reconstituted the collegiate church; thus music at Ripon was very limited. However the changes to the church and its music generally during this turbulent period were so profound that it is relevant to provide a brief outline.

Henry VIII had started the upheaval by the Act of Supremacy in 1534, which abolished papal authority over the English Church, and made himself and his heirs *the only Supreme Head in earth of the Church of England*. This in itself had no effect on church music which continued for a time unchanged, as did the liturgy. However, between 1536 and 1540 he went on to dissolve all the monasteries in the land, which significantly altered the musical and liturgical scene. The smaller monasteries did not have great choral resources, but many of the larger ones had organs, organists and skilled choirs. Most of these simply disappeared, causing a great musical loss over the whole country.

Those former monastic churches that were already cathedrals, such as Canterbury, Durham and Winchester, were the few not closed. These monasteries were dissolved and re-founded as secular cathedrals, becoming the so-called cathedrals of the new foundation. Many of the previous priors became deans, and those monks who acknowledged Henry as head of the Church of England became members of the cathedral clergy. The cathedrals of the old foundation, such as Exeter, York and Lincoln, had always been secular cathedrals and so were unchanged. In both sets of cathedrals the choirs not only continued but flourished. Henry VIII died in January 1547 and was succeeded by his son Edward VI.

One of the objects of the Reformation was to make worship more accessible to the people and to encourage congregational participation. The services were to be simplified, and the reading of the scriptures and the preaching of the word of God in English were to become all important. Thomas Cranmer's first English Prayer Book of 1549 was the legally enforced worship manual required by the Act of Uniformity, and was issued throughout the land, providing a whole new liturgy for the Church of England. The new service of Holy Communion was broadly similar to the old mass, but the seven Offices were condensed into two longer services, matins and evensong. The new matins was drawn from the texts of the old matins (lauds) and prime, and the new evensong from those of vespers and compline. Most importantly, all was in English, and so Latin texts became obsolete, requiring rapid composition of music set to English words. A notable example of this was John Merbecke's 'Book of Common Prayer Noted', published in 1550, which contained a setting of the Eucharist used in some churches to this day.

In 1552 the 1549 prayer book was replaced by a second one, again compiled by Cranmer. This was radically more Protestant and many parts of the services previously sung were now to be *said or sung in a plain tune after the manner of distinct reading.* Earlier, Erasmus (a Dutch scholar and humanist, 1466-1536) had written that *modern church music is so composed that the congregation cannot understand a word.* Cranmer and the church authorities also considered that English church music was *luxuriantly overgrown,* and were determined to change this. The importance of music in worship was played down, polyphony discouraged, and simple one syllable one note music promoted.

Archbishop Holgate delivered an injunction to the Dean and Chapter of York in 1552: *We will and command that there be none other note sung or used in the said church at any service there to be had, saving square note plain, so that every syllable may be plainly and distinctly pronounced, and without any reports or repeatings which may induce any obscureness to the hearers.* The use of organs was also discouraged and sometimes forbidden, Holgate decreeing: *forsomuch as playing of the organs ought and must be ceased and no more used within the church of York.*

The whole approach to church music and musicians is well illustrated by a Royal Injunction of 1550 given to St George's Chapel, Windsor: *whereas heretofore, when descant, prick-song and organs were too much used and had in price in the church, great search was made for cunning men in that faculty, among whom there were many that had joined with such cunning evil conditions as pride, contention, railing, drunkenness, contempt of their superiors, or such like vice, We now intending to have Almighty God praised with gentle and quiet sober minds and with honest hearts ... do enjoin that when the room of any of the clerks shall be void the dean and prebendaries of the church shall make search for quiet and honest men.*

One more of Edward's injunctions is worthy of a mention. In 1547, before he dissolved the collegiate church of Ripon, he decreed that, whereas previously all choristers had been tonsured, in future they were to have a normal, if short, haircut. Therefore all of the choristers' heads were completely shaven to allow the new hair to grow normally, and so for some weeks every chorister in England was completely bald.

Edward VI was succeeded by Mary I, a Catholic, in July 1553. Protestant worship was replaced by worship as it was *most commonly used in the realm of England in the last year of the reign of King Henry VIII,* that is, the restoration of the sevenfold daily Office, together with the Sarum Latin Mass. This was short-lived, however, for Mary died on 17th November 1558 and Elizabeth I came to the throne. Elizabeth was a moderate Protestant who desired religious stability and concord. One of her major achievements, early in her reign, was the establishment of the Church of England based on the Thirty Nine Articles of 1563. She staunchly supported church music and had little sympathy for the Puritans, who deplored *the beauty of holiness* and sought to abolish church furnishings, vestments, organs, choirs and all non-congregational singing. A revised version of the English Prayer Book was issued in 1559 bearing many similarities to that of 1552. Holy communion, matins and evensong were in English, but the great difference was that choral music in church and cathedral was to be encouraged.

Despite the support of queen and church, however, there was a significant decline in the standard of church music during the early years of Elizabeth's reign. The main reason was inflation, the cost of living more than doubling between 1550 and 1600. The stipends of church musicians remained at pre-Reformation levels, and consequently many left. Some had to take a number of other jobs to make ends meet, and slackness and incompetence became widespread. In 1575 Thomas Whythorne, director of music to Archbishop Parker's private chapel at Lambeth wrote: *First for the church, ye do and shall see it so slenderly maintained in the cathedral churches and colleges, that when the old store of the musicians be worn out which were bred when the music of the church was maintained (which is like to be in short time), ye shall have few or none remaining.*

People in the north of England were somewhat slow to accept the queen's religious changes and the steady march of Protestantism. Indeed the Rising of the North in 1569 was a largely religious rebellion by northern Catholics, many of whom were subsequently hanged in Ripon market place. It gradually became clear that to bring about their acquiescence to the Reformation, systematic instruction was required rather than force. Therefore, towards the end of Elizabeth's reign plans were drawn up to establish a university in Ripon. In 1596 a prospectus proposed the creation of *an Ecclesiastical Colledge,* to be endowed with a significant number of clerical and secular academics. This was intended to be a centre of learning and true religion, and thereby influence the whole of the north of England. The choice of Ripon as its location was perhaps a reflection of the importance of this ancient town and the fact that it was a prominent and long-standing centre of religion, even though the collegiate church had been dissolved a few decades before. This enterprise gained support from both archbishops and the nobility, but unfortunately the queen did not exhibit much enthusiasm. Its advocates *never obtained anything but fair unperformed promises from Queen Elizabeth,* and nothing came of this ambitious venture. After Elizabeth died, the project was revived, but again it failed to gain support and the plans were discarded.

With the ascent of James I to the throne in March 1603 the general attitude to cathedral music gradually became much more favourable, although the puritan element was still evident with its anti-music and anti-clergy stance. William Bastwick wrote of the clergy, *One would think that hell were let loose and that devils in surplices, in hoods, in copes, in rochets, and with four-square cow turds upon their heads were come among us and had beshit us all.* However the established church largely ignored the puritan extremists; organs were restored, choirs were again supported and musical standards significantly raised. A 'high church' element appeared at this time, gradually increasing and culminating in the appointment of William Laud as Archbishop of Canterbury in 1633. He was a strong proponent of church music of the highest quality, encouraging both choirs and organists alike. Into this very positive atmosphere the collegiate church of Ripon, together with its music, was reconstituted by James I in 1604.

Chapter 4

A ROYAL CHARTER
1604 – 1641

On 2nd August 1604 James I, encouraged by his wife, Anne of Denmark, issued the first of three charters, or letters patent, reconstituting the church in Ripon into a collegiate church with all its original endowments. This charter can still be seen framed and mounted on the north wall of the chapter house. The second and third charters, issued in 1608 and 1610, adjusted and augmented the income of the chapter because of difficulties in re-acquiring old endowments. The result was a collegiate church with a re-established chapter of a dean, sub-dean and six prebendaries. The importance of reinstating the choral foundation was also recognised by the King, for the 1604 charter, translated by J.T. Fowler in 1916, states:

> *And further, We will that in the church aforesaid there shall be from time to time perpetually and continually incumbent seven vicars or clerks choral called vicars choral or called singing men, one organist, and eight querestri, in English called queresters, who shall be in the church aforesaid to celebrate Divine Offices as in the Collegiate Church of Westminster is now usual and customary.*

The first dean was Moses Fowler (1604-1607), who with the chapter submitted a petition to James in 1605. This sought to reinstate endowments, and in support of this listed the yearly stipends of the *members of Ripon Churche*. They included six choristers at 2 marks each and eight clerks choral at 8 marks each (despite the fact that the James charter, issued one year earlier, stipulated eight choristers and seven clerks choral). If these singers were all in post by this time, it indicated a very active recruitment campaign, for it must have been extremely difficult to re-establish the music, considering that there had been no choir and no organist at the minster for fifty-six years.

The next dean was Anthony Higgin (1608-1624) and it was he who built up an extensive library which he bequeathed to the minster. It was from this collection that the cathedral acquired the famous Caxtons sold in 1960 to purchase a new choir school. Dean Higgin also attempted to regularise the singing men, and on 20th September 1608 the chapter published a set of statutes defining their responsibilities and outlining how they should behave.

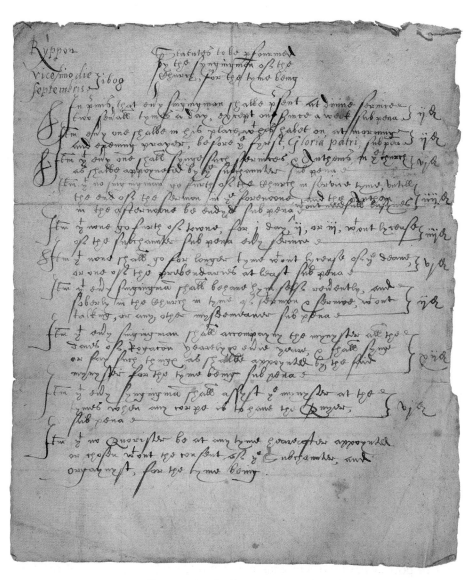

Statutes for the Syngingmen 1608.

Statutes to be perfourmed by the syngingmen of the Church, for the tyme being.

In primis that euery singingman shalbe present at diuine seruice two seuerall tymes a day, except one seruice a week, sub pena.

Item euery one shalbe in his place, with his habet on, at morning and euening prayer, before the fyrst Gloria patri, sub pena.

Item that euery one shall synge such seruices, & Anthems, in the church as shalbe appoyneted by the subchaunter, sub pena.

Item that no singingman go furth of the Church in service tyme, vntill the end of the sermon in the forenoone, and the Anthem in the afternoone be endyd, without needful busynes, sub pena.

Item that none go furth of towne, for i day, ij, or iij, without lycense of the subchaunter, sub pena euary seruice.

Item that none shall go for longer tyme without lycense of the deane, or one of the prebendaries at least, sub pena.

Item that euary singingman shall behaue hym self reuerently, and soberly in the Church in tyme of sermon and seruice, without talking, or any other mysdemeaner, sub pena.

Item that euary singingman shall accompayny the mynyster all the daies of Rogacion yearely & euerie yeare, & shall synge or say such thinges as shalbe appoynted by the said mynyster for the tyme being, sub pena.

Item that euary syngingman shall assyst the mynyster at the tymes when any corps is to haue the Quyer, sub pena.

Item that no Quorister be at any tyme heareafter appoynted or chosen without the consent of the Subchaunter, and Orgaynyst, for the tyme being.

The final item mentions the *Orgaynyst*, but as far as we know, no organist was in post at the time. Previous publications have suggested that the first organist following the 1604 reconstitution, John Wanlass, was not installed until 1662. However, scrutiny of the chapter archives indicates that he was, in fact, appointed in 1613. This would certainly make sense since the music was up and running by then, and it seems unlikely that the Dean and Chapter waited fifty eight years to acquire an organist. Precisely how long John Wanlass stayed as organist is not clear (Ref. Chapter 12). The next recorded organist, Henry Wanlass (thought to be John's son) was appointed in 1662.

The James I charter had given the chapter the right to make rules, statutes and constitutions for the government of the minster, and Dean Thomas Dod, appointed in 1635, decided this should be done. Accordingly he called a chapter meeting on 13th June of that year, at which a formal set of statutes was drawn up.

First the annual salaries of the various officers of the minster were defined (see below). Unlike his medieval predecessors, the organist was paid a salary commensurate with his senior position in the choral establishment. This comprised the precentor and his assistant, who no longer sang in the choir, the organist, six singing men and six choristers. Four of the singing men received £8 and the other two £4; the reason for this difference is unclear. From this time onwards, the title vicar choral was given to the precentor and his assistant only; the men of the choir were lay clerks and referred to as singing men or singers.

Annual Salaries of Officers of the Minster in 1635

The Precentor	*£14*	*0*	*0*
The other Vicar Choral	*£13*	*6*	*8*
The Organist and Master of the Boys	*£16*	*0*	*0*
Four Singing men each	*£ 8*	*0*	*0*
Other two Singing men each	*£ 4*	*0*	*0*
Each of the six Choristers	*£ 2*	*0*	*0*

There then follow separate sets of rules for the vicars choral, organist, singing men and choristers. These are reproduced here in full because they constitute the first complete set of statutes at Ripon Minster written for the governance of an organist and choir consisting entirely of professional lay musicians. They also give a glimpse of the ways in which some of the people of the time thought and behaved.

The Vicars Choral, Singers and Choristers

1. *The Residentiary shall carefully note any neglect of duty on their part and reprove them for it.*

2. *If either of the Vicars is absent from Morning or Evening Prayer he shall pay a drachma each day; and if any of the Singers he shall pay two pence. These fines may be increased at the discretion of the Residentiary, and shall be deducted from the salaries of the defaulters when they are paid, and distributed, if thought well, amongst the more diligent.*

3. *The Organist as Master of the Boys shall correct any negligence on their part.*

Orders for the Vicars and Organist

1. *That ye Sub-Chanter and ye Organist do agree about ye Services and ye Anthems to be sung (after Evening prayer for ye next morning, and after Morning prayer for ye Evening) that ye irriverent and indecent running to and fro of ye Boys in Service time may be prevented. And if ye Service or Anthem appointed cannot be sung by reason of ye absence of any of ye singing men, let it be omitted for that time, but let him that is absent be mulcted (fined) for every such default Fower pence unless he give to ye Residentiary a just and nessary cause of his absence.*

2. *That ye Sub-Chantor do duly note ye absence of ye singing men, and certify them to ye Residentiary, that their Mulcts may be taken, and deposed according to ye statute.*

3. *That ye Vicars do diligently Catechize ye youth of ye Towne, half an hour before Evening prayer every Sunday.*

4. *That ye Vicars and Singing men do carry themselves reverently in Service time attending to ye preacher, not leaning upon their elbows, and sleeping, upon pain of such mulcts as ye Residentiary in his Discretion shall impose upon them.*

5. *That every of ye Vicars and Singing men do keep in good repair both their desks for their Books and their Cubboards,*

for their Surplices with Locks, Keys and Bands; otherwise if ye Residentiary cause them to be repaired or amended let ye charge be deducted out of their wages.

6. *That every Singing man keep his book in his own Desk, and turn it himself.*

7. *If by default or negligence of any of ye Singing men his book or any part of it be soiled or spoiled let him prick* (copy) *it anew himself or let ye Residentiary cause it to be done by another, and pay for it out of their wages.*

Orders for ye Choristers

1. *That they be all present at Morning and Evening prayer unless any of ym have leave of Absence given him by ye Residentiary.*

2. *That they carry themselves reverently in Service & Sermon time. Kneeling upon their knees in time of prayer not leaning upon their Elbows, standing up at ye Creed, Gospel, and Gloria Patri, Bowing at ye name of Jesus; attending to ye Preacher not jangling one with another. If any of those things being faulty, and often times admonished and corrected by their Master, they do not reform themselves, let any of them so faulty be removed from their places, and others put in.*

3. *That they keep in good repair with locks and keys and Bands both their Desks for their books, and their Cubboards and their Supercloths; which if they neglect to do let ye Residentiary cause ym to be mended, and deduct ye cost out of ye wages.*

4. *That no other boys be suffered to crowde into ye Choristers seats, or if any do, that ye Verger do forthwith remove ym, but if there be any Boys, which have learned to Sing, and may after come to be chosen choristers, they may be suffered to Stand at ye end of ye seat, and to look on ye Books, but not to sing, unless their master who teacheth them, do certify that they are fit to sing.*

Item 4 in the *Orders for ye Choristers* is an early reference to the system of young boys serving as probationers prior to full choristership.

Chapter 5

CIVIL WAR & RESTORATION
1642 – 1699

In 1642 the civil war began and during the following two years all choral establishments in England were closed down. The collegiate church at Ripon was again dissolved and its members dispossessed of their income. Prayer books and music books were destroyed and organs demolished; it was written of Westminster Abbey: *Whereas there was wont to be heard nothing almost but roaring boys, tooting and squeaking organ pipes and the cathedral catches of Morley, and I know not what trash; now ... the bellowing organs are demolished and pulled down, and the treble, or rather trouble, and bass singers, chanters or enchanters driven out.* All professional choirs were disbanded for the next eighteen years, the only time since the arrival of Augustine in 597 that the singing of praises to God in choir was totally silenced throughout the land.

In 1660 the Stuart monarchy was restored, and Charles II set about repairing the damage done during the civil war, often struggling to maintain a balance between the still disparate factions within the clergy. The Book of Common Prayer of 1662 was introduced, establishing a unified liturgy throughout the church, and the choral foundations, including that at Ripon, were reconstituted. After a long time without any music, however, there were major problems. While the organists and adult singers of old were still available (albeit out of practice), the previous boy choristers were now adults. There were none left who had been brought up with, and trained in, the singing of church music, and thus a whole new treble line had to be established. The organists had difficulty in finding suitable boys; they then had to train them and ensure a new input of choristers in the following years.

When the treble line was weak, men altos often had to sing the top line. At both Durham and York sackbut players were employed for about twenty years after the Restoration to support the singers; it is quite possible that similar arrangements were used at Ripon. Some former organists and singers were re-employed, and the rebuilding of the organs and copying of music began, although this was not always straightforward. The musicologist, Dr Charles Burney, makes the following observations in his 'General History of Music':

As to organs, the difficulty of procuring them upon short notice seems greater than of finding either persons or music to perform, for, except Loosemore of Exeter, Thamer of Peterborough and Preston of York, scarce a tolerable organ builder could be found in the whole kingdom.

The problems at Ripon were compounded by the collapse of the central spire in 1660, which put a severe strain on the finances and delayed both the appointment of an organist and the rebuilding of the organ (Ref. Chapter 13). After an eighteen year break questions and disagreements frequently arose regarding the attendance of the choir, fees for certain services, and suchlike. The new dean was John Wilkins, a very able man and the brother-in-law of Oliver Cromwell. On 30th May 1663 he called a chapter meeting to sort matters out. It was decided that if any of the singing men were absent without leave from the residentiary, they should be fined 4d. If the organist failed to correct any choristers for their absence from divine service or for any other *negligence and disorder in them* he should be fined at the discretion of the residentiary.

In response to some unrest amongst the musicians the Dean and Chapter also determined the fees the choir should receive for singing at funerals. The organist should have 2 shillings, four singing men 1s. 6d. each and the other two singing men 1s. each; the six choristers *two shillings amongst*. These rates were for the full choir, but the family of the deceased was given the option of only having *An Half Quire*, in which case *each of ye partys above mentioned shall have the half of their former proportion respectively*. This fee structure did not quell the dissatisfaction however, for in June 1667 the chapter ordered *that notwithstanding the orders made at the great chapter in 1663 concerning ye regulating ye fees and dews of ye Quire, that they are now permitted and allowed to demand and receive whatsoever fees and dews shall appear to be legally belonging unto them*.

Despite these problems, this was a time of great optimism after the austere years of the Commonwealth. It was the age of the English baroque, encouraged by Charles II's love of French and Italian styles of church music. This was the time of Henry Purcell and John Blow, of verse anthems with symphonies and ritornelli, of florid solo passages calling for a different style of singing. The Italian violin replaced the English viol, and both organ and strings were used for accompaniment in church.

Music at Ripon evidently flourished during this period. The organ was upgraded in 1677 by William Preston of York under the direction of William Sorrell, the organist. A new larger instrument was built in 1695 by Gerhard Schmidt, under the then organist Thomas Preston, for the old organ was proving inadequate. The choir evidently performed well during these decades; Dr Edmund Diggle, one of the prebendaries, had not attended the minster to preach his course during 1675, nor had he attended chapter meetings. He was fined £10, of which £4 was divided amongst the members of the choir who had *diligently attended to their duties* during the year. Dr Diggle was also absent from the minster for the whole year in 1677 and again in 1684, and on each occasion a goodly portion of his fine was given to the choir as a reward for commendable service.

Thomas Preston was appointed organist of Ripon in 1690, and his activities also reflected the positive approach to music at the minster during this time. In 1696 it is recorded that *Mr Preston, Organist, having produced a note of eight song books by him pricked for ye Quire and one for ye Organ, amounting to £12, to be paid at three payments, and out of ye fabric rents.* He was given 21s. 6d. in 1699 and 40 shillings in 1700 *for writing of several anthems in the song books of the church as a gratuity for his pains therein.* Thomas Preston seems to have been determined that his choir regularly sang new and contemporary music as befitted a leading musical establishment of the day. He composed a good deal of music himself. (Ref. Chapters 14 and 15).

Not everything was perfect however. In 1696 Thomas Umpleby, singing man, who had previously been admonished because of his unsatisfactory behaviour was threatened with dismissal, but continued in post with a reduction of £2 in his £8 annual salary. His conduct apparently improved, for the following year, *upon his making his submission on his knees,* his salary was restored to £8. In 1710 the chapter resolved that this same Thomas Umpleby, *being grown old and unserviceable, his salary be reduced from £8 to £6 during pleasure.* Perhaps this story is a reflection of the times, for in the last two decades of the seventeenth and on into the eighteenth century, the standard of English choral music fell dramatically, probably to its lowest level ever.

Chapter 6

EIGHTEENTH CENTURY INDIFFERENCE
1700 – 1834

The Restoration period effectively came to an end with the deaths of Henry Purcell in 1695 and John Blow in 1708. Church music thereafter went into a long and gradual decline. It would be many years before any composer would achieve the stature of either of these two figures. Even the best church musicians of the eighteenth and early part of the nineteenth centuries are only remembered today through the inclusion of one or two of their compositions on music lists.

With the accession of George I in 1714, England no longer had a monarch who was interested in maintaining the pre-eminence of the Chapel Royal. In fact it had already been reduced in size following the death of Charles II in 1685. The string band had been dismissed and Purcell was already turning his attention to composing masques and operas. Whereas most of the important composers of the sixteenth and seventeenth centuries (Tallis, Byrd, Mundy, Blow, Purcell, Humphreys) had been Gentlemen of the Chapel Royal, the names of very few 'Gentlemen' in the eighteenth century would be recognised today.

By the 1730s the standard of English church music had fallen to a sorry state. Inflation had led to a significant reduction in purchasing power, but church musicians' salaries remained static. Chapter papers show that the remuneration of the lay clerks and choristers at Ripon Minster in 1830 was almost the same as it had been in 1635. There was a general apathy and indifference within the church. The boys and men recruited into the choir were evidently of a low calibre, and generally came from poor backgrounds and had little compunction to give of their best. As an insight into the standard of lay clerks at this time, the story of Handel requiring singers to rehearse his 'Messiah' while delayed at Chester before departing for Dublin, is of interest. *I was told you could sing at sight,* said Handel to the lay clerk. *I can, but not at first sight* came the reply.

The eighteenth century exhibited a waning attitude towards religion and the place of the Church in society, which did nothing to enhance cathedral music. Beauty, dignity and the striving for perfection in the services were no longer considered important. Matins and evensong were only said or sung because there was a statutory requirement to do so. In fact, matins and evensong were sometimes neither said nor sung simply because clergy failed to turn up. The Eucharist was also considered unimportant being celebrated infrequently and irregularly. The attitude was evidently to get through the services as quickly as possible, and therefore only the simplest and shortest of settings and anthems were sung. There was no enthusiasm and only sheer routine maintained the moribund momentum of the daily round of choral services.

Cathedrals and minsters such as Ripon were not valued as places for daily worship, but became impressive locations for grandiose civic occasions, prestigious funerals, and suchlike. Clergy were frequently absent, even those who were supposedly in residence. It was not uncommon for priests to hold livings hundreds of miles apart; famously, the Dean of Carlisle was also Rector of St George's, Hanover Square in London. Approximately 70% of clergy lived outside their parishes and were represented by curates.

Church musicians regularly failed to attend, as they usually had other jobs which to them took precedence over singing in the minster. The Dean and Chapter chose to ignore this absenteeism, or even failed to notice it as they themselves were often absent. Reports of the frequent comings and goings of the Ripon choristers during service, either to sort out what was being sung, or perhaps pump the organ, typified the general disorder. Certainly no attempt was made to form a decent procession into service; lay clerks simply threw on a surplice over their work clothes, and waited around in the stalls until the minor canon arrived.

Recruitment of choristers was greatly hampered by the poor attitude to children in general during this period. They were basically considered unimportant, schooling being non-existent for most of them who were expected to work long hours from an early age. It is probably true that the number of choristers at every choral foundation in England fell during this time.

The problems were compounded by the population's taste in music during the eighteenth century. There was a growing interest in secular music, Italian opera being particularly fashionable. This later gave way to the popularity of oratorios, especially those of Handel, which, at the time, were performed in theatres, not in churches. Subscription concerts, daily concerts in the pleasure gardens at Vauxhall, and the growth of choral societies were all features of the age. Mozart and Haydn paid extended visits to England, and the appetite for new music was insatiable. Church music, however, was seriously neglected.

The foremost composers of the sixteenth and seventeenth centuries had all started out as choristers and had gone on to write inspired liturgical music. Of the few notable eighteenth century English composers however, only a limited number had been boy choristers, such as Maurice Greene and William Boyce at St Paul's, and only a minority composed music for the daily office. The repertoire of the Ripon Minster choir during this century, like that of all cathedral and church choirs in England, was restricted to a relatively small batch of uninspired music written by a handful of largely uninspired contemporary composers.

The Hon. John Byng, later to become Lord Torrington, travelled the country between 1781 and 1794 visiting many cathedrals. He recorded his observations in a diary and wrote of the pitiable state of cathedral music. At Christ Church, Oxford, he found *evening prayers miserably performed*, at Worcester *matins very ill performed,* and at Lincoln the litany was chanted *by two lay-vicars with voices like bulls.* Byng visited Ripon on 8th June 1792, but unfortunately was unable to give an opinion on the music because *at 10 o'clock I repaired to the minster where service was going to begin; but as there was no chaunting today I fancied it too damp; so only walked around the inside where I saw some few old defaced monuments.* It is probably fair to say that, had he heard a sung service, Byng's comments concerning Ripon would have expressed similar derogatory sentiments as pertained to other choral establishments.

One interesting report of this time is a description of the Rogationtide Procession at Ripon, an ancient custom observed every year until, along with other traditions, it was discontinued by Dean Webber in 1830. This account was written in 1795 by John Hardcastle, one of the choristers, and the length of the route, together with the time it must have taken, would probably horrify today's choristers.

Perambulation day at Ripon. The day appointed for this service was always on Monday, Tuesday or Wednesday before Holy Thursday: any one of these days it was to be done. The choir and the vicar met as on other days for service at ten o'clock, with ten blue-coat boys, with branches of plane or sap tree. The service was gone through as on other days until we came to the collect, then we came out of the choir, and the blue-coat boys met us at the choir doors with their branches of plane trees. Then the choir formed themselves, the blue-coat boys with their branches in their hands, Henry Hamilton, the Dean Waddilove's verger, with his mace, then the song-boys, then the song-men, then the clergyman in whose week it happened to be. The first Psalm by the choir was the 25th Psalm, begun at the choir doors, and sung down the body of the church, down Bedern Bank and Bondgate, till about the centre. Then we entered a field where the Gospel for the fifth Sunday after Easter was read by the clergyman. Then we went down Eckler Lane to Borish Bridge, where we commenced singing the 134th Psalm, and sung it to the centre of Skelgate to the Holy Lamb. Then we commenced with the 65th Psalm and sung it to the top of Skelgate, down Westgate as far as Mr. Humfries'. Then the clergyman went to a field belonging to Mrs. Lucas, at back of Pickill Hall, and read the same Gospel. Then we commenced singing Park Street, 103rd Psalm, down Westgate, across the Market Place, past the Cross, down the Middle Street, down North Street, to the end of it. Then we sang no more till we came at Magdalens, where the clergyman entered a field back of Magdalens Chapel and read the same Gospel, and the choir went round by the chapel to meet the clergyman, and then commenced in the field where the chapel stands. Then the 67th Psalm to the centre of Stammergate or above the draw well, and ending the Psalms with the Gloria Patri, then began chanting the Litany, the clergyman chanting his own part and the choir responding to him in the usual forms as at church. And we chanted the Litany all the rest of the way, entering the gate at the east end of the church, round the churchyard, by the school steps, and up where the sap trees stand, and out of the stile at the west end of the church up the body, chanting the Litany, and into the choir, and so concluded the prayers in the usual form, and then went home and got our dinners if we had any.

Dean Webber, who has been described as *consistently disliking anything of interest* also abrogated Candlemas in 1830. This was another ancient Ripon tradition whereby on 2nd February each year, to celebrate the Feast of the Purification of the Blessed Virgin Mary, the cathedral was illuminated by candle-light, and after evensong the congregation, themselves holding candles, would process around the body of the church. As was reported of a gentleman in 1790 *that having visited Harrowgate for his health a few years before, he resided for some time at that pleasant market town Ripon where, on the Sunday before Candlemas-day, he observed that the collegiate church, a fine ancient building, was one continued blaze of light all the afternoon from an immense number of candles.* The origin of this custom is not clear, but it dates back to the medieval church. Candlemas at Ripon was prohibited in 1571, but the concept survived the Reformation and it was revived at an unknown later date. Although abolished again by Dean Webber in 1830, it was restored by Dean Llewelyn Hughes in 1964. It has continued ever since and is an eagerly anticipated event in the cathedral's calendar, albeit celebrated with a special Eucharist rather than at evensong.

Another Ripon custom of the eighteenth century took place each Christmas Day when *the singing boys come into the church with large baskets full of red apples with a sprig of Rosemary stuck in each.* The apples symbolised life and the rosemary death. The choristers presented the fruit to members of the congregation who then rewarded the boys with 2d., 4d. or 6d. *according to the quality of the lady or gentleman.* This tradition too was discontinued in 1838, but later in the nineteenth century the dean would present the choristers with a sovereign at Christmas. This practice also disappeared for a time, but both customs were revived in 1990, although now the apples are given to children in the congregation without exchange of pennies, and the choristers each receive a £1 coin from the dean.

The lamentable state of cathedral music in England continued into the nineteenth century, and provision for the schooling, housing and general well-being of the choristers was similarly deplorable. Maria Hackett, born in 1783, saw the wretched conditions in which the boys lived, and determined to improve matters. Her sustained letter-writing campaign, which began early in the nineteenth century, firstly involving the Dean and Chapter of St Paul's, and then other cathedrals, initially met with considerable indifference. Not to be deterred, however, she began visiting cathedrals in person, compiling information about each one. She became known as 'the choristers' friend' because she took an interest in their welfare and, on her visits, brought them presents.

Maria Hackett wrote to Dean Waddilove of Ripon in 1818 enquiring about the choristers' education. He did not reply until 1824, but had to admit that the Dean and Chapter provided nothing towards the boys' schooling other than in music. Their duties in choir did not allow them to attend local schools, even though Ripon had an ancient grammar school and Jepson's Hospital school. This situation held for most choristers in England, the only formal education coming from the choirmaster who taught them music, but nothing else. Over the years Miss Hackett's campaigning contributed significantly to improvements in the care and education of the choristers in nearly all the major choral establishments in England.

In 1833 a group of Anglican clergymen at Oxford University began what became known as the Oxford Movement, which advocated reform of the Church of England and restoration of practices abandoned since the Reformation. It stressed the importance of higher standards of worship, including music, and brought about many changes throughout the second half of the nineteenth century. Other reformers were also active around this time. The Rev Dr John Jebb made a survey of all choral establishments and, in a series of hard hitting lectures, and in his book 'Jebb on The Choral Service of the Church' (1843), pointed out the sorry state of affairs. S.S. Wesley also wrote 'A Few Words on Cathedral Music with a Plan of Reform' (1849) and was fearless in his criticisms.

The need for major church reform was also recognised in 1835 when the Ecclesiastical Commissioners were established. They brought about a re-distribution of the payments made to clergy, reducing the annual salaries paid to bishops, and improving the stipends of curates and vicars in poorly endowed benefices. Previous annual salaries of bishops were between £30,000 and £50,000, but the first Bishop of Ripon was paid £4,500. They also restricted the number of livings held by individuals and changed the rules regarding residentiary clergy.

The first half of the nineteenth century saw the beginnings of a more positive approach to education, to church music and musicians, and to worship in general, and this coincided with the creation of the new Diocese of Ripon and the elevation of the minster to cathedral status.

Chapter 7

THE MINSTER BECOMES A CATHEDRAL
1835 – 1899

By an order in council of King William IV dated 5th October 1836 Ripon was constituted an episcopal see, thus creating the new Diocese of Ripon, and the ancient collegiate church of Ripon was elevated to a cathedral church. Ripon became the first new diocese to be established in England since the Reformation. The dean was James Webber, appointed in 1828; the dean and prebendaries were thenceforth known as dean and residentiary canons. Likewise George Bates, appointed in 1829, became the first organist and master of the choristers of Ripon Cathedral.

Charles Thomas Longley (previously the headmaster of Harrow School) became the first Bishop of Ripon and was enthroned in the cathedral on Friday 11th November 1836. A new palace was built, and George Bates became the bishop's private organist responsible for playing the instrument in the palace chapel when required. Likewise, the cathedral choir was occasionally called to sing in the chapel, and from time to time performed informally for guests in the palace, especially at Christmas.

The elevation of Ripon Minster to a cathedral coincided with a time of great social change and improving attitudes towards religion and education. By 1850 there was a strong desire to change the slipshod approach to worship of the previous century and promote serious and beautiful choral liturgy. Whereas Georgian choristers had taken their seats in the choir before the service when they felt like it, ordered processionals and recessionals became the rule. Georgian choristers had worn open fronted surplices over their everyday clothes, now cassocks and unsplit surplices were introduced so that all secular clothing was covered. The repertoire sung by cathedral choirs, including that at Ripon, broadened considerably. This was achieved by the re-discovery and publication of a good deal of fine choral music from the sixteenth and seventeenth centuries, and by the introduction of compositions by composers such as S.S. Wesley, Goss, Ouseley, Stainer and later Stanford.

Cathedral chapters required that the daily offices should be improved musically and called on their choirs to attain a higher standard. The number of boys and men in almost all choirs had fallen during the eighteenth century and this needed to be reversed so that cathedrals might have a *full and efficient choir ... in order that the choral services may be conducted with augmented power and effect.* The more positive approach of the nineteenth century encouraged this, and nearly every cathedral increased its chorister numbers, Ripon expanding from eight boy choristers in 1862 to twelve in 1880.

Prior to Ripon Minster becoming a cathedral, all the services had been held in the choir and the nave was empty. New side aisles had been added in the sixteenth century but they too were empty (see illustration of The Nave, circa 1840). Cathedral status brought a growing number of services, and evidently from the late 1850s onwards some of these were held in the nave. When Gilbert Scott commenced his major restoration work in 1862, he started on the Bromflet stalls, and it is thought that during this time the oak pews in the choir were moved into the nave. When all the restoration work was completed nine years later and the pews were back in the choir, the nave was provided with permanent wooden chairs in about 1872 (see illustration of The Nave, circa 1880).

Throughout this century many cathedral choirs sang matins and evensong on most days of the week. Ripon, however, was different. A report to the Ecclesiastical Commissioners sent by the Dean and Chapter in 1835, just before the minster became a cathedral, stated there was a daily morning service but this was choral on Mondays, Tuesdays, Saturdays and Sundays only. On other mornings *the prayers are read in the chapter house to the few individuals who attend them.* As for evening services, those which were held on weekdays were all said; the only choral evening services were held on Saturdays and Sundays. Daily choral matins and evensong were not established at Ripon until 1875, although it seems that the number of choral services had been gradually increasing for some years because, in 1869, a petition to chapter by members of the choir asked for an increase in pay due to the extra work created by the additional evening services. In the early nineteenth century choral Eucharist was infrequent in all cathedrals, and only became a regular part of worship later. In Ripon weekly communion services on Sundays did not become a fixture until 1875, but it is not clear when they became choral.

Perhaps the greatest positive change for choristers after 1850 was recognition of the importance of their general education, non-existent during the previous century. Some cathedrals established schools specifically for their choristers, employing schoolmasters to teach them; others made arrangements for the boys to go to local schools. In 1876, shortly after the arrival of Dean William

The Nave, circa 1840.

The Nave, circa 1880.

Fremantle, he and the chapter established a school for the choristers, purchasing the old premises of the Ripon Grammar School in High St Agnesgate. The new choir school comprised classrooms, a song school, some boarding facilities, and a headmaster's house. The Reverend James Cornford was appointed headmaster and choir chaplain, but was soon succeeded as headmaster by Samuel Jacob, father of Naomi Jacob, the novelist.

To receive a choral scholarship, parents of choristers boarding at the choir school had to sign an agreement with the Dean and Chapter. It read:

I (name of parent) hereby agree that my son shall conform to the Rules and Regulations laid down by the Dean and Chapter for the management of the Choir and School.

And, in consideration of the Dean and Chapter paying the larger portion of the school fees, I also agree to pay thirteen pounds per annum, (exclusive of laundry and other incidentals), in three equal instalments in advance, at the beginning of each Term.

It is understood by this agreement that in return for the great advantages which will accrue to the boy as a member of the Cathedral Choir, his services shall be continued as long as the Dean and Chapter require.

A daily timetable was drawn up giving space for schoolwork as well as for singing. Five and a half hours per day were allowed for schooling, but of this one hour was for bible study, and one and a half hours for prep. This left three hours per day for teaching all other subjects and, as it appears that schooling took place on only four days a week, a mere twelve hours a week was assigned to the boys' general education. This compared with four hours singing each day – two practices and two services – seven days a week.

Ripon Cathedral Choir School
Timetable c. 1880

7.00 - 7.45	Private coaching
7.45 - 8.00	Play
8.00 - 9.00	Prayers & breakfast
9.00 - 10.00	Bible lesson
10.00 - 11.00	Cathedral service

11.00 - 12.00	Practice
12.30 - 1.00	Dinner
1.30 - 3.45	School
3.45 - 4.05	Play
4.05 - 5.00	Cathedral service
5.00 - 6.00	Practice
6.00 - 6.30	Tea
6.30 - 8.00	Preparation
8.15	Prayers & bed (supper)

By 1890 extensive repairs were required to the old school buildings, so the Dean and Chapter proposed to demolish them and build a new choir school on the same site. John Oldrid Scott, the son of Sir George Gilbert Scott, was appointed architect, and his initial plans included a schoolroom, two studies, two dining rooms, stores and kitchen. It appears that he did not include dormitories, but these appeared in a second set of plans dated 1891. The estimated cost of the new choir school was £3,600, and the advisory committee set up by the Dean and Chapter reported back in 1892, intimating that this sum was not affordable. At the same time, disagreements arose between the Dean and Chapter and Samuel Jacob, the choir school headmaster, over money owed to him by the cathedral; as a result, on 27th July 1894, Jacob resigned. The consequence was that the Dean and Chapter closed the choir school in 1894. Thereafter the choirboys were educated at the Bluecoat School, The Cathedral Boys' School (Junior Section), The Wesleyan School, or Trinity School, then later (at 11 years) transferred to either the Grammar School or Modern School, Clotherholme Road. The old choir school buildings and headmaster's house were demolished, and a song school was erected in about 1897. Some 65 years later, this became the present cathedral hall.

Ripon chapter papers of 1864 give an account of the duties and responsibilities of the organist and choir members of that period. The organist was George Bates and his annual salary in 1862 was £74. His duties were as follows:

To attend the services on Sunday morning and evening and on Monday, Tuesday, Thursday and Saturday mornings. Also on festival days and at any other time when requested by the Precentor or the Dean or, in his absence, the Canon in Residence.

He is under the direction of the precentor to instruct the choristers in music so that they may sing by note. And also diligently to teach those who may be in training for any vacancies that may occur. And he is to practise the choir for one hour each Monday and Saturday and at any time when thought necessary by the precentor and use every exertion in his power to give effect to the choir and maintain the decent solemnities of public worship.

The choir members of 1862 are also described, together with their duties and salaries:

The choir consists of 6 songmen and 8 boys who are required to attend the choral services and are under the same control as the organist.

The stipends of 4 of the songmen are £45 each, one £40 and the other £35. The latter as teacher or singing master of the boys has an additional stipend of £12, to practise them one hour every day except Sunday under the direction of the precentor.

The stipends of 2 of the boys are £7 a year each, 2 others £5, the remaining 4 £4. They attend the choral services and also in addition one hour a day, Sunday excepted, to practise.

There are also 2 boys in training to supply vacancies who attend an hour every Wednesday and Friday to be taught. Fare allowed £1 6s. 0d. a year each.

It seems the organist took a full choir practice for one hour twice a week, but one of the songmen was also singing master of the choristers, and he took a boys' practice for one hour every day from Monday to Saturday. The choristers, therefore, practised for one hour each day Tuesday to Friday, and for two hours on Mondays and Saturdays. This together with all the choral services – evensong was becoming more regular by this time as well as frequent matins – meant a heavy workload for the boys. Two probationers were employed attending boys' practice twice a week only.

By 1860 it had become the custom for the dean to invite the cathedral choir to the deanery during Advent to entertain guests by *the rehearsal of select programmes suited to the Christmas season.* This event was extremely popular, so in 1866 Dean Goode arranged for the concert to be held in the Public Rooms so that more people could attend. This particular concert was an outstanding success, being judged *a highlight of the year.*

There were in all five choruses which were rendered with a degree of precision and harmonious effect attainable only in a concerto of voices well trained together and judiciously balanced. But the most delightful of these was the echo chorus 'At the Night Raven's Dismal Voice', in which the still small echo from an adjacent room, just loud enough to fall upon the listening ear with the exquisite softness of a distant reverberation, completely took the audience by surprise, who listened in breathless ecstasy to what seemed a sweet delusion – a melodious whisper in the air, a mocking voice in the far-off distance.

In the solos, perhaps the sweetest and most touching was 'The Pit Boy's Song' which was rendered by the clear pleasing treble of Master Groves in a manner that could not fail to touch the heart with compassion.

Despite the positive approach, not everything was sweetness and light. Samuel Joy, precentor from 1875 to 1878, wrote *choirs are proverbially crooked things to manage*, and inevitably there was trouble from time to time. Samuel Joy wrote a letter to the dean concerning difficulties he was having with the choir and the apparent lack of support that he was getting from the Dean and Chapter:

My dear Mr Dean,

Perhaps I can best explain myself by giving instances – let me take one or two.

Last summer the choirmen asked from you to be excused from the Sunday 25th September service. The arrangement was made with them without my being allowed to have any voice whatever in it. The result was that when in September I carried out, or tried to carry out your wish in reassembling the choir, I was at once met by the private arrangement which they said they had made with you not to meet again until October. Not only the men, but the boys too were quite quick enough to see the position, & although I ordered them to come, they too thought fit to absent themselves in a body.

Let me take another instance in the anomaly of Hullah's position. Mr. Cornford expels a boy from the choristers' school. He says that it is done with your consent, & yet I who by the statutes am responsible for the boys know absolutely nothing about it until, a couple of months later, it by accident oozes out – and what is the practical result? The whole choir see a boy who is known to be expelled from the school occupying a leading position in the choir.

Now Mr. Barber's absence (utterly unknown to me except from a few words dropped by his father) just serves to show the hopeless disorder into which the choir must fall if the control vested in me by yourself & the chapter is to be thus set aside first in one direction & then in another.

The inevitable results of this breach of discipline are: (1) for the next 10 days (probably longer) the whole choir is maimed. I am afraid I cannot, as you suggest, write to a sister choir and take away at a few days notice one of the voices on which they are relying. We must limp on as best we can with mutilated services until either Mr. Barber returns or we can by advertisement & competition get another voice.

But (2) there is a more serious evil behind – & it is this – the other singing men will reasonably wonder why Mr. B. is to be exceptionally treated, and to have a leave of absence which is denied to them, & of course it is impossible to enter with them into the explanation of Mr. Barber's absence.

It is not clear how the Dean responded to this letter, but Samuel Joy resigned very shortly afterwards.

Henry Dutton applied for the post of alto lay clerk at Ripon Cathedral late in 1875. These posts were much sought after, and he was one of forty candidates. He was successful and took up his appointment in January 1876. After only a few years at Ripon he moved to St Paul's Cathedral where he occupied his stall until his death in 1947, aged 92. A fellow vicar choral at St Paul's commented later on Dutton's determination to continue singing, saying that he would have been paid for staying away; *He was stubborn, he would come into service. If he felt like singing we would stand*

RIPON CATHEDRAL,—in consequence of the election of Mr. Dutton to a lay clerk-ship in St. Paul's Cathedral, there will shortly be a VACANCY for an ALTO VOICE in the Choir at Ripon Cathedral. One fully qualified to take the Solo and Verse Parts in the daily services required. Stipend £85 to £90. For full particulars apply to J. F. A. Coppin, Esq., Chapter Clerk, Ripon, to whom applications, with testimonials, must be sent.

Advertisement reproduced from The Musical Times, 1st November, 1877 on his toe. Perhaps Ripon Cathedral choir was thankful that Henry Dutton chose to move to London.

In 1879 a Royal Commission was set up to enquire into the condition of cathedrals and collegiate churches in England and Wales, and assess how well they were fulfilling their purposes. Both the organist, Edwin Crow, and the lay clerks were invited to make submissions to the Commission, and they did so in 1880, drawing attention to the parlous financial state in which they found themselves. The lay clerks pointed out that their duties *are undeniably the most arduous and continuous of any in the cathedral service, and although every other office in the cathedral, from that of the dean to the verger, is a foundation or life appointment, that of a lay clerk at Ripon Cathedral is held only at the pleasure of the Dean and Chapter ... and we submit that lay clerks should be placed upon the foundation, and their duties and salary clearly defined in the statutes.*

Considering that the lay clerks are responsible for the greater part of a cathedral service their present remuneration is very inadequate; it should be sufficient to enable them to bring up their families respectably (say a minimum of £150 per year) without being compelled to seek additional employment.

At this time both matins and evensong were sung every day of the week (with the possible exception of Wednesdays), and on Sundays matins was extended to include an ante-communion. Clearly this was a commitment that must have made finding a second job extremely difficult.

The lay clerks concluded by claiming that they *should be made secure against penury in their old age, and that adequate provision should be made for their superannuation; as it is at present the position of a lay clerk is, in our case, both in emolument and in the matter of superannuation, inferior to that of a verger.* This letter was signed by the lay clerks in post at the time:

Parson Pearce	*William Fletcher*
John Thursfield	*Herbert Parratt*
Walter Taylor	*A Vacant Stall (by death)*

Edwin Crow began his letter by supporting the submissions of the lay clerks: *There is at present absolutely no provision for them in old age. They are liable to be dismissed when their voices are worn out without pension or any kind of provision against absolute destitution. This acts disastrously on our music, since all our best men seek and obtain appointments in more fortunate cathedrals.* Crow went on to point out *the want of a house for the organist* and also *that all 12 boys and 6 men form a choir only half as large as it ought to be.* He concluded, *I am happy to be able to say that there is nothing to complain of in the working of the cathedral arrangements. Poverty alone is our difficulty.*

These submissions seem to have had some effect, but although the remuneration of the organist and lay clerks was increased shortly afterwards, the increment was minimal, and the question of pensions for lay clerks remains an outstanding issue to this day. The provision of a house for the organist by the Dean and Chapter was not forthcoming until the 1960s, and Edwin Crow's concluding remark *Poverty alone is our difficulty* might well be said today.

The first festival of what was known as the North Eastern Cathedral Choirs' Association (later to become the Northern Three Choirs) took place in the summer of 1881 at York Minster. The choirs of York, Durham and Ripon Cathedrals were joined by many of the more prestigious Parish Churches in the three dioceses and it is reported that a total of 915 voices performed the cantata 'St John the Evangelist' composed for the occasion by Dr Philip

Pencil drawing by Jim Gott of the Oldrid Scott nave stalls, 1899.

Armes, organist of Durham Cathedral (1862-1907). John Naylor, the organist of York Minster and Edwin Crow of Ripon shared with Philip Armes the duties of conducting and playing the organ.

In July 1883, the North Eastern Cathedral Choirs Festival was held at Ripon Cathedral for the first time. The three choirs sang a joint evensong and the Magnificat and Nunc Dimittis were sung to a setting in A major which Edwin Crow had written specially for the occasion (Ref. Chapter 12, page 124). In the evening the choirs sang a church oratorio entitled 'Phillippi' by Dr Gladstone. The Musical Times of 1st August, 1884, tells us that on this occasion there were 351 singers.

In 1886 the City of Ripon organised a 'Millenary Festival' to celebrate the thousandth anniversary of the year 886 when, it was believed, King Alfred the Great granted a charter to the city. The festival commenced on Wednesday 25th August with a special service in the cathedral. The Ripon Cathedral choir was joined by the choirs of York and Durham under the direction of Dr Crow (Ref. Chapter 14). There followed a whole week of luncheons, meetings, banquets, torchlight processions and pageants which were meticulously recorded in a large book entitled 'The Ripon Millenary Record'. Typical Victorian enthusiasm for period revival, particularly in matters medieval and gothic, made the narrative rather more important than historical accuracy (it is highly unlikely that any such charter was granted) and the festival was a great success.

In 1899 Dean Fremantle opened a subscription list to raise money for repairs and improvements to the cathedral. Because of the increasing number of nave services, the old rudimentary choir desks and benches in the nave were replaced by imposing finely carved oak stalls designed by J. Oldrid Scott (See illustration opposite). The original music desks were used in 1962 to furnish the new choir practice room in the cathedral undercroft, and they remain there in regular use. The Oldrid Scott stalls fulfilled their purpose until 1990 when they were replaced with lightweight moveable units.

Chapter 8

A DIFFICULT PERIOD WITH TWO WORLD WARS
1900 – 1953

The first year of the new century evidently passed normally at Ripon Cathedral and the music provided for Christmas 1900 by the organist Edwin Crow and his choir was well received. However, although he had no inkling of it, this was to be Dr Crow's last Christmas at the cathedral.

Over the years Crow had experienced problems with the lay clerks (what choirmaster hasn't?), many of whom were elderly and opinionated. Matters came to a head when they went behind the organist's back and poured out their woes to the precentor, Samuel Reed, claiming that Dr Crow was mistreating them at choir practices. Instead of talking to Crow himself, the precentor went straight to the Dean and Chapter and reported verbatim what the lay clerks had said about the organist – evidently he had even shouted at them! There may have been more serious allegations, but there is no evidence of this either in the records or the correspondence.

The minutes of a Dean and Chapter meeting in late May 1901 contained the resolution *The Chapter of the Cathedral, having had before them a complaint of the choirmen in February last and that as this is the culmination of a long series of facts which indicate that Dr Crow is unable to conduct the work desired by the Chapter to their satisfaction, resolve that the time has come to terminate the connection with him as organist. They hereby resolve to give Dr Crow notice of the termination of his engagement. Should Dr Crow prefer to resign his appointment, the Dean and Chapter will, on his leaving Ripon and signing a Warrant and Memorandum (to be prepared by the Chapter Clerk) give him a gratuity of £200.*

There is no record of the Dean and Chapter having written to Dr Crow at this point, but evidently, in early July he was summoned to a meeting by the chapter clerk at which he was informed of their decision.

Edwin Crow must have been devastated, but after the initial impact he wrote in his flowing hand a long personal letter to the dean, telling him how shocked he was and pointing out that, in his long period of service as organist and choirmaster, he had never before been summoned by the Dean and Chapter for unsatisfactory performance of his duties.

He went on to state *I admit speaking strongly to the choirmen, who are indolent, regarding their lack of discipline and neglect to prepare new and difficult music by private study. Their consequent shocking performance has rendered plain speaking by the choirmaster a real necessity. Many times have I reported these difficulties to the Precentor; but to no avail. There were no such problems when Samuel Joy was the Precentor. I appeal to you as a Christian man and beg you to withdraw this undeserved and disgraceful termination to my cathedral life. I think you cannot have realised what it means to a man of 60 years from an honourable position, with a family depending on him, to make a fresh start in life.*

The Dean and Chapter, however, declined to change their decision, and after what must have been a good deal of agonising and with the inducement of a gratuity of £200 (although it is evident that the restrictive terms attached to it, that he must cease all music teaching in Ripon, had not at this stage been expounded to him), Dr Crow decided to resign and thus avoid the stigma of being dismissed. Doubtless with a heavy heart, he wrote his letter of resignation on Thursday 1st August 1901:

It is twenty eight years since I was appointed organist of Ripon Cathedral ... and I feel the time is approaching that I should retire.

I am not sure what the Statutes say, but I would like to be released of my duties in six months time.

The following day Dean Fremantle wrote an interesting and somewhat enigmatic note to the chapter clerk, Mr J. Whitham:

Accept Crow's resignation with a formal letter, but write privately re. 'other matters' so he is aware of the terms of the resolution. This is to avoid anything disreputable re. Crow appearing in our books.

It is not known to what the words *anything disreputable re Crow* refer. Was the dean in possession of some fact about Crow and his behaviour which was very serious, or was he anxious that the shabby way in which he and the chapter had handled the affair should not be put into writing? The only clue is a surviving letter written by Mrs Crow that implies that at some time, probably in the late 1890s, Crow's relationship with her had deteriorated, so that he left their original family home in The Crescent, Ripon and they were living apart. There is certainly no evidence of an extramarital affair, nor indeed of Crow and his wife Emily having divorced, but in those days, the merest hint of

58

the breakdown of a marriage, especially involving persons holding important offices within the church, carried with it a stigma which the Dean and Chapter may well have found intolerable. If so, it seems possible that Crow's minor problems with the choir were exaggerated by the Dean and Chapter and used as an excuse to dispense with his services.

If there was something seriously sinister about Crow's behaviour, his wife certainly did not know about it because on 27th July Mrs Emily Crow wrote an impassioned letter to the chapter clerk asking *What has he done ... any great wrong?* On 2nd August she wrote to him again expressing concern at *not being able to pay the rent and go on living in Ripon.*

After Edwin Crow had written his letter of resignation – and effectively burned his boats – the chapter clerk told him the precise terms and conditions to which he must agree to receive the £200. These were embodied in a document which the Dean and Chapter euphemistically called a Warrant and Memorandum which read:

In consideration of the sum of £200 being paid to Dr Edwin Crow ... he will not at any time in the ten years from this date carry out the profession of teacher of music, or any other business or profession, within ten miles of the Ripon Market Place.

The effect of this harsh proviso was that not only did the Dean and Chapter deprive Dr Crow of his livelihood as organist of Ripon Cathedral (the salary for which, as the Dean and Chapter were well aware, included no provision for a pension), but they also sought to deprive him of earning a living at the one profession for which he was qualified, that of teaching music. It is not surprising that Edwin Crow refused the terms. He had a number of private music pupils in and around Ripon and taught two or three days a week at a girls' private school, Skellfield School, run by a Miss Boycott.

In late September the dean went personally to see Miss Boycott. Deans were powerful men in those days and he was evidently successful in prevailing upon her to terminate Dr Crow's employment at the school from the end of that year. From this point onwards the affair hotted up and the correspondence flew thick and fast.

On 12th October 1901 Dean Fremantle wrote to the chapter clerk *I want to be sure re the Warrant & Memorandum that Crow cannot teach in Ripon. The new candidates for the post of organist are asking about it.* On 23rd November Dr Crow wrote a letter to the chapter clerk reiterating that *I cannot possibly give up my teaching practices in Ripon.* He goes on to refer to *congregational support* and states that if the matter is not satisfactorily resolved, he will resort to legal action.

The Dean and Chapter records on this matter, filed in an old brown envelope marked 'The Crow Affair' contain:

A letter dated 9th January 1902 from Edmundson & Cowland of Ripon, Crow's solicitors, to the chapter clerk, stating *As it is too late to remedy the existing state of things, we think it is only fair to give you notice of the action that will be taken against the Dean in this matter and it will be for him to consider in the meantime whether it is wise to persevere in his present action.*

A further letter dated the following day from the solicitors to the chapter clerk intimates that court action will go ahead and asking for confirmation *that the Dean will accept service of proceedings.* Evidently the chapter clerk claimed that the dean had some special exemption because on 14th January another letter from Edmundson & Cowland refuted the suggestion that the dean was immune from legal proceedings against him and asked the chapter clerk *to kindly inform us if you will accept service of Writ on the Dean's behalf.*

The last item of correspondence on the file is a letter to the chapter clerk dated 8th April 1902 from Edmundson & Cowland, which states *There is not the slightest doubt that Dr Crow's decision to resign was brought about by the intimation in your letter that he would receive a present from the Chapter in recognition of his past services.*

And there the Dean and Chapter records end.

It seems certain that Dr Crow did not give up his private pupils in Ripon, but we do not know whether Miss Boycott continued to follow the dictates of her name or reinstated Edwin Crow as a teacher at her school. Nor do we know the outcome of the threatened legal proceedings. In view, however, of the resignation under duress, coupled with the dean's ill-advised action in visiting Miss Boycott, it is reasonable to assume that the matter was settled out of court and some payment made to Dr Crow. The records show that the Dean and Chapter did pay an amount of £30 to Mrs Crow and a further £30 to her daughter. Further researches reveal that Edwin Crow was appointed organist of Thirsk Parish Church in 1903, so he evidently left Ripon and moved to the Thirsk area where it is hoped that he found some music pupils.

To say that the dean's high-handed attitude and actions were probably not untypical of senior clergymen of that era, is not to find them elevating.

However, as far as the general public was concerned, Dr Crow had simply decided to resign, and this was confirmed in an article in the Ripon Gazette dated 15th August 1901:

RESIGNATION OF THE RIPON CATHEDRAL ORGANIST

The announcement of the resignation of Dr E. J. Crow as organist of Ripon Cathedral has been received with surprise as well as regret by all who know the efficiency with which he has carried out his duties for the long period of nearly 28 years.

On 23rd November, there followed a long tribute to Dr Crow's *refined and cultured taste* and his constant *striving for perfection in the cathedral choir* and all that he had achieved.

The Dean and Chapter announced the appointment of Charles Harry Moody as the new organist in October 1901, to commence his duties in January 1902. The following year Moody took the Ripon Cathedral choir to a festival gathering of the choirs of York, Durham and Ripon. The Musical Times of 1st August 1903 reported that *the Festival of the North Eastern Cathedral Choirs was held on 15th of July of this year in York Minster. The duties of conductor and organist were shared by Mr Tertius Noble of York and Mr Charles Moody of Ripon.*

Shortly after his arrival at Ripon Charles Moody started work on the 'Ripon Chant Book', which was published by Novello & Company Ltd in October 1907; it contained just over 300 chants, some by Ripon composers (Ref. Chapter 15).

In October 1910 the Dean and Chapter decided to organise a re-union for former choir boys, providing a meal for them, together with the precentor, succentor and organist. This led to the formation of the Ripon Cathedral Choir Old Boys' Association the following year by the Rev Ernest Henry Swann, the precentor, and Charles Moody (Ref. Chapter 17).

On Tuesday 14th July 1914 Britain declared war on Germany, and recruitment and mobilisation of troops began on a massive scale. Not a city, town or village escaped the devastating effects of the Great War and Ripon was no exception. Within months several thousand troops were billeted in the city, and work started on building an army camp north of Ripon. By the spring of 1915 there was a huge encampment with tents, huts, roads and sewers, effectively a military town with all its own facilities, including an electricity generating station and a light railway connecting it to the Littlethorpe siding of the Ripon main line. At its height the Ripon army camp had a population of some 30,000 troops and this had a major effect on the city. Hitherto, Ripon had been a rather sleepy place and in the first decade of the new century had suffered severely from lack of trade and prosperity. Large numbers of men from Ripon joined up, including many from the cathedral choir.

Charles Moody made strenuous efforts to keep the choir singing, and some retired lay clerks were brought back to replace those who had gone to the war. Senior boys whose voices had broken helped with the alto line and some musical clergy were cajoled into singing. At the time war broke out the choir was singing matins (at 10.00 am) and evensong (at 5 pm) on Mondays, Tuesdays, Thursdays, Fridays and Saturdays and two, sometimes three (choral communion was sung once a month at 11.45 am), services on Sunday every week. These choral weekday services took place for some forty two weeks in the year with choral services on forty six Sundays. While some minor curtailment of weekday matins occurred, Charles Moody managed to continue choral services at Ripon Cathedral throughout the war. He also worked tirelessly helping with the entertainment of troops at the camp, and supporting organists and clergy in various parts of the diocese. He travelled extensively giving organ recitals and talks on various subjects including The Cistercian Order and Fountains Abbey, Ripon Cathedral, English church music and bell ringing (yet another of his wide ranging interests).

After the Armistice on Monday 11th November 1918 a 'Service of Thanksgiving for Peace' was held on Sunday 6th June 1919. The cathedral was packed to overflowing and many in the congregation were parents for whom the price of peace was the loss of their sons. Things slowly returned to normal but Ripon kept a significant military presence. Splendid church parades and services at the cathedral, with the organ and a military band, became a regular feature which continues to this day. Several decades later a minor canon told the story of hundreds of immaculately turned out soldiers marching into the cathedral through the west doors and down the central aisle to take their seats in the nave. The sergeant major noticed that one young private was still wearing his cap and went up to him, saying in a less than discreet voice, *'ave you no respect lad? You're in God's 'ouse, get your bleedin' cap off.*

The services, music, clergy, staff and congregation at Ripon Cathedral were never immune from what was happening in the secular world outside. In a scribbled note inserted by Charles Moody in the margin of the choir attendance book of 1919, against the details of the music for evensong on 27th September was written *National Strike – no organ until settled.*

On Monday 20th August 1923 Queen Mary, who was staying with her old friends the Vyners at nearby Fountains Hall, visited the cathedral where she was given a tour of the building. A surviving photograph of this occasion shows the queen leaving by the west door accompanied by Dean Mansfield Owen.

THE QUEEN THANKING THE DEAN OF RIPON (DR. MANSFIELD OWEN) AFTER HER VISIT TO RIPON CATHEDRAL, AUGUST 20th, 1923.

Reproduced by permission of the "Yorkshire Evening Post."

When the old choir school in High St Agnesgate had been closed in 1894, the choristers went to be educated, and some to board, at Jepson's Hospital Bluecoat School (see illustration below), which Zacarias Jepson had established and endowed in 1672 *for the education of orphan boys or sons of poor tradesmen of Ripon.*

Staff and pupils of Jepson's Hospital Bluecoat School, circa 1915.

In 1904 the Dean and Chapter agreed that they would pay the fees for all the choristers, including probationers, at Jepson's School. The twelve choristers were also to be given annual payments according to their seniority. Three boys were to receive £4 each, three boys £5, three £6 and the three most senior boys £8.

A set of *Rules and Regulations for Choir Boy Boarders at Jepson's School* was issued on Thursday 18th May 1922 as follows:

1. That no choir practice shall interfere with the boarders' meals at 8.15 and 4.30 on week days, and on Sundays at 12.30.

2. That the boarders shall be in by 9 pm.

3. That the Dean and Chapter will confer with the Head Master before fixing the dates for the choir holidays.

4. That in the case of slight illnesses which do not need the services of a Doctor but necessitate the boy being kept indoors at the school, the Master shall send a note to the Organist at once explaining the nature of the illness, and the Organist shall notify the Precentor.

5. That when new boarders are elected the Dean and Chapter shall give the Master seven days notice before their arrival.

6. That no boy shall be elected a chorister unless he produces a Doctor's certificate stating that he is strong enough to stand school life and the training that is involved in belonging to a cathedral choir.

7. That no boy shall be sent to the school until he has passed the third Standard and can read well.

8. That if any parent is in default with the payment due, the Master shall report the case to the Dean and Chapter within one month.

9. That all complaints shall be made by the Master to the Dean or Canon in Residence.

> *Approved*
> *Charles Mansfield Owen*   *Arthur H. Watson*
> *Ronald Macpherson*   *Charles H. Moody*
> *R. Parkin*   *May 18th 1922*

Bearing in mind the punishing daily schedule of early morning rehearsal, then matins and evensong, plus full choir practice twice a week, together with surviving the rigours of a martinet choirmaster, clause 6 was clearly essential.

During the 1920s the finances of Jepson's School became increasingly precarious; in 1927 the trustees decided that the school was no longer viable, and it was closed. The old school buildings in Water Skellgate were later demolished (being replaced with what is now the Ripon Conservative Club) and all the pupils, including the choristers, were transferred to the grammar school. Thereafter most of the choristers aged eleven years and over were educated there, the Dean and Chapter paying their fees.

Singing occupied a major part of the choristers' day in the 1930s. Each weekday, except Wednesdays, the boys assembled for an hour's practice at 8.30 am. After a short break they robed, and at 10.00 am sang matins. Then the boys were taken to the grammar school in a four-wheeled horse-drawn wagonette, arriving a little after 11.00 am just in time for the last lesson of the morning. It has been said that the choristers received only a part-time education. The boys assembled once more for evensong at 5.00 pm, although occasionally there was a short rehearsal at 4.30 pm. Evensong was sung each weekday except Wednesday, and also every Saturday. On Mondays and Fridays it was followed by a full choir practice which lasted an hour. Matins was sung at 10.00 am each Sunday, often with the litany, and occasionally followed by choral communion. Evensong on Sunday was at 5.00 pm.

Through the week the choristers wore their ordinary school uniforms, but on Sundays they had to wear Eton suits and mortarboards. The two head choristers sported red tassels on their mortarboards, contrasting with the black ones worn by the other boys (See illustration of Eric Witts, Head Chorister 1933-1934 on following page).

On Saturday 26th April 1930 Canon James Tuckey, a residentiary canon at Ripon, wrote to the BBC to enquire about broadcasting a service from Ripon Cathedral. They replied saying they thought this an excellent idea. Further correspondence regarding the service and possible dates ensued, but all came to nought. On 20th November 1930 Canon Tuckey wrote to the BBC: *After being offered several dates for broadcasts, I feel I ought to tell you that although the majority of the Chapter was strongly in favour of accepting your most generous offer, as the Dean was so strongly against broadcasting a service, we felt we could not carry it in the face of his opposition. He is a splendid man but he is old and cannot adapt himself to the advance of science and*

Head chorister Eric Witts, 1933.   *Eric in his Cantoris Stall, 2006.*

the advantages offered to the religious life of the nation. Bishop Burroughs of Ripon remarked of Dean Owen: *he makes the not inconsistent boast that he is the most conservative Dean in England. Methinks he does not claim too much.* So, in early 1932, Bishop Burroughs decided to take the question of a radio broadcast from Ripon into his own hands and, using his contacts with the BBC, steam-rollered his idea through. This groundbreaking event took place on Sunday 18th September, and was announced in the Radio Times as *A Religious Service for Cyclists & Wayfarers from Ripon Cathedral.*

This first radio broadcast from the cathedral was evidently a great success, so in 1934 the BBC put out two more broadcasts: a talk given by Charles Moody on Wednesday 31st January entitled 'What the North owes to the early Cistercians', and on 26th March a programme entitled 'The Music of the Church'.

On Sunday 20th May 1934 two programmes were broadcast from Ripon Cathedral one after the other. The first was a 'Religious Service', tuned into by assembled congregations in various parishes in the diocese, huddled round specially issued 'amplified wireless sets'. The second was a 'Broadcast to America' in co-operation with the Columbia Broadcasting Corporation. This latter programme commenced with a peal of the cathedral bells, followed by the town crier and the mayor from outside the town hall, continuing with a short choral service from the cathedral and an address by the bishop, ending with a curfew from the hornblower. The Bishop of Ripon gave a short address on each of the two broadcasts which were well received, but the producer and executives of the BBC had reservations. They admonished Bishop Burroughs for including in his address an appeal for money to build new churches in the diocese. Their displeasure was expressed in a letter to the bishop and a memo on the subject stated *If we allow this sort of thing to happen, the Non-Conformists, Papists and Jews will want to get in on the act.* Dean Owen, influenced by these broadcasts, soon became favourably inclined to the idea of featuring on the radio. Indeed he personally offered to give every possible assistance to the BBC for the upcoming Palm Sunday service, due to be broadcast from Ripon Cathedral on 5th April 1936. In July of the same year the choirs of Ripon, York, Durham and Newcastle Cathedrals combined to sing a festival evensong at Ripon which was also broadcast.

The four cathedral organists, 1934.

Ripon Cathedral first hosted the Festival of the National Federation of Cathedral Old Choristers' Associations in 1922 and then again in 1934, when over a hundred old cathedral choirboys from all over England descended on the city. Special choral services, an organ recital and visits to local beauty spots, including Fountains Abbey, took place with Charles Moody acting as the historical advisor and guide.

The first joint festival evensong of the cathedral choirs of York, Durham and Ripon was held at York in 1881. Thereafter these North Eastern Cathedral Choirs festivals rotated between the three cathedrals almost every year, save for an interruption during the Great War. In September of 1934, the event was held at Durham and, probably because of Charles Moody's friendship with William Ellis, the Newcastle Cathedral choir were invited to participate. On this occasion, a photograph of the four organists was taken (see previous page). These are, from left to right, Edward Bairstow (York), John Dykes Bower (Durham), Charles Moody (Ripon) and William Ellis (Newcastle).

Just before war was declared on Sunday 3rd September 1939 widespread bombing of major cities in Britain was anticipated. Consequently large-scale evacuation of school children took place. A 12 year old boy, Eric Record (who retired to Ripon many years later and is now a keen supporter of Ripon Cathedral and its music), was a pupil at Leeds Grammar School and was evacuated to Ripon along with about 80 boys and some of the teachers. The evacuees attended Ripon Grammar School; accommodation was limited, so the Leeds contingent took part in sports and extracurricular activities in the mornings whilst the classrooms were being used by the Ripon boys, and they changed over for the afternoons. One of the Leeds Grammar School teachers was Herbert Bardgett, the music master, who was well known as the successful chorus master of the renowned Huddersfield Choral Society whose then chief conductor was Sir Malcolm Sargent. Herbert Bardgett gathered together a group of the Leeds boys who were musical and could sing, and used some spare time in the mornings to fashion them into a choir. After two months of rehearsal they were invited by Charles Moody to sing choral matins in the cathedral once a week with the Ripon lay clerks. On these occasions Dr Moody conducted the choir and Herbert Bardgett played the organ. Eric recalls that he and his fellow Leeds choristers were terrified of Moody who was always very stern and intolerant of any mistakes. The Leeds boys borrowed the Ripon cassocks, discovering various interesting items in the pockets. Eric remembers well a large and sticky lump of chewing gum which took a long time to remove from his hand, not to mention from the copy of Stanford's Te Deum in C, to which he also became particularly attached!

The Leeds Grammar School boys' stay in Ripon continued until just before Christmas of 1939 when the so-called 'phoney war period' was deemed to be over, and most of the evacuated children went back to their own homes and schools.

The Second World War had a similar, although perhaps not quite so drastic, effect upon the cathedral and choir as the First World War. Several men in the choir were called up, but Charles Moody had seen it all before and again managed to maintain the daily choral services.

In the midst of the war, however, Ripon Cathedral had its own conflict. The trouble started at the annual parochial church meeting held on Tuesday 4th May 1943 when the Mayor of Ripon, Alderman A. Nettleton, suggested the introduction of more congregational singing in the cathedral at Sunday services. He said that people love to sing and that they should be given the opportunity to do so during cathedral services. After all, he continued, *God listens to the crow as much as to the nightingale.* There was some sympathy with this proposal and Dean Birchenough suggested that Mr. Nettleton bring it up at the next parochial church council meeting. This was duly done, and at the PCC meeting on Tuesday 1st June a resolution, asking the Dean and Chapter to consider *making the Sunday services at the cathedral more congregational* and that *at these services either settings or anthems should be used but not both,* was passed by thirty-nine votes for to only one against.

The Dean and Chapter discussed this resolution at the chapter meeting on Tuesday 15th June. The idea was evidently well received and it was unanimously agreed that the canticles at both morning and evening services on Sundays would in future be sung to chants instead of settings. On hearing this, Dr Moody wrote a letter to the Dean and Chapter asking for the whole matter to be reconsidered, but he was summoned to meet the dean and canons on Tuesday 6th July and informed that they were resolved and that the matter was settled.

There followed a torrent of correspondence, both private and in the press, putting forward arguments for and against the Dean and Chapter's decision. Dr Moody wrote extensively deploring the chapter's decree and received many letters of support from senior ecclesiastical figures, including the Dean of Gloucester and even the Bishop of Ripon, Dr Lunt. Many musicians and well-known public dignitaries sent letters to The Times and other national newspapers in support of Dr Moody. Cosmo Lang, the recently retired Archbishop of Canterbury, and other notable churchmen likewise wrote deploring the ruling. The Ripon Cathedral Choir Old Boys' Association, at their annual meeting on Saturday 9th October 1943, unanimously agreed to oppose the Dean and Chapter and wrote a letter to them accordingly. A similar letter was written by the Royal College of Organists, but still the Dean and Chapter declined to reconsider.

An eminent musician of the day, Ralph Vaughan Williams, wrote a letter to Charles Moody which read as follows:

> *Dear Dr Moody,*
>
> *It would be a terrible thing if the Cathedral Tradition were to disappear and I hope very much that you win your fight with the Dean and Chapter.*
>
> *These people do not seem to realise that music has also its nobilities and its indecencies. I wonder what they would say if it were suggested that a chapter from a pornographic novel should be substituted for the First Lesson? or that the Lord's Prayer should be re-written in the style of American journalism? And yet they permit, and even encourage, such indecencies in music for the sake of bringing people into church.*
>
> *I admit, and I know that you agree, that people should have a share in the service, but there is no more reason why they should join in the Anthems or Canticles than in the Absolution or the 'comfortable words'. And further, I think the idea of a choir service is a noble one, where the people come only to listen and to meditate. Would not a practical solution be to have a choir service every Sunday at 10 am and 3 pm and congregational services at 11 am and 6.30 pm?*
>
> *We must beat this ecclesiastical totalitarianism somehow, but we can only do so by confining ourselves to what is really noble in our cathedral repertory. You know of course as well as I do that many of our canticles and anthems are vicious, theatrical, mechanical, or intolerably smug. Unless we can root these out of our services we shall give the enemy cause to blaspheme.*
>
> *Please make any use you like of this letter.*
> *Yours sincerely, Ralph Vaughan Williams*

On this subject, Charles Moody asserted that, at this stage of the proceedings, he offered to co-operate by providing congregational services on Sundays as well as choral matins and evensong, as Vaughan Williams had suggested, but this proposal was rejected.

Meanwhile the precentor, Hugh Williams, and the organist, Charles Moody, had to implement the ruling that the Te Deum and Benedictus or Jubilate at matins and the Magnificat and Nunc Dimittis at evensong had to be sung to ordinary chants. It is said that, as a gesture of his annoyance, Dr Moody used the same single chant (Pelham Humphrey in C – No 226 in the Ripon Cathedral Chant Book of 1907 – the melody of which only employs two notes, C and B) for the Te Deum, Benedictus, Magnificat and Nunc Dimittis Sunday after Sunday. Rumour has it, however, that this tactic rebounded on Moody because the choir became sick and tired of this boring chant long before the congregation (who evidently quite liked it!), so different chants were introduced to relieve the monotony.

It was apparent that the argument was not going to be settled amicably and it ended up going to court. An action brought by the Royal College of Organists through the Attorney-General came before Mr. Justice Uthwatt in the Chancery Division on Tuesday 13th February 1945. It was agreed that statute XIII para. 2 of the Ripon Cathedral Statutes of 1836 stated that *There shall be full choral services every Sunday morning and evening throughout the year.* The arguments in court centred around the interpretation of the phrase *full choral services.* Did this mean full settings of the canticles as claimed by the Royal College of Organists, or would canticles set to chants satisfy the statutory requirement as alleged by the chapter? The RCO fielded three eminent church musicians as witnesses, Sir Ivor Atkins, Sir Edward Bairstow and Sir Percy Buck, who all stated that, to them, full choral services meant settings and not chants. The Dean and Chapter argued that control of the worship in the cathedral lay with them and them alone. Judgement was given on Wednesday 21st March 1945 when Mr Justice Uthwatt pronounced that this was not a matter for the secular court, but one for an ecclesiastical court and he therefore declined to give a ruling one way or the other.

The scene was set for the Royal College of Organists to take the case to an ecclesiastical court, but the extensive and controversial publicity accompanying the dispute led the dean to call a special meeting of the chapter on 29th May 1945 at which a compromise was negotiated. The chapter agreed that the Te Deum should be sung to a setting on Sunday mornings, provided that the precentor and the organist were willing to co-operate *by withdrawing the charges of illegal action on the part of the chapter, by cessation of all public controversy on this matter and by being willing to play tunes to hymns in a lower key.* During the dispute Dr Moody, to demonstrate his displeasure at the Dean and Chapter's ruling, had evidently played hymns at Sunday congregational services transposed up so high that very few could sing them. The matter was settled on the basis of this agreement, but a good deal of damage had been done and relations between the organist (and the precentor who had supported him) and Dean Birchenough and the chapter were never quite the same again. Rumour, probably apocryphal, has it that on the first Sunday after the compromise deal had been agreed the precentor and Dr Moody chose as the opening hymn 'The strife is o'er'.

It is worthy of note that the choral canticles versus congregational chants affair affected the music policy at Ripon for many years. Even twenty years later, during the early days of organist Ronald Perrin, appointed in 1966, only one of the canticles at matins, usually the Te Deum, was sung to a setting. The other canticle, whether the Benedictus or Jubilate, was always sung to a chant. It was not until the mid 1970s, when there were regular choral Eucharists in addition to matins, that both the matins canticles were sung to settings.

In the statutes connected with the establishment of Ripon Minster as a cathedral in 1836, there appears to be no stipulation that choral matins should be sung daily, although the 1604 Charter refers to 'daily choral services'. The music lists for 1934 indicate that matins was sung at Ripon Cathedral every weekday, except Wednesdays, throughout the year, with the exception of choir holidays. Indeed, The Times newspaper of Tuesday 11th September of that same year carried a short report of the annual meeting of the Federation of Cathedral Old Choristers' Associations at their national festival in Ripon when *they expressed their deep appreciation to the Dean and Chapter of Ripon Cathedral, and six other cathedral and collegiate churches, in maintaining musical services twice daily in accordance with the unbroken custom of the centuries.* They went on to *express their deep concern for the fact that the majority of Deans and Chapters of other establishments, including some of the wealthiest and best endowed, had adopted a different policy and abandoned the choral rendering of matins and to some extent evensong also.*

However the provisions of the 1944 Education Act finally took their toll at Ripon Cathedral in 1946 and daily choral matins ceased. In the choir attendance book on the page for Tuesday 18th June 1946 there is a short but poignant entry in Dr Charles Moody's handwriting which reads *Boys exempt henceforth from matins*. It appears that the men continued to sing occasional mid week matins but this was discontinued after the summer of that year. This is confirmed by an article in the Ripon Gazette of Thursday 30th January 1947 headed 'A Blow to Music' which stated *During the past few months the morning choral services at the cathedral have had to be abandoned except on Saturdays and Sundays, owing to the demands of the new Education Act.*

The screen that divides the choir from the nave has always been closely associated with music at Ripon. From the earliest days it was the place where the organ stood (records of 1408 refer to *an organ on the purpytal screen)* and through its fine central arch the clergy and choir have processed into services for generations. It is thought that the present screen, probably fourteenth century in origin, was installed at Ripon about 1480. There seems little doubt that from the beginning of its time at the minster, the niches of the screen were empty. When, in 1945, the Dean and Chapter installed figures in the three niches over the entrance arch to the south choir aisle, these were so well received that it was decided to place figures in the choir screen. Mr Esmond Burton, who had created the choir aisle figures, was commissioned to design and sculpt them. Sensing the inseparable link between the screen and the music, the sculptor created a series of angels playing a variety of medieval musical instruments, with two others reading or singing from their books, and these fill the twenty

The choir screen.

four upper tier niches. In the eight larger niches of the lower tier Burton created seated figures of important persons connected with Ripon, but St Wilfrid was not included.

All the figures were completed and installed by the early summer of 1947 and on Saturday 28th June the Princess Royal attended a service of dedication at which she unveiled the new statues. At this time all the figures were the colour of the natural stone from which they were carved. It was not until the summer of 1958 that the formidable task of painting and gilding the figures, always envisaged by Esmond Burton, was finally completed.

These figures have been admired and enjoyed by countless worshippers and visitors for over sixty years and are one of the most popular features of the cathedral, much beloved of cameramen and television producers. Thankfully this significant addition to beautifying the cathedral was undertaken at the end of the first half of the twentieth century. Had the project been delayed, with the current restrictions on even the slightest changes to the fabric of ancient cathedrals, the choir screen niches would probably still be empty.

Dr Moody and his choirboys taken in front of the screen in about 1950.

Major repairs and improvements to the organ were completed, and inauguration recitals were given in the summer of 1950 by three celebrated organists, namely Lady Susi Jeans, Dr John Dykes Bower of St Paul's Cathedral, and Sir William Harris of St George's Chapel, Windsor. On 21st June 1950 a Four Cathedral Choirs Festival was also held at Ripon, when the choirs of York, Durham, Newcastle and Ripon combined to sing choral evensong. This was a very impressive occasion; the organist was Francis Jackson of York Minster.

A new Dean, Llewelyn Hughes, was appointed in 1951. He was a kindly Welshman and a charismatic preacher, who had been chaplain to Field Marshal Montgomery during the war and later became Chaplain General to the forces. On his arrival at Ripon he realised that, in view of the average age of the chapter, the introduction of some young blood was needed.

He was a key factor in appointing the Reverend Duncan Thomson as the new succentor in 1953 and, a year later, the energetic Harry Graham, who soon became Archdeacon of Richmond. Harry Graham's fund-raising efforts and the

F Llewelyn Hughes, Dean 1951-1968.

'Repair Ripon' campaign, which he promoted almost single-handedly to finance the restoration work on the fabric, were extremely successful.

Dr Charles Moody retired due to increasing ill health in December 1953, and his successor was the 30 year old Lionel Dakers. Harry Graham, Duncan Thomson and Lionel Dakers were all young and enthusiastic, and they set about revitalising the music at Ripon Cathedral.

Chapter 9

THE NEW CHOIR SCHOOL
1954 – 1960

Duncan Thomson was born in London on Saturday 20th December 1924. He was educated at Highgate School from where he won a scholarship to Corpus Christi College, Oxford, to read classics and theology. While at Oxford he maintained his keen interest in music, and it was at a series of university lectures on the history of music given by Sir Hugh Allen that he met Stephana Wilson, who was herself reading music at Lady Margaret Hall. The couple were married at Romsey Abbey on 11th April 1950, and so commenced the extremely fruitful partnership of a gifted, energetic and devoted couple, to whom Ripon Cathedral, and particularly the choir school, owe an immeasurable debt of gratitude.

Duncan Thomson had gone to theological college in London in 1948 and it was during this time that he sang as a vicar choral in the choir of St Paul's Cathedral where he met Alfred Deller (later to become the celebrated counter-tenor) who was also in the choir, and they formed a lifelong friendship.

He was ordained deacon in Gloucester Cathedral in 1951, and then priest the following year taking up a curacy at Northleach in the Diocese of Gloucester. In April 1953 Duncan Thomson responded to two advertisements which appeared in The Church Times. One was for a succentor at Ripon Cathedral and the other for a curate in the Yorkshire Dales. Letters of application were dispatched and, whilst waiting for a response, the Thomsons decided to travel to Yorkshire to look over both places.

At Ripon Cathedral they met Canon Bartlett, who was extremely welcoming and genial and took them round the ancient building. The following day they planned to go to the Dales church where the vacant curacy had been advertised, but Canon Bartlett turned to Duncan and said, *My dear boy, you can't possibly go there; the vicar's had twelve curates in twenty years.* Later that day Canon Bartlett advised the Thomsons that he had sent a telegram to the dean, who was on holiday. The dean promptly responded, saying *Hold the Thomsons, I'll be back tomorrow.* Dean Llewelyn Hughes always referred to this as 'God's Telegram', because when the Thomsons met him and his wife, Dorothy, it instantly became clear that they were going to work well together. Stephana

Thomson specifically recalls that it was this factor, rather than the job or the music or the fine cathedral, that clinched matters.

So Duncan Thomson was appointed succentor of Ripon Cathedral. The young couple left Northleach on Tuesday 2nd June 1953, after watching the coronation of the new Queen Elizabeth II on a black and white television in a neighbour's barn. They set off in a little 1939 Vauxhall car and drove north to start their new life in Ripon. The boot and back seat were both filled with the Thomsons' possessions, including a coop containing two laying hens and a hive of bees. Driving through the Midlands, first one, then a considerable number of the bees appeared flying around inside the car, and it soon became clear that they had eaten their way through the cardboard with which the hive exit had been blocked. Stephana was very alarmed (being allergic to bee stings) but Duncan swathed her in his bee hat, veil and gloves and drove on unperturbed until he saw a notice saying 'Honey for Sale'. By great good fortune the beekeeper was at home and successfully blocked the exit to the hive with a solid piece of timber which could not easily be dislodged.

The weary travellers finally reached Ripon late that evening, and a few days later they were joined by their two children, Christina and Isabel. The family lived at 17 High St Agnesgate, on the south side of the cathedral, almost opposite the song school, and Stephana Thomson remembers the house as being rather cramped and decorated throughout with brown paint. The hens and the bees were housed at the bottom of the garden, but the neighbours were unhappy with this and new homes had to be found for them.

The precentor was John Marshall, a Scotsman, who evidently welcomed the arrival of this bright young singing succentor from the south, and was content to let him precent most of the services and deal with the music. Indeed, when John Marshall left the cathedral in 1956 to take up a post in Edinburgh, Duncan succeeded him as precentor, but this involved little change in his duties as he had already been fulfilling this role.

Charles Moody, who had been organist at Ripon for over 50 years, was by now a sick man, and his duties were being carried out by his young pupil, Paul Mace, who had been given special release from his national service at Catterick Camp in order to deputise at the cathedral. It was said that Mace sometimes played the organ in his army boots, which can have done little for an accurate pedal technique, but he discharged his responsibilities very capably.

After Oxford University and St Paul's Cathedral, Duncan Thomson felt there was room for improvement in the standard of music at Ripon. An opportunity came a year later when Charles Moody retired. His successor was Lionel Dakers who, at the age of thirty, was one of the youngest cathedral organists in England. He found a choir that was very run down, and a Dean and Chapter who did not all see the need for a professional and well-trained choir at the cathedral. The repertoire was dominated by compositions from the Victorian era, and Dakers set about purging the choir library, burning a good deal of the old music.

In the same year, 1954, the Reverend Henry (Harry) Burrans Graham was appointed a minor canon at Ripon. He was an enthusiastic outgoing character who had spent his pre-ordination years working as a financial adviser and fund-raiser for the Conservative Party. He was a great lover of church music and recognised the important part it played in worship. While not always diplomatic, he came as a breath of fresh air to the cathedral, and his 'Repair Ripon' campaign was one of the first co-ordinated and well-promoted cathedral fund raising operations in England; within three years it had raised over £150,000 for urgent renovation of the fabric.

Stone carving of the head of Archdeacon Harry Graham on the wall of the restored chapter house

And so it was that in Duncan Thomson, Harry Graham and Lionel Dakers, Ripon had acquired three like-minded energetic young men who were determined to work together to improve the music at the cathedral. When Dakers left in 1957 to go to Exeter, he was succeeded by Philip Marshall who was equally resolved to enhance the singing. Even when Duncan Thomson resigned as precentor in 1957 to become the chaplain at Aysgarth School, he maintained his close association with the cathedral and his drive to enrich its music.

Since grammar school entry had become conditional upon success in the 11 plus examination, the cathedral could no longer offer payment of fees as an incentive to aspiring choristers. In a speech to the Federation of Cathedral Old Choristers' Associations at Chester on 27th October 1951, Charles Moody first suggested that the Dean and Chapter of Ripon Cathedral should consider selling some of the valuable books which were languishing in the cathedral library, in order to finance the founding of a new residential choir school. These old books included three printed in London by William Caxton between 1478 and 1482 which formed part of a large collection of books that had been left to Ripon Cathedral by Dean Anthony Higgin on his death in 1624. They were discovered in the summer of 1820 by Dr Thomas Frogmore Dibdin, a library historian, when he was *rummaging amongst the dusty books in the Lady Loft Library*. This discovery, together with the existence of other valuable old books, was confirmed when the cathedral library was examined and catalogued by Jean Mortimer of Leeds University in 1950-1952.

Charles Moody had repeated his plea for selling the Caxtons to help set up a choir school when he wrote an article which was published in the Church Times in the summer of 1952, and so, when Duncan Thomson, Lionel Dakers and Harry Graham came together to consider ways of improving the singing at the cathedral, the solution was obvious.

Thus it was that Harry Graham, encouraged by Duncan Thomson and Philip Marshall, and with the support of Canons Bartlett and Wilkinson, persuaded the Dean and Chapter to sell some of their books in order to help establish a new choir school in Ripon. Two of the Caxtons, together with nine other books, were sold at Sotheby's on 31st May 1960. The first Caxton, a 'Vocabulary and Conversation Book in French and English' printed in 1480, fetched £23,000. The second was 'The Epitome of the Pearl of Eloquence', a popular handbook, written in Latin, on rhetoric. This was printed by Caxton in about 1482 and achieved £12,000. These, together with other old books, raised a total of £45,000 towards the setting up of the new school. The estimated total cost of this project was £65,000, and the balance was raised by the tireless and dedicated efforts of Harry Graham who used his persuasive personality to win over local landowners and businessmen.

It was envisaged that the new choir school would have approximately seventy to eighty pupils including the choristers, and provide facilities for both boarders and day boys. It would be a preparatory school and offer a sound general education, as well as specialist music tuition, both vocal and instrumental, for children up to the age of thirteen.

It so happened that, during his time at the cathedral, Duncan Thomson had taught divinity at St Olave's, a small independent school in Ripon. This had been founded by Selwyn Wilson in 1924, and occupied a large brick building off Whitcliffe Lane which had previously been part of the grandstand for the then Ripon Racecourse. By 1959 Selwyn Wilson's health was deteriorating and he was keen to retire. Accordingly, Harry Graham went to see him and established that he was amenable to selling the school in its entirety as a going concern.

The Rt Rev John Moorman, appointed Bishop of Ripon in 1959, recognised the importance of music in the liturgy and was very supportive of the choir school scheme. He himself had been a chorister at Adel Parish Church, where there is a fine woodcarving of him as a choir boy. Also in 1959, Canon Sampson came to Ripon Cathedral. He had been vicar at Leeds Parish Church, with its long-standing tradition of church music, and he likewise encouraged this undertaking.

Stephana Thomson, in an article she wrote in 1990 entitled 'Thoughts on 30 years in a Cathedral Choir School', recalled that *On All Saints Day, 1st November 1959, Canon Harry Graham, Archdeacon of Richmond, visited Aysgarth School to see Duncan and me. He confirmed that the Dean and Chapter had agreed to sell the Caxtons and to purchase St Olave's School.* Duncan Thomson was invited to return to the cathedral as precentor and to be headmaster of the new Ripon Cathedral Choir School, with Stephana undertaking the organisation of the school music, and the co-ordination of the matrons and domestic staff.

The Ripon Cathedral Choir School.

There were approximately 95 boys between the ages of 7 and 13 at St Olave's School, most of whom were boarders. The staff comprised:

Mr G. La Trobe Foster; the senior master and a great character. He taught mathematics and ran the school scout troop.

Miss 'Ma' White; an elderly lady who taught French. She had previously been a governess to various aristocratic houses in Europe.

Mr and Mrs Mans; both taught various subjects. It was said of them that *he was as charming as she was acerbic*.

Wilfred Parnaby; taught gymnastics and sports, which comprised cricket, football and boxing.

Mr Peter Stevenson; an affable bachelor housemaster who taught general subjects and games.

Miss Beecroft; who taught the younger boys.

In addition to the teaching staff, there was an elderly matron called Miss Harmer, who was in her seventies and somewhat lame. She had a young girl as an assistant. There was a daily housekeeper, Mrs Trotter, a clergy widow from the Dales. She was much liked by both staff and boys. Also two wonderful cooks, Madge Harrison and Mrs Benson, who were renowned for their Yorkshire puddings and apple pies. Three other domestic staff came from a home in Ripon for women with learning difficulties.

Duncan and Stephana Thomson and their five children moved into the premises in August 1960, and the new Ripon Cathedral Choir School opened its doors in early September of that year. Most of the pupils and staff of St Olave's were retained and initially things continued much as before.

It cannot be overstressed that the founding of a cathedral choir school at Ripon, at a time when some cathedrals were struggling with their choir schools, and others were being closed, was a major achievement and a tribute to all those concerned.

Thanks to Harry Graham and Duncan Thomson, several people were persuaded to endow choral scholarships, which paid for half of the choristers' school fees and musical education, and these were named after their benefactors. Although Dean Hughes was not initially enthusiastic, once persuaded to proceed with the new choir school, he gave it his full support, and thus there was also a 'Dean's Chorister'.

By 1967, there was a considerable number of scholarships:

Sir Frederick Ackroyd
Coulthirst
Charles Crabtree
Adeline Crabtree
Mary Crabtree
The Dean's Scholarship
Daphne Durham
Edgecombe
Hamilton-Brown
Hargreaves
Lady Doris Martin
Pamela Murphy
Vera Penrose-May
Sir John Priestman – two Scholarships
Canon R. J. Wood
Governors' Scholarships
Sir George Martin, Major Roger Ingham and Sir Richard and Lady Graham also provided financial support for scholarships.

The founding governors of the new cathedral choir school were:
Rev Canon W. E. Wilkinson, Chairman
R. W. Thompson, Esq. JP, MA, Vice Chairman, Headmaster of Aysgarth School
Miss Joan Cullingworth, Headmistress of the Girls' High School, Ripon
J. I. T. Houghton, Esq., Manager of the Midland Bank, Ripon
Mrs F. R. Ingham (Edna, wife of Major Roger Ingham of Bellwood Hall)
S. M. Kirkman, Esq. FCA.
Lady Doris Martin
Dr John Shone, MRCS, LMSSA.

The first voice trials were undertaken by Philip Marshall and Duncan Thomson in March 1961. They agreed that they were looking for bright intelligent boys with a good ear and musical potential. The successful candidates became choristers at the cathedral and boarder pupils at the choir school. All the boys of the existing cathedral choir were invited to continue singing, and four agreed to do so, Stephen Orton, David Elsey, and brothers John and Colin Yarker. Roger Hemingway, one of the new intake of choristers, recalls that *as a very inexperienced novice, I and my fellow new choristers looked up to the four original old hands, who were very kind and helpful to we new boys.* Stephen Orton is now an internationally renowned cellist.

Life at the new choir school settled into a routine and the daily timetable was:

6.45 am Wake-up call.

7.00 am Instrumental practice.

7.50 am Breakfast cooked by Stephana Thomson for the whole school, assisted by two volunteer boys who fetched and carried the food on a large wheeled trolley.

8.20 am Morning choir practice for the choristers. Non-choristers were free to play or catch up with prep.

9.00 am Prayers in the gym. Duncan Thomson took a short assembly service every day except Sunday. This consisted of a hymn, a reading by a boy, and prayers, followed by a short religious or topical talk. After this came the announcements, when the practical arrangements for the day were explained. A small musical ensemble, or as it later became the orchestra, always played a short piece after assembly on Wednesdays, and then stayed on for the first period to practise.

9.20 am-1 pm Lessons, which were in one hour slots, with a short mid-morning break for juice and a bun or biscuit.

1.10 pm A good solid lunch was served – meat and vegetables (fish on Fridays) and a pudding.

1.45 pm In the early years of the school, every boy had to have a rest and reading time on his bed until 2.05 pm, but eventually this time became used for other activities.

2.05 pm Games; football (soccer or rugby) in the autumn and winter terms, cricket in the summer term.

3.50 pm Low tea; this comprised tea or fruit juice and a home made cake or buttered scone.

4.00 pm Choir practice at the cathedral. Day boys went home.

5.00 pm Choral Evensong; non-chorister boarders had other activities such as art, class singing, music lessons, instrumental practice, or extra prep.

6.15 pm High tea; a cooked meal with brown bread and jam and occasionally cake.

6.45 pm   The youngest prepared for bed, and lights out was at 7.30 pm.

The older boys had one or two preps. In the later years there might be some television for a treat.

9.00 pm   All supposedly in bed and silent with lights out.

Stephana Thomson comments *The above may sound somewhat austere, but it must be remembered that this was 1961. Life's expectations were very different from those today. Old choristers and other pupils interviewed all speak well of their days at the choir school and have largely happy memories. They state that with care, imagination and a bit of cunning, they had a great deal of fun.*

Old choristers particularly recall that Wednesdays were a 'plain day' (i.e. evensong was said not sung) so matches were played in the afternoon when parents came, and afterwards special low tea was provided for all, including the visitors. Also on Sundays there was a much appreciated opportunity for a later start to the day; that is until 1971 when Dean Edwin Le Grice introduced Choral Eucharist.

Duncan Thomson.

85

In his speech day address to the school in July 1961 Duncan Thomson thanked all the staff by name:

Full-Time Teachers	Part-Time Teachers
Mr La Trobe Foster	Dr Marshall, singing
Mr and Mrs Mans	Miss Hyde
Miss White	Mr Jackson
Mr Sherbourne	Mr Lawrence Gibbon
Mr Tarrant	Mr John Langdon
Miss Beecroft	Mr Wilfred Parnaby
Miss Hewitt	

Duncan Thomson's handwritten notes for this address then contain the following words:

Finally, I wish to mention my wife. How she has coped this year without going off her head, I do not know. She was born in a Winchester College House and now she has come back to that sort of life. Stephana has put in a tremendous amount of hard work in the background and if anything has been achieved in this first year, much of the credit is hers.

Duncan Thomson strengthened the choir school establishment with new energetic young staff. 1963 saw the arrival of Robin Davidson, who had been a chorister at Truro Cathedral, as the resident classics master (English and Latin), and he was also appointed cantoris alto lay clerk in the cathedral choir. A few months later Alan Dance, from London, was appointed assistant organist at the cathedral and a full-time teacher (history and games) and resident housemaster at the choir school. In 1966 the headmaster further added to his young team by engaging Simon Deller (the son of Alfred Deller) and his wife Mollie. Simon taught the older boys and was appointed cantoris bass lay clerk in the cathedral choir, and Mollie taught the reception and junior classes. It was these young people who, with the Thomsons, became the dynamic core of the new choir school. They worked hard together but also enjoyed each other's company. Every Sunday evening Stephana would cook a traditional roast dinner, and they would all meet in the headmaster's lounge for sherry before repairing to the dining room. After the meal they discussed the forthcoming events at the school, and whiled away the remainder of the evening singing madrigals.

The subjects taught in 1961 were those that had been inherited from St Olave's, and included English, history, Latin, mathematics (arithmetic, algebra and geometry), French, scripture and geography. General science lessons started in 1964, and these were taken by Mr La Trobe Foster (Fozzy as he was known by the boys). They later developed into the three separate subjects of physics, chemistry and biology.

There were regular gymnastics sessions twice a week and games periods daily for every pupil. Games included football and cricket, but boxing did not survive. Music tuition comprised instruction in piano, violin, cello, flute, clarinet, French horn, trumpet, and later double bass, oboe, bassoon and trombone. Subsequently this was extended to include harp, guitar, percussion and saxophone. A highly professional band of part-time peripatetic music staff came to the school, and choristers were expected to learn the piano and a second instrument. Non-choristers were likewise encouraged to take music lessons, several of them also learning two instruments.

Choir school staff and pupils in 1964.

Over the 48 years since its foundation in 1960, many have served on the staff of the cathedral choir school. With the help of numerous people, particularly Stephana Thomson, Richard Moore and Rachael Evans, the writers have attempted to compile a list of the names of the longer-serving members of staff and this appears in the appendix.

The Choir, 1937.

Choir boys with tape recorder, circa 1955.

The Choir, July 1957.

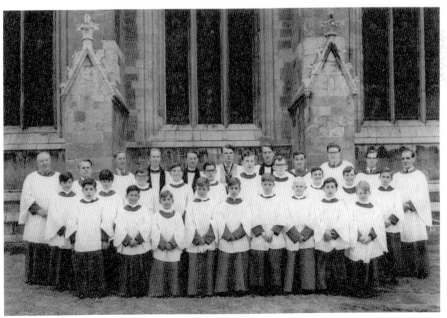

The Choir, 1964.

The Choir, circa 1968.

The Choir, 1972.

The Choir, 1974.

The Choir, July 1981.

The Choir, May 1989.

The Choir, 2006.

Chapter 10

RENAISSANCE AT RIPON
1961 – 2008

The establishment of the new choir school and its associated choral scholarships in 1960 undoubtedly started a renaissance at Ripon, and brought numerous benefits.

In 1959, before the new choir school was up and running, the precentor and organist decided that the choir should have a rehearsal room within the cathedral. Here they could also robe before processing into services, and thus avoid having to walk up to the south transept porch from the old song school in all weathers.

The site chosen was in the Norman crypt, known as the undercroft, situated beneath the chapter house. For many centuries this had been used as a charnel-house and was known by choristers of Crow and Moody's eras as 'the bone house'. It was a spooky place although most of the old bones had been cleared and re-interred in the graveyard in 1865.

The undercroft was in two sections, east and west, and initially contained both bones and some old stone tomb vaults. After the bones had been removed from the east section it became a mortuary chapel and store room, and later, in 1984-1985, was refurbished as the Chapel of the Resurrection. Here are the memorial plaques to Harry Graham and Duncan Thomson, both prominent in establishing the new choir school. It was the west section, still containing the old tomb vaults and memorial plaques, that was earmarked for the new choir practice room, also incorporating vestry facilities and the music library. This transformation was a considerable task, and took nearly two years to complete.

First, the old vaults had to be cleared, and the story is recounted by two of the cathedral stone masons at that time, Jack Yarker and Dave McKay. Evidently, the lead coffins were still largely intact, but the old timber ones had disintegrated. A former chorister, Frank Lowley, who had become an undertaker, kindly supplied eight new coffins. Two large pits were excavated in the graveyard to the south-east of the cathedral where all the coffins were to be re-interred. Regulations required that this should take place during the hours of darkness, so one night in the early autumn of 1961 all six of the stone masons spent several hours lifting the coffins out of the undercroft and reburying them in the churchyard. This was done by the light of hurricane lamps and when, by the early hours of the morning, all the coffins were in place the clergy, clad in their cassocks and white surplices, looking ghostly in the lamp light, stood round the pits to perform the reburial service. When this was finished, the masons filled in the grave pits and tidied up.

At the time that the reburial service was taking place, however, a workman on night duty happened to be cycling past the cathedral. When he saw lights in the churchyard and white clad apparitions standing around the open grave, he promptly fell off his bicycle and ran away terrified. After regaining his composure he recovered his bicycle and pedalled furiously to Ripon Police Station where he informed the officer on duty that *grave robbers are at work in the churchyard at the east end of the cathedral.* Fortunately the police knew of the planned nocturnal operations and were able to reassure the trembling fellow that all was well.

Once the vaults had been cleared, it was necessary to reinforce the undercroft foundations, especially at the bases of the stone pillars. Cupboards and shelves were then installed, and the new choir vestry and practice room was first used

The nave choir stalls, circa 1885.

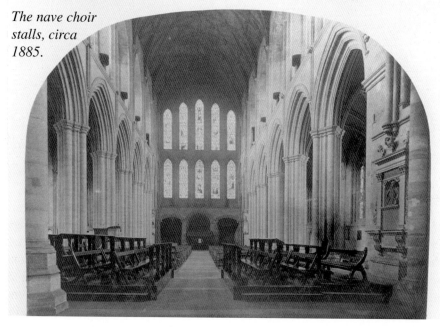

in late 1962. The music desks of the pre-1899 nave choir stalls (see photo opposite page) had been kept in store and were installed in the new choir practice room.

The organ was partly rebuilt to the design of the organist, Philip Marshall, in 1963 at a cost of £12,000, when significant additions and changes to the instrument were made (Ref. Chapter 13).

The choir's repertoire was gradually being expanded, including the introduction of music from the Tudor period. The story is told that, about this time, during an unaccompanied motet, the cantoris boys made an error causing confusion amongst the other voices. As a result, the whole piece almost ground to a halt, but due to a cadence a few bars later and the courageous conducting of Philip Marshall, the voices were brought back into line and the anthem concluded with a splendid monophonic chord sung with a confidence born of relief. At this point the senior cantoris lay clerk turned to the precentor, Duncan Thomson, and said *I wonder what God thought about that.* Duncan calmly retorted, *O don't worry about it, God's not here today – the dean's standing in for him.*

In 1966 Dr Philip Marshall took up his new appointment at Lincoln Cathedral, and Ronald Perrin, who had previously been assistant to Francis Jackson at York Minster, succeeded him.

On the Sunday before Christmas 1969, Ronald Perrin introduced 'A Ceremony of Carols' by Benjamin Britten. The choristers, holding lighted candles, processed into the darkened nave through the west door singing the plainsong *Hodie Christus natus est.* The remaining carols were also sung by candlelight, with harp accompaniment, as Britten intended. Though he did not realise it at the time, Ronald Perrin was establishing another tradition at Ripon Cathedral, and this event has taken place every year since. It is appropriate to add that in 2006 the boys and the girls sang the 'Ceremony' together for the first time, under the direction of Andrew Bryden.

The Nineteen Seventies

In autumn 1971 Dean Edwin Le Grice introduced Choral Eucharist on one Sunday every month, and the times of services were changed to accommodate this. The new choral communion was sung at 9.15 am followed by matins at 11.00 am. Thus choristers and lay clerks attended a full choir practice at 8.30 am, and on choral communion Sundays sang three services. In 1976 the Choral Eucharist became a weekly event, sung at 9.30 am with matins (usually without a sermon) at 11.30 am.

The nave altar had been placed in the crossing immediately beneath the central tower since the early 1950s, but in about 1972 it was moved to a position just west of the nave choir stalls. These were later angled towards the congregation to improve the audibility of the choir in the nave.

Increasing problems with the cathedral heating led Dean Le Grice to try to retain heat in the choir by erecting a large curtain in the open space beneath the arch between the nave and the choir. ICI Fibres of Harrogate donated the large amount of material required and the curtain was installed in early 1975, being hung from the top of the arch down to and around the organ case and choir screen (See illustration on following page). It was regarded by many as an intrusion which ruined the prospect from the nave looking east. Letters were written to the press, and Sir John Betjeman became involved. However its appalling appearance was not the only problem. The organ, as part of its normal function, sucks in air to operate the bellows and hence the pipes; when the full organ was being played the large volumes of air released caused the curtain to billow out towards the nave. Hence the curtain became known by many as the 'Sacred Spinnaker'. It was not a success, however, and was taken down in about 1978.

A long-serving chorister and lay clerk at Ripon Cathedral retired in 1977. Charles Bielby (known as Charlie) joined the choir as a boy in 1926, and when his voice broke he developed into a fine tenor and became a lay clerk. He was a good musician, and Philip Marshall said that *Charlie's singing of the solo part in 'This is the record of John' by Orlando Gibbons brought tears to my eyes*. Charlie was a kindly man and very helpful to young choirboys and lay clerks alike. By the time he retired (spending more time on his much loved hobby of fishing) he had been in the cathedral choir for over 50 years and served under four organists.

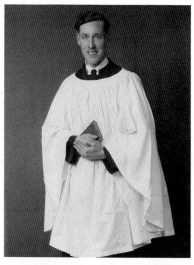

Charles Bielby circa 1946.

The governors of the cathedral choir school faced increasing pressure from many parents that their daughters, as well as their sons, should become

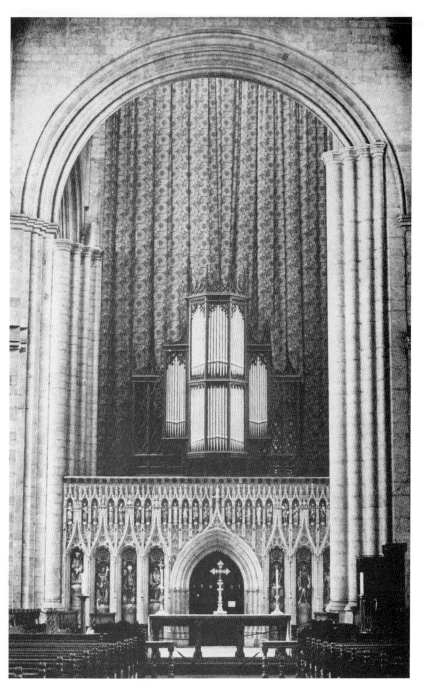

The 'Sacred Spinnaker'.

97

pupils, and it was decided in the spring of 1978 that the school would be co-educational. This involved providing extra facilities and it was some months before the girl pupils were able to be admitted. Seven years later in 1985, the headmaster, Robert Horton, and the governors decided to accommodate girl boarders at the school and additional dormitories were provided.

On Monday 12th March 1979 Duncan Thomson (precentor and headmaster) was interviewed by the music historian, Peter Phillips, on the subject of Ripon Cathedral and its choir school. The 1 hr 27 mins recording of this interview is held by The British Library in their National Sound Archives and provides a fascinating insight into the music policy at Ripon Cathedral and the running of the school at that time. It was during this interview that Duncan Thomson mentioned that *We are blest with three residentiary canons at Ripon who could almost sing a verse anthem between them.* An extract of the interview formed part of a lengthy article, entitled 'The Golden Age Regained' by Peter Phillips, which appeared in the January 1980 issue of 'Early Music'.

The Nineteen Eighties

At the start of this decade, Duncan Thomson had been precentor of Ripon Cathedral and headmaster of the choir school for nearly twenty years and it is appropriate to say a little more about this remarkable man and his equally remarkable wife. He was a well educated, scholarly, yet very pragmatic person, steeped in a love of church and classical music and imbued with a pleasant personality and a great sense of humour, underpinned with common sense. He ran the newly established Ripon Cathedral Choir School on the lines of a private prep school of the day, with no-nonsense discipline and a commitment to honesty, hard work and play, all infused with politeness and consideration for others.

Duncan and Stephana Thomson operated as a team and ran the choir school with a firm but kind and caring attitude. They knew the boys' names, traits, and personalities and cultivated good relations with the parents.

Duncan was of the old school and ran his school accordingly, but this was not the whole story. Whilst he did not take kindly to what he termed *newfangled educational ideas*, he was in many ways ahead of his time. One example of this occurred in the spring of 1968. The school magazine of that year reported that, in an effort to introduce the boys to the principles of commerce, the headmaster had set up 'The Redbank Brewing Company' (Redbank was an area near to the choir school). There was a chairman, plus two directors, and a company secretary by the name of The Reverend D. Thomson. The registered office of the company was the Headmaster's Study. The issued capital was 20 ordinary shares of one shilling; one share was held by each member of form VI, the remainder by the headmaster. A formal prospectus was issued which read as follows:

Each new member of Form VI shall have the right to purchase one share. The aim of the company is to produce good quality ginger beer, there being no shortage of raw materials which are mainly sugar and ginger. The company's trading position is potentially good. There is a constant demand for the company's product from the pupils of the cathedral choir school, Ripon, at two shillings a gallon. Vintage brews may well fetch a higher price. A final dividend is paid in July; an interim dividend may be paid at the end of each term. The company's brewery is situated in the school science laboratory.

In July 1968 the headmaster issued an annual report which was printed in the magazine:

Annual Report to Shareholders

The Company has operated in very favourable circumstances. The ginger beer plant was loaned to the Company free of charge and the raw materials have been forthcoming with no costs involved.

The Company produced nine gallons of drinkable ginger beer which was sold to the choir school for two shillings a gallon.

There are thus no charges to be set against the trading profit of eighteen shillings.

Consequently a final dividend of nine pence will be paid on each ordinary share, leaving three shillings for the reserve account.

The Company looks forward to a similar profitable year in 1968-1969.

Duncan Thomson,
Company Secretary.

In the period that Duncan Thomson was headmaster he certainly put the choir school on the map, as the list of scholarships demonstrates (Ref. Appendix). Because he was the choir school headmaster and also the cathedral precentor, he was able to co-ordinate and balance, as perhaps never before or since, the educational demands of the school and the choral responsibilities at the cathedral. Duncan and Stephana Thomson gathered around them a team of able and committed staff, many of whom stayed at the school for long periods (Ref. Appendix), and they ran and developed the choir school for twenty-three years.

Towards the end of 1982, however, Duncan became ill. His health deteriorated and he died on Tuesday 12th April 1983, which marked the end of a remarkable era.

Robert Horton was born at Watford in February 1952 and became a choral scholar at Canterbury Cathedral. He was a housemaster at the Westminster Abbey Choir School, then at Kings College School, Cambridge and later Westminster Under School, London, where he taught maths and science. He was appointed headmaster at Ripon Cathedral Choir School in September 1983 and came with his wife Ann and their two children. Ann taught languages and was also the school matron, co-ordinating the domestic staff. Robert Horton, known as Bob, took up his duties with commitment and vision, showing a deep interest in all aspects of school life. He and Ann were well-liked by both staff and pupils, and they were particularly kind to Stephana Thomson, ensuring that she continued to be involved with the school as a cello and piano teacher. The choir school magazine of 1984 refers to changes whereby the headmaster reduced the timetable of lessons by one hour, and doubled the time that pupils had to do their prep.

Bob Horton was a capable baritone with a good knowledge of the English cathedral music repertoire. Consequently, because of the *ad hoc* arrangements for fielding a full team of lay clerks, he often found himself able to keep a close eye on choristers' behaviour during services, standing right behind them in the men's stalls.

On Thursday 4th April 1985 Her Majesty the Queen and Prince Philip visited Ripon Cathedral for the Royal Maundy Service. The Ripon choir and clergy were resplendent in new cassocks of a slightly different shade of red to those previously worn. This was due to the fact that when a member of the Queen's staff had visited Ripon to make arrangements for this event, it was discovered that the cassocks (changed from blue to red back in 1909) were in fact Royal Scarlet. This colour can only be worn by the clergy and choirs of Royal Foundations, such as the Chapel Royal and Westminster Abbey. Thus the Queen not only issued money to deserving pensioners but also fresh robes to the deserving choristers, who, thanks to Her Majesty's generosity and appreciation of their singing, also received Maundy money.

The royal theme continued the following year when, on Sunday 1st June, a service in the cathedral marked the 1,100th anniversary of the supposed granting of the first Royal Charter to Ripon in 886 by King Alfred. This was attended by Her Majesty the Queen Mother, and a new anthem, 'Let God be Gracious', was composed for the occasion by the organist Ronald Perrin. The headmaster of the choir school, Robert Horton (who understood the value of children performing in public) commissioned the composer Alan Ridout to write an opera for children, based on a libretto by Alan Wicks, dealing with the rising of the northern earls in 1569, which was entitled 'The White Doe'. A cast of over 80 boys and girls from the school took part in the world première performed in the cathedral on Wednesday 3rd December 1986. The opera was produced by a senior member of the choir school staff, Moira Smith. The musical director was Robert Marsh, head of music at the school and assistant organist of the cathedral. With Ronald Perrin, the cathedral organist, on the Makin electronic organ, the solo harp was played by David Watkins (Principal, London Philharmonic Orchestra). The orchestra, including members of the English Northern Philharmonia, with Stephana Thomson, cello, Christine Butterworth, flute, and Robert Thompson, percussion, was led by David Greed.

The White Doe was later recorded and issued by the Abbey Recording Co. The front sleeve of the LP has a photograph of the cast taken outside Markenfield Hall, the eleventh century moated manor house near Ripon, the home of Thomas Markenfield, who took part in the northern uprising in 1569.

In May 1987, the choir school headmaster, Robert Horton, unexpectedly resigned. The senior resident housemaster, Edward Childs, stepped into the breach and played an invaluable role until the dean and governors were able to make arrangements for Ian McDougall, a recently retired housemaster from Sedbergh School, to take over for the interregnum.

The North Eastern Cathedral Choirs' Festival, first held in 1881, became an annual event later known as the Northern Three Choirs' Festival. Initially a joint service of evensong was sung at York, Ripon and Durham on a rotating basis. During the 1980s, however, the festivals expanded to include an organ recital and concert, and when held at Ripon in 1987, it had grown into a three-day event. There was an organ recital on the evening of Thursday 23 July, and the following day the choirs sang a festival evensong. On Saturday, Choral

Eucharist was sung at 11.30 am to Louis Vierne's double organ mass, and a concert of choral and organ music was held in the evening. Similar festivals took place until 1995, after which they gradually reduced in scale and reverted to the three choirs coming together each year for a joint evensong.

On Mothering Sunday 1987 another musical tradition at Ripon Cathedral was born; the singing of Mendelssohn's anthem 'Hear my Prayer', with its popular treble solo (Ref. Chapter 14).

At Christmas 1987 a television spectacular 'Rejoice' took place at Ripon Cathedral, produced by Yorkshire Television. The cathedral choir was joined by the Huddersfield Choral Society and the Black Dyke Mills Band. Ronald Perrin conducted and Simon Lindley from Leeds Parish Church played the Makin organ. The guest celebrities were Dame Janet Baker, Brian Kay, and Robert Hardy (see illustration below).

Richard Moore came as the new headmaster of the choir school in January 1988. Born at Forest Hill, Lewisham, in 1937, and educated at local schools, he won a scholarship to Oxford to read English. He was a master, and later headmaster, at Selwyn House boys' boarding school, Broadstairs, before moving to be joint headmaster at Scaitcliffe School, Englefield Green in 1977.

Richard, with his wife Sheila and their children, quickly settled in at Ripon making the school very much their home. Sheila, a qualified nurse, took over matron duties and co-ordinated the domestic staff.

Soon after his arrival Richard Moore recognised the need for pre-prep facilities, which were set up a year later. He changed the choristers' voice trials venue from the formal setting of the cathedral (with anxious parents sitting on the cold stone ledge around the chapter house whilst their sons were auditioned in the undercroft) to the more welcoming choir school. While the boys were being auditioned, parents were shown around the school and entertained by the headmaster and his wife to tea and biscuits. It was also Richard Moore who encouraged and organised the first choir tours abroad (to Normandy in 1990, and to northern France and Luxembourg in April 1994). Richard Moore also played a major part in the foundation of the Ripon Cathedral Girls' Choir (Ref. Chapter 11).

The Nineteen Nineties

In 1990 the old carved oak stalls in the nave (See illustration page 106), which had been there for ninety-one years, were replaced with new lightweight mobile choir stalls, with matching nave altar. Designed and constructed by Illingworth & Co. of Bristol, they are of light oak and built on platforms incorporating castors. Money was raised by a cathedral appeal and a generous donation from the Charles and Elsie Sykes Memorial Trust. The new stalls can be moved to different locations in the nave, providing a flexible layout for the increasing number of events. The old stalls were sold to specialist dealers in ecclesiastical furnishings, also in Bristol, but it has not been possible to trace the identity or location of the church to which they went.

In July 1990 Ripon hosted the Federation of Cathedral Old Choristers' Associations Annual Festival for the fourth time. This was attended by a large number of delegates from the United Kingdom and abroad, who were accommodated at the Ripon College. The festival banquet was also held there, with Dean Christopher Campling and Ronald Perrin as the main speakers.

By late 1994 Ronald Perrin had been organist at Ripon Cathedral for 28 years, but his health was deteriorating, and problems were arising. He resigned in 1994, when Dean Campling bestowed on him the title of 'Organist Titulaire'. The new organist, Kerry Beaumont, was no stranger to Ripon as he had been a chorister at the cathedral from 1965 – 1970. No one was more pleased about his appointment than Ronald Perrin, who had been the choirmaster when young

Beaumont was a chorister, and had given this gifted boy his first organ lessons. Appropriately, on the morning of Sunday 29th October 1995 Kerry Beaumont conducted the first performance of Ronald Perrin's *Missa Sancti Petri* in the cathedral with the composer present.

The most important occurrence of the late 1990s was the founding of the girls' choir, which proved to be such a major contribution to the renaissance at Ripon that it deserves a chapter of its own (Ref. Chapter 11).

On Friday 12th November 1999 a recital was given to an invited audience in the cathedral library by Kerry Beaumont to inaugurate the virginals, presented to the cathedral by a former lay clerk. This instrument was a copy of an Italian virginals of the seventeenth century and had been made by Morley of London in 1956. The donor had arranged for Kerry Beaumont to visit Morley's workshops where the instrument had been upgraded with new jacks and plectra and re-voiced in accordance with his requirements. The evening was a great success except that, during a particularly demanding piece by John Bull which required a robust keyboard technique, Kerry broke off the central C sharp of the keyboard and had to conclude the piece without it, a remarkable achievement. During the interval, Kerry produced a tube of superglue that enabled the music of the second half to be performed without difficult contortions. The virginals has since been used at small chamber concerts of baroque music, as a continuo with small orchestral groups and in oratorios performed in the cathedral.

The Second Millennium

A new mobile console for the organ, enabling the instrument to be played from any position in the nave, was given to the cathedral by a benefactor in the year 2000. It was built by Harrison & Harrison of Durham in the summer of that year and finally installed, commissioned and played for the first time at the Service of Nine Lessons and Carols on Christmas Eve (Ref. Chapter 13).

At the end of the summer term 2000 Richard Moore, who had been headmaster of the choir school for nearly 18 years, decided to retire. Several farewell events took place celebrating all that Richard and Sheila had achieved for the school. They retired to a cottage in Exelby, near Bedale.

During the ensuing interregnum Canon Robert Western, previously at Sedbergh School, was appointed acting headmaster, and held the fort until Richard Pepys arrived in September 2001. Richard, born in 1951 at Southsea in Hampshire and educated at Huishe Episcopi School and Westminster College, North Hinksley, had obtained a degree in education. He had taught science, chemistry and IT at several schools and had been a housemaster at Highfield School, Liphook before coming to Ripon.

Richard Pepys and his wife Jane, who was responsible for the matrons and domestic staff, quickly settled at the school. With his friendly informal manner Richard was always approachable, and while he did not make drastic changes, he dispensed with old-fashioned form orders (often regarded as a league table by parents) and reintroduced rugby, which had lapsed.

Richard Pepys, throughout his time as headmaster, showed a keen sense of the *opus dei* and the vital part played by the choristers. He regularly attended services, particularly midweek evensongs, sometimes in the depths of winter when only two or three others made up the congregation. His presence and unstinting support of the choristers was important and much appreciated.

In June 2004 Ripon Cathedral lost one of its most faithful servants. No account of the history of music at Ripon Cathedral during the second half of the twentieth century would be complete without a tribute to Kelvin Gott. He was born in Ripon in 1939, joining the cathedral choir as a boy in 1946 when Dr Moody was organist. A photograph of Moody and his choirboys, taken in front of the choir screen in about 1950, shows Kelvin, the middle boy in the back row.

In addition to his musical talents, Kelvin showed artistic aptitude. He took after his father Jim, a well-known Ripon postman famed for his superb drawings of the interior of Ripon Cathedral (see illustration following page). At the age of eighteen, Kelvin won a scholarship to the Slade School of Art in London, and during his time there he became a deputy vicar choral in St Paul's Cathedral choir.

Kelvin sang in Ripon Cathedral choir as a lay clerk for many years. He had the facility of being able to sing either alto or bass with equal accuracy and musicality, and was regarded by the organists as a major asset. On numerous occasions when a lay clerk was unable to attend a service, Kelvin helped out. He greatly admired Dr Marshall, with whom he developed a lasting friendship which continued long after the latter's move to Lincoln Cathedral.

Kelvin, an accomplished string player (particularly of the cello and double bass), performed with the Harrogate Chamber Orchestra and the Pro Musica

'In the Nave', pencil drawing by Jim Gott.

Orchestra (see illustration). He also appeared at concerts in the cathedral with the St Cecilia Orchestra under the baton of Xenophon Kelsey.

Kelvin was a teacher, and later deputy headmaster, at Breckenbrough Special School for Intelligent but Maladjusted Boys. He also assisted and taught intermittently at the choir school where he was responsible for coaching the string quartets, which varied in ability according to the resources available. A paragraph in the 1994-1995 choir school magazine stated *We hope that Mr Gott will soon be coaching more quartets, but at present there is no viola player sufficiently experienced to play chamber music.* Kelvin

Kelvin Gott, 1939 – 2004.

was also a Magistrate on the Ripon Bench, and when he retired, became a guide, and later the archivist, at Ripley Castle.

Kelvin Gott died in June 2004 after a total of 58 years in the choir. A service of thanksgiving for his remarkable life and major contribution to the music at Ripon took place on Sunday 26th September. The cathedral was filled with many of his wide range of friends, and the service concluded with one of his favourite anthems, 'The Spirit of the Lord', by Edward Elgar.

Richard Pepys resigned as headmaster in November 2007, and Patricia Burton was appointed acting head teacher. Born in Kirkby Hill, Richmond, Yorkshire in 1949 and educated at Casterton School and Fulneck, she took her degree at Durham College.

On Sunday 30th December 2007 the evening service held in the north transept with hymns and carols was accompanied on the piano by Joy Calvert, who had been a pupil of Dr Moody. Every year since 1982, when the Christmas services are over and the choir has gone on holiday, the hymns have been accompanied by Joy. The dean presented her with a beautiful glass bowl in appreciation of her dedicated service.

The Ripon Cathedral choir was honoured on 13th May 2008 to be invited to join St Paul's Cathedral choir for the annual service of the 'Festival of the Sons of the Clergy', first held in old St Paul's in 1655.

Simon and Mollie Deller started their married life together in 1966 teaching at Ripon Cathedral Choir School under the headmaster Duncan Thomson (Ref. Chapter 9). In 1969 they took up appointments in the south, and Simon later became the headmaster of the Guildford Cathedral Choir School. When he retired in 1998, he and Mollie returned to North Yorkshire and purchased a cottage in Kirkby Malzeard. Within a short time of their arrival, Simon again became a bass lay clerk in the cathedral choir where his fine voice and musical expertise greatly enhanced the singing. He served in the Ripon choir for ten years, becoming the senior lay clerk and, in 2004, lay succentor. He retired in July 2008 and in recognition of his services to Ripon Cathedral, Dean Keith Jukes made him an honorary minor canon.

Save for the interruptions caused by the Reformation and Dissolution, the Civil War and Commonwealth, the eighteenth century indifference and the two world wars, there had been a precentor at Ripon since the year 1230 (Ref. list of names on pages 279-281). In 1999 the post became vacant, but no appointment was made for nearly ten years. Happily, however, on Sunday 18th May 2008, the Rev Paul Greenwell was installed as canon residentiary and precentor, being a full member of the chapter.

The Ripon Music Custodians, instituted in January 2006, and are now well established and growing in numbers, currently providing over £25,000 each year for the Music Foundation.

The year 2009 marks the 1,300th anniversary of the death of St Wilfrid, and numerous special events are planned. This year will also see major maintenance work on the organ.

Chapter 11

THE GIRLS' CHOIR

Although the Ripon Cathedral Choir School was only for boys, the daughters of the first headmaster, Duncan Thomson, were for a time educated at the school, as were those of a number of clergymen and some of the choir school teachers. Moreover, from the setting up of the pre-prep in the mid seventies, parents wanted both their sons and daughters to attend. Girls were subsequently admitted to the pre-prep, and pressure then grew for the school to accept older girls.

In 1978 the Dean and Chapter and governors decided that the choir school should become co-educational, and from 1979 onwards girls were admitted. Their numbers quickly increased, and they began to make a significant contribution to school life, both academically and musically. The headmaster, Richard Moore, and his staff recognised the girls' keen interest in singing, and they began to participate in school choirs. Several girls started to take singing lessons, and the annual school concerts subsequently included girl soloists. Richard Moore felt that a further outlet for the girls' singing talents was needed, and when Kerry Beaumont arrived as organist in October 1994, it provided a perfect opportunity. Kerry had gained considerable experience of training girls' choirs during his time in Canada and the United States, and he was eager to establish such a choir at Ripon Cathedral, as were the Dean and Chapter. An item in the choir school magazine of 1994-1995 summed up the position.

Before Dean Campling retired, he and the chapter had agreed upon the desirability of a girls' choir at the cathedral, and Kerry Beaumont, the newly appointed organist, was enthusiastic and accepted that it would be his musicianship and toil that would bring a girls' choir into being.

Thus Kerry Beaumont, Richard Moore and the Dean and Chapter met to discuss how girls might become choristers at Ripon Cathedral. The first challenge was that of funding; all were aware of the potentially huge cost of such a venture, and the whole enterprise was only feasible if it was not mandatory for the girls to be educated at the choir school. This would relieve the chapter of finding many thousands of pounds annually to fund scholarships, and also give a greater number of girls the opportunity to sing in the choir; several girls wanted to join, but did not want to move from their existing schools. However, Kerry Beaumont was particularly keen to include girls from the choir school who wished to become choristers, so Richard Moore suggested that the Dean and Chapter could grant such girls a 20 per cent scholarship. This was welcomed as an excellent idea; it helped with the recruitment of new pupils to the school, and provided an additional incentive for girls already there to audition for the choir.

Kerry had reservations about the vocal stamina of girls aged eight to thirteen, and felt that if girls from a broader age range were allowed to sing, it would establish a stronger soprano line. So it was decided that girls would be admitted from age eight and would leave at the end of the academic year in which they turned fifteen, thus allowing them to finish before experiencing the pressures of GCSE .

The number of girl chorister places was set at twenty-two. Kerry wanted to have a few more girls than boys. Whereas boys' voices tended to be at their best just before they changed at around twelve and thirteen, girls voices peaked a little later at fourteen and upwards. Also with parents transporting the majority of girls to and from the cathedral, there would be unavoidable absences. Kerry commented *Twenty-two was probably a compromise between my wanting more and the chapter wanting less, but it turned out to be just the right number, as the succeeding years proved. The twenty-two girls who entered the choir in 1996 as founding members proved in little over a year that they could fill the cathedral's reverberant cavity with a rich soprano line to complement the six full time lay clerks.*

The complex question of how to absorb a second choir into an existing cathedral choral foundation took time to consider, bearing in mind that one of the strengths of the existing choir of men and boys was the frequency with which they all sang together. Should the girls be given equal parity with the boys and be responsible for singing half of the services, or should the boys sing most of the time with the girls singing less frequently? The organist expressed fears that the boys would lose their edge and their familiarity with the repertoire, particularly the singing of the psalms, if the number of services they sang was significantly curtailed. The headmaster, however, pointed out the benefits of reducing the boys' workload, and referred to various guidelines relating to children's hours of work. The existing schedule of eight sung services weekly put a considerable restriction on the boys' free time as well as their *exeat* weekends. Indeed, unease at the demands being made on the boy choristers had been expressed at a recent school inspection. The final consideration was that the girls' parents would bear the brunt of transporting them to and from the cathedral; it was important that this was not too onerous a responsibility. So it was decided that the girls would sing one or two services each week with rehearsals on Wednesday and Saturday evenings.

One possibility, voiced but quickly dismissed, was that the girls and the boys sing together for all services, as in Edinburgh and Manchester. Kerry opposed this practice as fundamentally detrimental to the boys' *esprit de corps*, quite apart from the excessive commitment it would require from the girls, plus the funding implications of such an arrangement. It was felt that, given the pressures to which boys are subjected by other boys, and the innate distraction the girls might cause, keeping the two choirs separate, except for special occasions, was the strongest way forward.

When asked recently about this issue Kerry said *I am sure that a great many other choirmasters feel the same way, and it is a policy to which I adhere even now. I believe that to combine the boys and girls in one choir would weaken the boys' sense of camaraderie, or 'this is a boy thing', and that our recruiting numbers would drop off. In any case the chapter entirely agreed with the views I put forward on the subject at the time, and we went ahead with the conviction that having two separate treble lines was the best way to retain the boys' choir. We were also conscious of the determined efforts and hard work put in only forty years earlier in the founding of the new choir*

The Girl Choristers, 2006.

school. Against formidable odds and financial difficulties the school had been established under the leadership of Precentor Duncan Thomson, and new boy chorister scholarships endowed. We were not about to instigate anything that would undermine the success of that comparatively recent venture.

The Dean and Chapter announced their intention of establishing a girls' choir at the cathedral in February 1996. It was generally greeted with enthusiasm, but there were negative reactions from a few head teachers in the area. At one girls' choir launch reception a prominent local headmaster was unsupportive of the opportunity offered to girls at his school. Others did not even reply to the invitation. In spite of this, many girls applied for choir places, and auditions took place in April, May and June 1996 (one memorable session lasting nearly five hours) undertaken by Kerry Beaumont, his assistant Robert Marsh, Richard Moore and a representative of the Dean and Chapter. The qualities looked for were identical to those required of the boys.

Among the founding members were girls from several Ripon schools together with girls from Richmond, Harrogate, Leeds, Thirsk, Northallerton and the surrounding villages. The first rehearsal took place on Wednesday 11th September 1996 at the choir school, and Kerry described this as *a joyous event.* After all the hard work he had put into this venture, one can well imagine his delight and satisfaction, standing in front of twenty-two eager young faces beaming with pride at having been chosen as one of Ripon Cathedral's first girl choristers, but tinged with apprehension as to what lay ahead.

Teams of reporters and cameramen from Yorkshire Television and BBC Look North attended this rehearsal. Several of the girls gave interviews, and the television news items generated a great deal of interest. Kerry reflected on the exciting day, *I think that probably some of the younger girls did not really understand the excitement which was buzzing about, but there was such positivism and optimism that the venture could not possibly fail.*

The question of the girls' robes remained. After careful consideration in consultation with Kerry's wife, Leslie, and his daughter Victoria (who was in the choir), it was decided they should wear red tabards (the same red as the boys' cassocks) over white cassocks with white ruffs. These vestments have been universally applauded since the day they were first worn, and the girls have often been photographed wearing these graceful garments.

The girls sang their first service in the cathedral on Sunday morning 17th November 1996. The music comprised the communion setting in F by Herbert

Sumsion, and the motet 'Panis Angelicus' by César Franck. One of the hymns 'Angel voices ever singing' seemed particularly appropriate. Kerry told how the words of this hymn were a great morale booster during practices before the first service, as he encouraged the girls to build their confidence by repeating the declamatory phrase at the end of the second verse 'Yes we can, Yes we can'. There were numerous tears in the packed congregation on the day, and Kerry, who conducted, and Robert Marsh, who played the organ, were delighted with the girls' singing.

Despite fears that some people might see this as weakening the special place the boy choristers hold in cathedral worship, there was a wealth of goodwill towards the girls' choir. As for the boys themselves, Kerry confirmed that *They were heroic in their acceptance of this new choir. The boys never complained and they always retained their seriousness and commitment to the daily office.* Some cathedrals had not been so fortunate. There were rumours of equal rights lawsuits, and of girls' choir recruitment literature being replaced by that which condemned the founding of girls' choirs as damaging to the tradition of boy choristers. In truth, in Ripon as in all cathedrals, the intention was never to undermine the role of boy choristers, but rather to extend this special musical and educational opportunity to girls.

The girls sang a second communion service on Sunday 15th December 1996 to Ireland in C with the motet 'This is the record of John' by Orlando Gibbons. That Christmas the two Services of Nine Lessons and Carols were sung by the boys and the girls together for the first time, each singing their own carols with the lay clerks. The combined choirs have sung at these carol services every year since. By the spring of 1997 the girls' choir was well established, and at their AGM in October, the hitherto 'Ripon Cathedral Choir Old Boys' Association' voted to change its name to 'The Ripon Cathedral Old Choristers' Association', thus opening its doors to female members.

From the outset, the parents have spent a considerable amount of time transporting their daughters to and from practices and services. As a result, parents regularly meet each other and many lasting friendships have been formed. Thus the close bond and *esprit de corps* that exists between the girl choristers extends to their mothers and fathers, and happily many of these friendships continue long after their daughters have left the choir.

The girls' choir has had great success, but rather more than its fair share of tragedy. In May 2001 one of the girls, Odette Coulson, while still a member of the choir, suffered a tragic accident and died. Three years later, in April

2004, Joanne Almack, a girl who had sung in the choir a few years before, also died. The mutual sense of loss, and fellowship and support expressed by both present and former girl choristers and their parents on these occasions was palpable. The keen interest in, and support of, the girls' choir consistently shown by Andrew and Arlene Coulson and other parents, continues to be a source of great encouragement and inspiration.

When Kerry Beaumont resigned as director of music in July 2002 he said *Being the director of the girls' choir was, for me at least, a thoroughly good and rewarding experience, and my own daughter sang under her father's direction.*

Following Simon Morley's brief tenure of office, Andrew Bryden was appointed director of music and took charge of the girl choristers in November 2003. Two years later, the age at which girls leave the choir was lowered to thirteen. The standard of singing of the younger girls had improved so much that those aged twelve and thirteen were performing to a level previously expected of girls of fourteen and fifteen. Moreover many girls had a sense of having achieved everything in the choir by age thirteen, and were merely 'treading water' in their last two years. Also, girl choristers who attended the choir school left at thirteen to go on to senior schools, and so, taking everything into account, lowering the leaving age was the obvious way forward.

Benjamin Britten's 'Ceremony of Carols' had been performed in the cathedral by the boys every Christmas since 1969. In 2006 Andrew Bryden decided that the girls and boys should sing this work together. This proved very successful, and they combined to sing the 'Ceremony' again at Christmas 2007.

The girls' choir has been warmly received by the cathedral community, and is considered to be a great asset to Ripon. The choristers have sung on radio and television, and regularly toured other parts of the United Kingdom. Several of the old girl choristers have gone on to study singing at college, having decided on careers in music. There is no doubt that the girls' choir at Ripon Cathedral has been an unqualified success, and a great debt of gratitude is owed to all those involved.

The authors wish to express their sincere thanks to Kerry Beaumont who provided most of the material for this chapter and was an invaluable source of advice. Thanks are also due to Richard Moore and Andrew Bryden for their help.

CHAPTER 12

ORGANISTS AND MASTERS OF THE CHORISTERS

We know from the records that an organ existed at Ripon Minster in 1399 because the fabric rolls of that year refer to *four pairs of bellows made for the new organ* (Ref. Chapter 13). It is likely that the organist, or *pulsator organorum,* would have been a priest skilled in the art of Gregorian chant who accompanied the plainsong on a rudimentary organ of only one or two ranks played from a basic keyboard of levers. We have to wait forty-eight years, however, before the name of an organist is first recorded.

THOMAS LITSTER (1447 – 1478)

Thomas Litster was a chantry priest skilled in playing the organ, which was probably a single manual instrument placed on top of the screen and facing into the choir, where nearly all the services were held.

The Chapter records of 1447 state:

> *Thomae Litster capellano pro missa cantanda in capella Beatae Mariae infra ecclesiam Ripon et ludendum super organicis per annum 10s.*

> *10 shillings a year for Thomas Litster the chaplain responsible for singing the mass in the chapel of Blessed Mary beneath the church of Ripon and playing on the organ.*

This is the first recorded payment to an organist at Ripon.

John E. West in his book 'Cathedral Organists' (1899) recorded the names of the seven known organists from the fifteenth century, and two of these were at Ripon. John Ingleton of Lincoln (1439) was the only listed organist before Thomas Litster.

LAWRENCE LANCASTER (1478 – 1511)

He was also a priest who, records confirm, received an annual payment of 10 shillings, plus 3s. 4d. for playing the organ at daily mass in the Chapel of St Mary.

JOHN WATSON (1511 – 1513)
WILLIAM SWAWE (1513 – 1520)

ADAM BAKHOUSE (1520 – 1540)

WILLIAM SOLBER (1540 – 1548)

Minster records of 1546 refer to *rent of 13s. 4d. payd yerlie to the organ player* who was William Solber. The use of the term 'rent' is interesting; it is thought that the sum of 13s. 4d. was in fact William Solber's annual salary, and that this was probably payable out of rental income that the canons were receiving from their properties and land.

Note. The existence of the above four organists had not hitherto been established, and they are not named in any previous books on Ripon Minster or its organs and organists. The names and dates in office of Watson, Swawe, Bakhouse and Solber came to light during researches for this book in the Chamberlains' Rolls of the period. In addition, further information has emerged regarding the periods in office of the subsequent organists, John Wanlass, Henry Wanlass, Mr Wilson, Alexander Shaw and William Sorrell, which supercedes dates quoted in previous sources.

1548 – 1604 Period of major disruption

The dissolution of the chantries and the college of canons at Ripon Minster was implemented on Easter Day 1548. As a result, the choral foundation ceased to exist and the organist and singers were all dismissed (Ref. Chapter 3). Music at Ripon was fallow until James I granted a charter to the minster in 1604. A Dean and Chapter and choral foundation were established but there is no evidence of an organist being appointed until nine years later.

JOHN WANLASS – Possibly Wanless (1613 – ??)

An 1869 document in the Dean and Chapter archives refers to the appointment of John Wanlass as organist in 1613, but there is some evidence that he soon moved on. There is reference, in West's book 'Cathedral Organists', to a John Wanlass being appointed organist at Lincoln Cathedral in 1616.

The chapter accounts for 1635 state that the organist's salary was £16 per annum, but we are not sure who the organist was. Whoever was in office at that time, however, was probably dismissed some time around 1643.

1643 – 1660 Period of major disruption

The Civil War started in 1642 and the collegiate church in Ripon, together with its choral foundation, was dissolved. In 1643 Ripon

Minster was extensively damaged by Parliamentary troops and parts of the organ torn down.

The Restoration of the monarchy in 1660 led to the reconstitution of the collegiate church and its music.

HENRY WANLASS (1662 – 1674)

It was not until two years after the Restoration that an organist was appointed, and perhaps this was because there was no organ (Ref. Chapters 5 and 13).

Henry Wanlass, who is thought to have been a chorister at Durham Cathedral, took up office as organist of Ripon Minster in May 1662. It is possible that he was the son of John Wanlass the previous organist.

The minster accounts for 4th October 1662 state that *Mr Wanlesse was paide for going to view ye organs of the Lord Darcey; two shillings* and it may be that this visit was to secure the loan of an instrument for the minster until such time as a new organ could be built or afforded.

Henry Wanlass was not a well man; in the chapter minutes of Wednesday 24th August 1670 it was recorded:

Consented and agreed that betwixt Mr Wanlass the organist and Mr Wilson one of the singing men, that Mr Wilson should and would, in consideration of the deafness and impotency of the said Mr Wanlass, both teach the choirboys and play upon the organs for and instead of Mr Wanlass, if the said Mr Wanlass would sing in his room and stead in the choir. This twelve month agreement was renewable for another year *if the said Mr Wanlass shall so long live.*

This confirms that in the early days, the organist was often recruited from among the vicars choral or later, as in this case, the singing men. Indeed at some cathedrals and collegiate establishments the new organist was evidently elected from their number by the vicars choral themselves.

Henry Wanlass died on 5th December 1674.

MR WILSON (1670 – 1674)

As referred to above, Mr Wilson was a singing man at Ripon Minster who assisted in playing the organ and training the choristers from August 1670 onwards.

On Thursday 4th June 1674 the chapter minutes record *for the house organ bought from Mr Wilson the late organist for the use of the next organist, £7.*

Perhaps Mr Wilson taught the choristers at his home, and there is no doubt that from 1670 onwards he was in effect organist and master of the choristers, although there is no record of him having been appointed to the substantive post. Mr Wilson probably left Ripon, or gave up the temporary arrangement, shortly before the death of Henry Wanlass.

ALEXANDER SHAW (1674 – 1677)

One of the first choristers at Durham after the Restoration, Alexander Shaw was the son of a bell ringer and clock winder at the cathedral. When his voice broke in 1663 he remained at Durham employed as a sackbut player.

Shaw came to Ripon as organist in 1674 and whilst in the post he was paid *9s. 6d. for pricking out songbooks for the choristers.*

In 1679 the Dean and Chapter agreed that *Mr Shaw late organist be payed for his playing for the last half year.* As he left in 1677, he evidently had to wait more than a year before being paid for his services in the last six months of his tenure.

After only three years at Ripon, Alexander Shaw returned to Durham Cathedral as organist and married the widow of the previous Durham organist, John Foster. Shaw was, however, removed from this post in 1681 due to *inappropriate behaviour*, and he died in 1706. A service and a small number of his anthems remain (Ref. Chapter 14).

WILLIAM SORRELL (1677 – 1682)

The chapter minutes contain three references to William Sorrell. On Monday 4th February 1677 the records state *To give unto William Preston, Organ Maker the sum of Tenne Pounds for making an organ … to have five stops … such as shall be approved by Mr Brownhill and Mr Sorrell.* In May of that year his appointment as organist was confirmed. On 31st May 1679 it was recorded that out of the fabric money *an annual allowance of five shillings be paid to Mr Sorrell for wire and his pains in repairing the organ.*

William Sorrell died in office and was buried in the minster on 15th March 1682 but the whereabouts of his tomb is not known.

JOHN HAWKINS (1682 – 1689)

It is believed that John Hawkins was a songman at York Minster but other than this, little is known about him.

At a chapter meeting on Saturday 27th May 1682 it was agreed that *At this*

Chapter Mr John Hawkins is admitted organist of this church.

He died in 1689 and was buried in the south choir aisle; no trace of his memorial plaque remains.

THOMAS PRESTON, THE ELDER (1690 – 1730)

Thomas Preston was born in 1663. His appointment as organist at Ripon was confirmed on Saturday 31st May 1690, and he held the post for forty years. He married Mary and they had twin children, Thomas and Frances.

Thomas Preston wrote several anthems and services, some of which have survived incomplete in manuscript form (Ref. Chapter 14).

Minster records of 1696, 1699 and 1700 refer to payments made to Thomas Preston for writing out music for the choir and organ (Ref. Chapter 5).

The chapter minutes of Saturday 29th May 1708 state that *Whereas the organ hath been much damaged by the fall of the trumpet stop amongst the small pipes which hath been repaired by Mr Thomas Preston the organist, for which this chapter is well satisfied, he deserves the sum of ten pounds.*

Thomas Preston died on 15th October 1730 aged 67 and was buried in the south transept.

THOMAS PRESTON, THE YOUNGER (1731 – 1748)

At a chapter meeting on Tuesday 25th May 1731 it was recorded that *Mr Thomas Preston, placed by the dean as organist of this church, is hereby confirmed in the same.*

This suggests that he took over the role of organist at the time of his father's death on the dean's instructions and his appointment was confirmed seven months later.

WILLIAM AYRTON (1748 – 1799)

Born in 1726, William Ayrton was the son of Edward Ayrton, who was Mayor of Ripon 1760-1761 and a successful chirurgeon (barber surgeon) in the town.

The Ayrtons were a musical family and both William and his older brother, Edmund, showed great promise and received lessons from James Nares, the organist at York Minster from 1734 to 1757.

Little is known of William despite the fact that he was organist of Ripon Minster for fifty-one years.

Edmund was appointed organist and *rector chori* of Southwell Minster in 1754. He subsequently moved to London, where, following service as a vicar choral of St Paul's and lay vicar of Westminster Abbey, he took up the post of Master of the Children at the Chapel Royal. In 1789 Dr Edmund Ayrton paid for a new stop to be added to the Ripon Minster organ by Donaldsons of York (Ref. Chapter 13).

William Ayrton died in office in 1799.

WILLIAM FRANCIS MORRELL AYRTON (1799 – 1805)

William Ayrton was succeeded by his son William F. M. Ayrton (born 1779) whose appointment was confirmed in a chapter minute of Tuesday 25th June 1799. Little is known about him except that he held the post for six years, then moved away from Ripon.

He died in 1850 at Abbot's Grange, Chester, aged 71 years.

NICHOLAS THOMAS DALL AYRTON (1805 – 1822)

Nicholas T. D. Ayrton, born in 1783, was the younger brother of William F.M. Ayrton, and became organist of Ripon Minster on 2nd June 1805.

It is only known that he died in office on Thursday 24th October 1822 at the comparatively young age of 39 years, and was buried in the churchyard adjacent to the east end of the minster.

JOHN HENRY BOND (1823 – 1829)

A list of the choristers at St Paul's Cathedral, compiled in 1787, includes a John Henry Bond. This list was referred to by Miss Maria Hackett, 'the choristers' friend' (Ref. Chapter 6), in her writings of June 1818 when she added that *John H. Bond is now the organist of Malton Parish Church in Yorkshire.* It seems likely that this was the same John Henry Bond who was appointed organist of Ripon Minster in 1823.

The exact date of Bond's appointment is not recorded, and one source suggests that he may have acted as organist on the death of Nicholas Ayrton. The chapter minutes of Saturday 14th June 1823, however, state that *Mr Bond, the organist, having given great attention to the improvement of the choir, particularly the boys, the dean makes him a donation of £3 in addition to the usual extra donation of £2 in the accounts.*

After six years in office, John Bond tendered his resignation on 30th June 1829.

GEORGE BATES (1829 – 1873)

Little is known of George Bates's early life, except that he was born in Halifax on 6th July 1802, and became a professional musician at a young age. In addition to his keyboard skills, he was an accomplished violinist and played with the York Festival Orchestra in early performances of the Beethoven symphonies.

When John Henry Bond resigned in 1829, the post of organist at Ripon was advertised. There were several applicants, but we do not know who auditioned the candidates. There remain in the Dean and Chapter archives, however, copies of the four testimonials, all dated early February 1829, written in support of George Bates.

The Reverend James Holme, Curate of Pannal and Low Harrogate, confirmed that he had known George Bates for several years, because he received cello lessons from him. Holme also stated that he (Bates) *had attended me in a very satisfactory manner and I have every reason to recommend him on account of his conduct and his qualifications as a musician.*

Mr R. Blackburn was the manager of The Promenade, Low Harrogate. This building was erected in 1806 to provide an assembly room for those 'taking the waters'. It later became the Town Hall, then the Town Hall Theatre, where Lillie Langtry, Oscar Wilde and other notable personalities appeared. It is now the Mercer Art Gallery on Swan Road. Blackburn wrote of George Bates *he has been engaged by me for five seasons at the Promenade as organist, and during that time has given general satisfaction … during his stay in Harrogate, Mr Bates has conducted himself so that his moral and general conduct stands irreproachable.*

The letter from Thomas Mason of Knaresborough was both short and (due to his scrawly handwriting) almost unreadable. He said *Mr Bates has attended in his professional capacity on the instruction of my daughter for nearly five years, and I have great satisfaction in recommending him.* Not a word as to the nature of 'the instruction' nor of Bates's musical abilities.

The last testimonial was from George White of Leeds and, like the curate's egg, was only good in parts. It is a document of masterly understatement and even at its best is hardly conducive to instilling confidence into the Dean and Chapter.

I have known Mr George Bates for several years as a good musician and he has played second to me (presumably on the violin as Bates was known to be a very competent performer on this instrument) *at various concerts. Of his organ performance I am not so well able to judge, having rarely heard him perform, but as he has had full practice for three years and is able to play a concerto on the pianoforte before the public, I imagine he is, or may soon be, quite competent for your situation.*

I shall conclude by the same recommendation that I gave to the late Dean, viz. to make a trial for a short time when you will be able to form your own opinion and act accordingly.

The last paragraph was probably 'name dropping' to enhance his credibility, but it also implies that George White advised the previous dean (Robert Waddilove) in 1823 when John Henry Bond was appointed organist.

Notwithstanding these testimonials, the Dean and Chapter appointed George Bates as organist at Ripon Minster. His stipend was *not less than £30 per year,* and two years later in 1831, the chapter minutes state *the £40 yearly income from the pew rents are to be given to the organist.*

George Bates was evidently very much the nineteenth century gentleman (See illustration previous page). He lived at No. 6 Park Street, Ripon, but there is little information about his family except that his wife, Mary, was organist at Holy Trinity.

His folio 'Sacred Music' which included a Te Deum and Jubilate, the hymn Veni Creator Spiritus and thirty chants was published by J. H. Jewell of London in about 1850 and ran to a second edition (see page 183). He also wrote several other pieces.

George Bates retired in 1873, and at a meeting of the chapter on Tuesday 8th July 1873 *It was resolved and ordered that an annuity of £30 should be paid to Mr Bates for his life from the date of his retirement from the office of organist.*

He died in Ripon on Sunday 22nd January 1881 and was buried in the churchyard at Holy Trinity, Ripon. On the wall of the north nave aisle of the cathedral there is a memorial plaque to George Bates (see opposite page) on which is engraved the opening bars of his 'Veni Creator', regularly sung at ordination services during the latter half of the nineteenth century.

EDWIN JOHN CROW,
Mus Doc Cantab, FCO.
(1874 – 1901)

Edwin Crow was born on 17th September 1841 at Sittingbourne, Kent. He was a chorister at Rochester Cathedral and became an articled pupil of the organist, John L. Hopkins. In 1858 he went to Leicester to study with G. A. Löhr, whom he succeeded as organist of Trinity Church. He was then organist successively at St Andrew's and St John's, in Leicester.

In 1868 he became a Fellow of the College of Organists (the College of Organists had been founded in 1864, but did not get its Royal Charter until 1910), and graduated Bachelor of Music at Cambridge in 1872.

Edwin Crow was appointed organist and master of the choristers at Ripon Cathedral in 1873 following an audition by Dr Edwin Monk, organist of York Minster. He took up his duties at Ripon on 1st January 1874 with an annual salary of £100. Dr Monk evidently told Edwin Crow, after he had got the job, that things at Ripon *could not ... be worse*. These words obviously proved true because soon after Crow had taken up his duties, he wrote to a friend *the music here at Ripon is abysmal.*

As a result of Crow's efforts, however, the standard of singing improved significantly, and within a few years the Ripon Cathedral choir had gained an enviable reputation. This is amply demonstrated by a letter that appeared in The Musical Times of Saturday 1st June 1878 in which the Reverend Samuel Joy, precentor at Ripon, replied to a glowing tribute from a reader who had written expressing his delight at the excellent standard of the choir. Samuel Joy heartily thanked the letter writer for his favourable comments, but pointed out that the real credit was due to Mr Crow, who he said was *an experienced and thorough musician of untiring patience, upon whom as choir master as well as organist, has devolved the actual work of training the choir.*

Edwin Crow originally lived in The Crescent, Ripon with his wife and daughter, and it is said that *he usually walked to the cathedral, only taking a horse-drawn cab when the weather was particularly inclement.*

In 1877 Crow was involved in choosing a firm to undertake the building of a new organ at Ripon, but he later fell foul of the Dean and Chapter and Sir George Gilbert Scott by suggesting the ancient choir screen should be removed. As a result he was excluded from the new organ implementation committee, but he did, however, have a hand in the design of the specification of the new organ (Ref. Chapter 13).

Edwin Crow was appointed music master at Ripon Grammar School, and in 1882 he became a Doctor of Music at Cambridge and an examiner for the Incorporated Society of Musicians and the College of Organists.

The choirs of York, Durham and Ripon Cathedrals came together for the first time at Ripon in July 1883. Edwin Crow wrote an evening service in A for this event and it was later published by Novello. In an article in The Musical Times of Monday 1st October 1883, a critic wrote, *Dr Crow's Evening Service in A is a composition of some importance and is evidently intended for large and well-trained choirs. Contrapuntal elaboration is freely employed in the voice parts and the accompaniment is for the most part independent. The exclusive use of triple time occasionally leads to some rather flippant effects; but on the whole the Organist of Ripon Cathedral may be congratulated upon the production of a fine original service, worthy to compare with the best of its contemporaries.*

From this and other music that he wrote, it is clear that Crow was a very professional and competent musician. His communion service in F won a College of Organists prize in 1872. In addition, he wrote a communion service in A, evening canticles in the keys of D and G, and a morning service (Te Deum and Jubilate) in C sung at the inauguration of the new cathedral organ on Sunday 24th April 1878.

Edwin Crow also wrote organ music and his set of 'Five Short Voluntaries' was published about 1890. The March (Number Five) became so popular that it was later published separately in its own right.

The Ripon Cathedral Oratorio Choir was founded by Crow and they gave regular concerts, including, in about 1885, what must have been one of the earliest performances of Brahms Requiem (completed in 1868) in the North of England.

In 1874 the Marquess of Ripon presented the Dean and Chapter with his original copy of the 'Ripon Psalter', dated 1418, containing the Psalms of David, some Antiphons, Te Deum, Benedictus, Benedicite, Magnificat, and the Litany. This ancient book, which had evidently been rebound in the late fifteenth century, also contained a Breviary and Missal with the Offices for the Octave of St Wilfrid at Ripon Minster. Written on the blank pages at the back of the book were discovered the words of two ballads; 'A Lytyll Ballet of ye Young Dukes Grace' (*circa* 1490) and 'Ballet of ye deth of ye Cardynall' (*circa* 1450). Dr Crow set both these ballads to music, scoring them for four voices, and records state that *they were sung by the choir of Ripon Cathedral in July 1874.*

Dr Crow's tenure at Ripon came to an end in unfortunate circumstances. The Ripon Gazette reported that he had resigned, but in fact he did so under pressure from the Dean and Chapter. The dean wrote to Crow threatening to dismiss him if he did not resign, and offering him a financial incentive to do so. He resigned, but the circumstances of the affair, described more fully in Chapter 8, evidently reflected badly on the Dean and Chapter.

After his departure from Ripon, Edwin J Crow became organist of Thirsk Parish Church and he died in Harrogate on Sunday 6th December 1908.

Eighteen years later, a notice appeared in the Musical Times of 1st July 1926:

THE LATE DR E.J. CROW, OF RIPON

Sir, – Will you kindly allow me to appeal to old choristers and pupils of my predecessor, Dr E. J. Crow, for subscriptions to a fund which is being raised to place a memorial in the cathedral? It is suggested that this shall take the form of a statue to be placed in the Rood Screen.

I shall be glad to receive and acknowledge donations, which should be endorsed 'Crow Memorial Fund.

Yours etc
Charles Moody
The Cathedral, Ripon

The proposal that the memorial to Dr Crow should be a statue of him in the ancient screen, which during his lifetime he had ardently wanted to dispose of, is difficult to understand, because Moody (a lover of church architecture and passionate about its preservation), knew full well about Crow's desire to remove the screen. Whatever the reason for his suggestion, the 'statue in the screen' idea was not pursued, but a memorial tablet to Edwin Crow was erected in the north nave aisle of the cathedral.

CHARLES HARRY MOODY,
CBE, D Mus, FSA, FRSA, Hon FRCO,
Hon RCM. (1902 – 1953)

Charles Harry Moody was born on 22nd March 1874 at Dennis Park, Stourbridge, Worcestershire, his father being the proprietor of a local newspaper. After studying for a time under G.W. Bates at Stourbridge Parish Church, he became an articled pupil of T. Westlake Morgan, who was organist of Bangor Cathedral; Moody was later assistant organist there.

In 1893 he was asked to take temporary charge of the choir at Worcester Cathedral. This was short-lived and soon afterwards he became the organist at St Michael's College, Tenbury. Whilst there, he was nominated by Sir John Stainer as a candidate for the post of organist at the fashionable and well-endowed church of St Luke's, Osnaburgh Crescent, North West London, to which he was later appointed.

Moody moved to Wells Cathedral in 1894 as assistant to Charles W. Lavington, and when the latter was taken ill in 1895, Moody became acting organist and choirmaster there. He was also appointed the private organist to the Bishop of Bath and Wells. His services were evidently appreciated, for when Lavington's successor, Percy C. Buck, was appointed in 1896, the Dean and Chapter of Wells wrote to Moody thanking him for his assistance and sending him a cheque for £30.

In December 1895, again on the recommendation of Sir John Stainer, Charles Moody was appointed organist and master of the choristers at Wigan Parish Church. This was a prestigious appointment; firstly because the Rector of Wigan was Chaplain to Queen Victoria (Wigan was one of the richest livings in England and the rectorship was in the gift of the Crown), and secondly because many previous organists of Wigan had gone on to leading positions in cathedral music.

Moody moved to Holy Trinity Church, Coventry in 1899, and his successor at Wigan Parish Church was the 25 year old Edward Bairstow, who subsequently became organist at Leeds Parish Church and then York Minster. Holy Trinity was a large and well-endowed church, where the renowned Revd Dr Walter F. Hook (later Dean Hook) had been the incumbent before moving to Leeds Parish Church, and was committed to maintaining a high standard of music.

Charles Moody was appointed organist and master of the choristers at Ripon Cathedral in 1901, having been auditioned, together with five other candidates, by Tertius Noble, organist of York Minster. He took up his post on Monday 20th January 1902 and, at the age of 28, was the youngest cathedral organist in England (See photograph opposite). His starting salary was £160 a year, increasing annually by £10 up to a maximum of £200.

It was reported in The Musical Times of 1st January 1902 that Mr C. H. Moody had entered upon his duties at Ripon Cathedral but *that the services are being sung without accompaniment as the organ is being rebuilt by Messrs Hill & Son.*

During the early years of his appointment Charles Moody set about compiling a Ripon Chant Book which was published by Novello & Co in 1907 (Ref. Chapter 15). This contained chants by at least 40 different organists of the day as well as by Rev E. H. Swann (succentor and later precentor of Ripon Cathedral) and Rev G. E. Alvis (succentor of Ripon Cathedral). In addition, there were several chants by Moody himself, but none by Edwin Crow or George Bates, nor any other previous organist of Ripon Minster.

In addition to his responsibilities at the cathedral, Charles Moody was appointed lecturer in music at the Ripon and Wakefield Diocesan Training College, and also conductor of the Ripon Choral Society. In 1905 he founded what was originally 'Mr Moody's Amateur Operatic Society', but the name was later changed to the 'Ripon Operatic Society', which still flourishes. Moody also taught music and piano at The Ripon Training College (later St Margaret's College) founded in 1862 to train school mistresses. One of Charles Moody's pupils at this college was Miss Joy Norton Dean who studied both piano and organ with him from about 1945 onwards. Over the years she became a personal friend and later Moody used to visit Joy and her family at their home in Nottingham. On her retirement, Joy Dean (later Mrs Joy Calvert) moved back to Ripon, and Charles Moody bequeathed most of his music, correspondence and memorabilia to her. The authors owe a particular debt to Joy who has made all of this material freely available.

Charles Moody conducted the Huddersfield Glee and Madrigal Society from 1912 to 1923 and became an external examiner for the Royal College of Music, the Royal Manchester College of Music, and the United Universities Board. He was also a freemason and in this capacity was later awarded the Masonic rank of Grand Organist of England.

Moody suffered problems with his back from an early age, and as a result had to wear a stiff corset – hence his very upright posture evident on many photographs. He was rejected for military service, but was given a commission in the old 1st Volunteer Battalion, Prince of Wales Regiment. Despite his physical restrictions he was goalkeeper for the Ripon hockey team for several years. It was his weak back which precluded him from walking long distances and he used a pedal cycle. However, in about 1951, Moody decided to splash out on a motor, not a car – his salary would not stretch to that – but what was called a 'Cyclemaster', a petrol engine powered bicycle. This was a state of the art machine at the time, and Charles Moody used it regularly around town and for trips to his beloved Fountains Abbey. Dr Moody and his moped became a well known sight in Ripon, and the choirboys, awaiting his arrival at the song school, could always hear him coming by the noise of his little engine.

Moody was a martinet, and in an article written in 1990 by Kelvin Gott, who was a chorister under Moody from 1946-1953, he recalls *Rehearsals at the song school were always an event. Not many boys fell asleep but if they showed the slightest sign of lapse in attention, he would hit the music stand with such force that it hurtled along the top of the piano. Hymn books were often used as a missile but mainly, if Moody saw or heard something he didn't like, he was up and along to that boy with lightning speed with a whirlwind of arms and legs. He had the boy by the ears, sometimes lifting him off the floor.* Nevertheless, the boys realised Dr Moody wanted nothing but the best and they respected him.

It was due to Charles Moody's energy and influence that, during the First World War and afterwards, Ripon was one of the few cathedrals that maintained a full round of daily choral services. Moody also spent much time organising music for the troops in and around Ripon, and for this he was awarded the CBE in 1920. That same year he was made an honorary Fellow of the Royal College of Organists. The choir attendance book on Wednesday 31st October 1923 notes, by Moody in his own hand, *the degree of Doctor of Music conferred upon CHM by the Archbishop of Canterbury at Lambeth Palace, London.* This was in recognition of his services to English church music over many years, but especially his unstinting efforts during the war.

Charles Moody enjoyed musical composition and, in addition to his sacred works, he wrote secular songs, mostly under the pseudonym of 'Coulthart Brayton'; Coulthart was an old Moody family name and Brayton was his wife's maiden name.

The Musical Times of 1st May 1924 contained a report on the performance of Bach's St Matthew Passion in Ripon Cathedral by the cathedral and oratorio choirs combined. The performance of large-scale choral works was a feature of Moody's long incumbency, and he introduced several contemporary compositions.

Moody was a man of wide-ranging interests and travelled extensively, including a visit to Ripon, Wisconsin in the United States of America, giving organ recitals and lectures on the English Church and its music, particularly the monastic orders. He also visited Canada, adjudicating at several music festivals and lecturing on English cathedrals and abbeys under the auspices of the National Council of Education of Canada. He was a respected historian and a passionate advocate for the preservation of church architecture and history. He was probably the first English cathedral organist to broadcast on national radio. On Wednesday 31st January 1934, Moody delivered a 15 minute talk on the BBC Home Service entitled 'What the North owes to the early Cistercians'. There is a letter to Moody from William Ellis, the then organist of Newcastle Cathedral, which reads:

> *Dear Charlie,*
>
> *Congratulations on your broadcast; it sounded as though you were in the room with me.*
>
> *Yours Bill.*

Moody subsequently broadcast again, this time on campanology.

Dr H. K. Andrews, Organist and Fellow of New College, Oxford from 1938-1955, commented to more than one of his students that *Charles Moody at Ripon Cathedral is one of the finest trainers of boys' voices in England.* Indeed, Moody wrote a book on the subject, entitled 'The Choir Boy in the Making'. This was first published by Oxford University Press in 1923, and was so successful that it ran to a second edition in 1939 and a second impression in 1944.

It is ironic that when the whole world was at war, a minor war should break out at Ripon between the Dean and Chapter and the cathedral organist. This caused quite a stir in the local and national press, and in musical and church circles. The full story is told in Chapter 8.

For the last thirty years of Moody's time at Ripon, he lived in a large house 'Woodbridge' in Priest Lane, next to the river Skell and immediately adjacent to the old ford. It was here that he gave piano and music theory lessons to his many private pupils.

Dr Moody became ill in 1951 and relied increasingly upon his deputies, particularly Alex Forrest (assistant organist 1947-1952), and one or two of his other competent pupils. Luckily, however, he was well enough to attend the special celebrations to mark his fifty years as organist of the cathedral in January 1952. He was given the Freedom of the City, and at the presentation ceremony in the Lawrence Café and Ballroom (since demolished, see illustration opposite), the cathedral choir sang several items, accompanied by Alex Forrest on the piano. To mark the occasion, the Mayor and Councillors commissioned a large portrait of Dr Moody which still hangs in the Town Hall (see below). In addition, he was given a Freeman's Scroll inscribed by local artist J. Porteus, a bracket clock, and a cheque for £800 from the cathedral congregation and friends.

The Lady Maud Warrender Award of Merit, together with £100, was bestowed upon Charles Moody in 1953 for services to church music. He retired in December of that year and was presented with two cheques; one for £1,233 6s. 7d. by the Mayor of Ripon, which had been collected by public subscriptions including donations from abroad, and another for £1,105 by the Dean and Chapter, on behalf of the cathedral. These were sizeable sums and reflected both the high esteem in which Charles Moody was held and the gratitude for his major contribution to the life of Ripon and its cathedral.

Charles Moody continued to write, and in 1959, when he was 85, his book 'Fountains Abbey and Fountains Hall' was published by Pitkins of London in their 'Pride of Britain' series. He still maintained an interest in his beloved Ripon Cathedral. When the new choir school was established in 1960, he took

great pride in this achievement as he had been campaigning for this for many years, and it had been his idea to sell the Caxton books to facilitate this. He later wrote a lengthy article 'A Choir School for Ripon' which was published in The Musical Times in July 1960.

Charles Moody's health continued to deteriorate and he died on 14th May 1965 at the age of 91. An inscribed stone on the north side of the choir screen arch serves as his memorial.

LIONEL FREDERICK DAKERS, CBE, B Mus, FRCO. (1954 – 1957)

Lionel Dakers was born in Rochester, Kent, in 1924. His father and grandfather ran W.H. Dakers & Sons, Estate Agents, which had branches in most of the Medway towns, and he was expected to follow in their footsteps. In 1931 he became a non-singing pupil at Rochester Cathedral Choir School. He showed an interest in music and commenced lessons with the organist Harold Bennett. The Rochester Cathedral Choir School closed in 1937, however, and young Dakers, by then 13, transferred to a school in Gravesend. Later he went to work as a trainee accountant, although he already had a job as organist at a local church and was studying for his Associateship of the Royal College of Organists.

In 1943 Lionel Dakers was called up for national service and due, apparently, to his flat feet he was assigned to the Education Corps, being posted to Beverley Barracks in Yorkshire. He later joined the Pay Corps and was sent to York. Here he came into contact with Sir Edward Bairstow (nearing the end of his long and distinguished career as organist at York Minster) and Francis Jackson, who was soon to become Bairstow's successor.

After a posting to Egypt, when he had the opportunity of playing the organ at Cairo Cathedral, Lionel Dakers left the army in 1947, having attained his FRCO. He subsequently commenced his studies at the Royal Academy of Music, and in January 1950 became assistant organist at St George's Chapel, Windsor, and Eton College.

Lionel Dakers was appointed organist and master of the choristers at Ripon Cathedral in 1954 and, at the age of 30, was one of the youngest cathedral organists in England.

In his autobiography 'Places Where They Sing', Dakers tells of his early days at Ripon where he found a choir that was very run down and a Dean and Chapter who did not all consider the music at the cathedral to be a high priority. He also had to cope with a critical Charles Moody attending some of the services to see how *the new young organist from the south* was getting on.

The new organist's first task was to set about improving the music at Ripon. The repertoire was dominated by compositions from the Victorian era, and it is said that he had several bonfires to purge the choir library. He was closely involved in the early plans for the new choir school, working with Duncan Thomson and Harry Graham on this undertaking (Ref. Chapter 9).

Lionel Dakers was a charming man with a warm personality and lively sense of humour. He was well liked by the boys and men in the choir, as well as by others in the wider cathedral community. Lionel was helped by his endearing wife, Elizabeth, and when, with the support of Harry Graham, he re-founded the Ripon Choral Society in 1955, it was she who became its accompanist.

Lionel Dakers left Ripon to take up his appointment as organist at Exeter Cathedral in 1957. Here he prospered and later became director of The Royal School of Church Music. He retired to Salisbury where he was made an honorary lay canon at the cathedral. He died at Salisbury on Monday 10th March 2003.

JOSEPH PHILIP MARSHALL, D Mus
Dunelm, FRCO, FTCL, ARCM. (1957 – 1966)

Philip Marshall was born at Brighouse in the West Riding of Yorkshire on Friday 24th June 1921. His father played the viola, and at first young Marshall took up the violin. When he was about four years old, the family moved to Mablethorpe, Lincolnshire, and Philip began to learn the piano. There was a harmonium at home, and it was not long before he started organ lessons with Frank Graves, organist of Alford Parish Church, who is said to have remarked *that young lad Marshall will be a cathedral organist one day – mark my words.* At the outbreak of the war in 1939 the family moved back to Brighouse, and here Marshall, aged 18, studied music theory with Whiteley Singleton, organist of St Martin's, Brighouse, who was a pupil of Sir Edward Bairstow of York Minster.

Philip Marshall was in the army from 1943 to 1948 and subsequently was head of music at Keighley Grammar School. He became a Fellow of the Royal College of Organists in 1946, winning the coveted Limpus, Harding and Reed prizes. In 1950 he was appointed assistant organist at Leeds Parish Church under Dr Melville Cook. He was also organist of All Souls', Haley Hill, Halifax, where he met Margaret whom he married in 1951. Later that year the Marshalls moved to Boston Stump, Lincolnshire where Philip became organist and taught at the grammar school. In 1955 he was awarded the degree of Doctor of Music by Durham University.

In 1957, following the resignation of Lionel Dakers, Philip Marshall was appointed organist at Ripon Cathedral. Soon after his arrival he befriended Charles Moody, by that time in his mid eighties. Philip Marshall would call upon him most Sundays after evensong, and while they smoked their pipes, Moody, a great raconteur, would reminisce about the music and clergy at his beloved Ripon Cathedral.

Philip Marshall was a superb musician and his improvisations, often based on a melody from one of the works of Sir Edward Elgar, were legendary. His accompaniment of the psalms was most sensitive and beautiful, skilfully reflecting the mood and words. It was said that *he didn't play the notes, he played the words,* although Philip once remarked *I could never manage 'a moth fretting a garment'.*

A skilled calligrapher, Philip Marshall compiled and handwrote the 'Ripon Chant Book', published in 1963 to mark the establishment of the new choir school in which he had played an important part (Ref. Chapter 9). His penmanship and musical skills were combined to remarkable effect in his several manuscripts of 'Rectus et Inversus Sed Upsydounium' an example of which appears in the illustration. This is a setting of the words 'God rest ye merry organists, let nothing you dismay' to the well known tune of the Christmas carol. The manuscript can be turned through 180 degrees and all the notes and harmonies read the same.

Rectus et Inversus Sed Upsydounium

He taught at Holy Trinity and Moorside junior schools, and became conductor of the Ripon Choral Society and the Harrogate String Orchestra.

Everything mechanical, from steam engines to organ mechanisms, always fascinated Philip. He and Philip Miles, head of music at Ripon Grammar School, dismantled the old pipe organ at Coltsgate Hill Methodist Chapel, Ripon, which was being closed. Working together for many months, assisted by senior boys, they transported everything to the grammar school where they rebuilt the organ in the assembly hall, some new parts being made by Philip himself.

In 1966 Philip Marshall accepted the appointment of organist at Lincoln Cathedral, where he served with great distinction for twenty years until his retirement in 1986. Philip often remarked, somewhat proudly, that, shortly before he left Ripon, it was he who auditioned, and recognised the potential of, a young chorister named Kerry Beaumont, who 28 years later was himself to become organist at Ripon.

In his later years Philip suffered from Parkinson's disease which progressively impaired the use of his right hand, but such was his fortitude that he learned to write with his left. His health, however, continued to deteriorate and he died in July 2005.

A moving tribute to Philip Marshall was given at his memorial service in Lincoln Cathedral by Dr Francis Jackson, with whose kind permission the following extracts are reproduced:

Philip was a consummate musician, who inspired great loyalty, respect and affection from choristers and instrumentalists young and old.

He was by nature reserved and sometimes appeared blunt, but conversation with him was always a pleasure. His friends found him a hilarious and pithy raconteur with brilliant impersonations and anecdotes of riveting quality.

Philip was deeply affected by music, sometimes being moved literally to tears whilst conducting large choral and orchestral resources in works such as Elgar's 'Dream of Gerontius'.

One of the most outstanding organ improvisers of his generation, he proved a hugely prolific composer, producing stylish choral and organ music as well as a fine piano concerto (with a particularly beautiful slow movement) and other works.

Throughout his long and distinguished career, and despite his formidable talents, Philip Marshall was always extremely modest. He would certainly have been astounded had one of his colleagues plucked up sufficient courage to tell him how much they admired him.

RONALD EDWARD PERRIN, MA (Oxon), FRCO, FTCL, LRAM. (1966 – 1994)

Ronald Perrin, known from an early age as 'Ron', was born in London on 13th April 1931. He was educated at Edmonton Grammar School and in 1949, won the prestigious Christopher Tatton Organ Scholarship to Christ Church, Oxford, where he studied with Dr Thomas Armstrong, reading for an honours degree in music. In 1951 he became a Fellow of the Royal College of Organists, a Fellow of Trinity College, London, and a Licentiate of the Royal Academy of Music.

After a period of National Service in Berlin, he spent a year at Leeds Parish Church, first as assistant and later acting organist. In 1954 he took up the post of suborganist at York Minster and served under Dr Francis Jackson for twelve years. Ron always regarded York as his spiritual home and had a lasting affection and admiration for Francis Jackson.

In 1966 Ronald Perrin was appointed organist and master of the choristers at Ripon Cathedral and he soon made his mark.

He was a brilliant organist with an outstanding technique and able to play very difficult pieces at what many regarded as a suicidal pace, often saying *I cannot play it any slower*. He took the psalms very briskly and the lay clerks often equated Ron with the famous Gerard Hoffnung cartoon of the organist at the console looking in his rear-view mirror and seeing a police car coming up behind to flag him down for speeding. Life in the choir, with Ron conducting unaccompanied polyphonic anthems, was never boring.

He was, for several years, conductor of the Ripon Choral Society and the Harrogate String Orchestra. In 1969 he introduced 'A Ceremony of Carols' by Benjamin Britten, which has been performed at Ripon Cathedral every Christmas since.

Ronald composed several lively and rhythmic settings of the canticles and some organ pieces, including one entitled 'Fileuse', which he included in one of the first commercial recordings of the organ at Ripon Cathedral in 1967. He wrote the flashy 'Spanish Toccata' in 1986 to show off the new orchestral trumpet stop, the pipes of which are mounted horizontally on the top of the swell box, facing westwards down the nave.

Ronald Perrin was a combination of a very private person and a hugely sociable one. On one occasion he was in the Turf Tavern of the Ripon Spa Hotel (often referred to as his second spiritual home) when he was persuaded to try to sing the top C in the 'Miserere' by Allegri. This took several attempts, and soon afterwards he was asked to leave the premises despite being a frequent customer.

Towards the end of his career Ronald Perrin's health deteriorated to such an extent that it affected his personality, and his relationship with the choir became difficult and strained. In 1994 he resigned, and in recognition of his services, the Dean and Chapter bestowed upon him the title 'Organist Titulaire'. This pleased him greatly and he was even more pleased when Kerry Beaumont, one of his old choristers and an ex-organ pupil, succeeded him.

Dr Simon Lindley, organist of Leeds Parish Church and a long time friend and admirer of Ronald Perrin, wrote an eloquent appreciation of him on his retirement, part of which is reproduced with his kind permission.

His long tenure at Ripon Cathedral has been the main focus of Mr Perrin's professional life, not that it has been a conventional, organ-loft bound, cloistered existence by anyone's stretch of the imagination. Fast cars, pastel-shade suits and flamboyant playing style are all part of his make-up and have been ours to enjoy.

He belongs to the now almost vanished school of cathedral organists who led their choirs from the keyboard. His always colourful accompaniments and vivid use of the many timbres of the superb Ripon instrument inspired many generations of choristers, who were sometimes bemused by the vagaries of his conducting style; but his ability to pull an evensong out of often very difficult circumstances on mid winter evenings (with adults held up in inclement weather conditions and influenza abounding in the boy choristers) is legendary.

His love of music is formidable and woe betide anyone whom he discovers going at this in a half-hearted manner.

Ron has certainly surrounded his many friends, colleagues and admirers, with his own 'symphony of praise' (a quotation from one of his compositions based on a poem by Dean Edwin Le Grice). Those of us who are privileged to know this mercurial, yet reserved, individual and are proud to call him friend, will want to join me in wishing him a very happy – and compositionally productive – retirement.

His retirement, however, was all too short. Ronald Perrin died on 5th September 1997, and is buried in Ripon Cemetery, his gravestone bearing a typical photograph of him when he was at the height of his powers.

KERRY JASON BEAUMONT, MA, Mus B, FRCO. (1994 – 2002)

Kerry Beaumont was born in Cambridge on 5th April 1957 of musical parents; his father was a teacher and composer who, for a period in about 1968, was a lay clerk in the Ripon Cathedral choir.

Kerry's primary education began at Ripon Cathedral Choir School, and at the age of 9 he became a chorister in the choir. He sang as a boy from 1966 to 1970, and was head chorister in his last year. During this time he began organ lessons with Ronald Perrin.

When Kerry was 13, his family moved to Canada, and his high school education was at the St Michael's Choir School, Toronto, during which time he was organ scholar at St Michael's Roman Catholic Cathedral. In 1975 he went to the Curtis Institute of Music, Philadelphia, Pennsylvania, where he obtained the degree of Bachelor of Music in organ performance. Further vocational training followed at Westminster Choir College, New Jersey, the Universitié de Laval, Quebec, and the Academie d'Été, Nice. He also studied organ improvisation with Antoine Reboulet in Quebec and Pierre Cochereau in Paris.

After a period of six years as director of music at the Episcopal Church of the Good Samaritan, Paoli, Pennsylvania, he returned to England. In 1990 he was appointed organist at St David's Cathedral, Wales and for some of his time there he was artistic director of the St David's Cathedral Festival.

Following his appointment in the summer of 1994, Kerry Beaumont took up the post of organist at Ripon Cathedral in October of that year, after the retirement of his old choirmaster and teacher Ronald Perrin. It was quickly realised that Kerry was an exceptionally gifted musician, as was demonstrated by his superb choir training and outstanding organ playing, especially his improvisations. Kerry had a most gentle, persuasive and warm personality which endeared him to everyone.

In 1996 on the joint initiative of Kerry and Richard Moore (the then headmaster of the choir school), and with the support of the retiring dean, Christopher Campling, and the chapter, the Ripon Cathedral Girls' Choir was founded (Ref. Chapter 11). It was due to Kerry's personality, his rapport with the girls, and his patient and hard work over many months that they were moulded into a successful choir.

Many CDs of organ and choral music were made during Kerry's seven years at Ripon, appearing under various labels and receiving excellent revues. It was typical of the man that, after assistant organist Robert Marsh resigned and was replaced by Andrew Bryden, Kerry was quick to recognise his new assistant's abilities and encouraged him to record a CD of organ music of his own.

Kerry was a prolific composer and while at Ripon he wrote many pieces for the cathedral choir (Ref. Chapter 15).

Soon after Kerry's appointment, Christopher Campling retired as dean and was succeeded by John Methuen in 1996. Over the ensuing years decanal difficulties developed which affected the whole cathedral community including the music department. Relations between the dean and the cathedral staff deteriorated, leading to the resignations of the bursar and chapter clerk. In July 2002 Kerry Beaumont reluctantly decided he could continue no longer and resigned. A great sense of loss was felt by the boy and girl choristers, the lay clerks and an overwhelming majority of those who worshipped at the cathedral. An emotional farewell party for Kerry and his wife Leslie, also a fine musician who taught the flute at the choir school, was held in the cathedral in August. A large number of people attended and, at the end of the evening, they were enraptured as Kerry vaulted over the stool of the nave console and played the organ for the last time.

Dean John Methuen was suspended by the Bishop of Ripon and Leeds in September 2004. He resigned and left Ripon Cathedral on 31st December 2005.

Kerry Beaumont taught for a period at two prestigious girls' schools in the south of England and in July 2006 was appointed director of music at Coventry Cathedral.

Following Kerry's departure from Ripon, his assistant, Andrew Bryden, became acting organist, fulfilling this role from September 2002 to April 2003.

SIMON MORLEY, ALCM, FTCL. (April – October 2003)

Simon Morley was born in Gloucestershire in 1964, and received his first organ lessons from John Belcher at St Peter's Church, Bournemouth. In 1983 he became assistant organist of Wimborne Minster, and four years later went to Trinity College of Music in London where he studied the organ with Christopher Stokes. During this time he was organ scholar at Westminster Abbey under Martin Neary and Andrew Lumsden.

Simon was appointed assistant organist of Truro Cathedral in 1990, serving under David Briggs for four years, and then as acting organist pending the arrival of Andrew Nethsingha. He was on the music staff of Truro School and Truro High School for Girls and was appointed to the Diocesan Liturgy Commission by the Bishop of Truro.

In 2000 Simon moved to Lincoln where he was assistant to Colin Walsh and had particular responsibility for the girls' choir.

Simon Morley was appointed director of music at Ripon Cathedral, taking up his duties in April 2003. He soon demonstrated his skills on the organ, both as a recitalist and accompanist. However, in early October 2003 he decided that the directorship of music at Ripon Cathedral was not for him, and he left at the end of that month.

ANDREW JOHN BRYDEN, B.Mus, FRCO, PGCE. (2003 to present day)

Born in Bridgend, South Wales on 25th September 1969, Andrew Bryden was educated at Ayr Academy. He won an organ scholarship to the University of Aberdeen where he studied with George McPhee, Timothy Byram-Wigfield and David Sanger, and graduated with an honours degree in music. For two years he was assistant organist at Aberdeen Cathedral.

Andrew went on to Leeds University where he obtained qualifications in teaching, and also, in 1993, his FRCO. During this time he was director of music at St John's Church, Ranmoor, Sheffield.

In 1994 Andrew was appointed organ scholar at Canterbury Cathedral, and also became head of music at the Montgomery Grant Maintained School and later head of academic music and organist at St Edmund's School, Canterbury.

Andrew Bryden came to Ripon in April 1998 following his appointment as assistant organist at the cathedral and director of music at the Ripon Cathedral Choir School. Here he was responsible for introducing the latest computer-based music software and electronic practice keyboards. At the cathedral he took a keen interest in the girls' choir and undertook some of their rehearsals. With his dry sense of humour, commitment to high standards, and often dour honesty, Andrew endeared himself to the boys' and girls' choirs alike.

When Kerry Beaumont resigned in July 2002, Andrew became acting director of music, fulfilling the role with great success. The substantive post was advertised, following which there was a huge response from many highly qualified and experienced organists, some of whom already held cathedral appointments. A shortlist of two emerged and Simon Morley was appointed. The other shortlisted candidate was Andrew Bryden, and so when Simon Morley resigned, the Dean and Chapter immediately appointed Andrew to the post.

He commenced his duties as director of music at Ripon Cathedral on Saturday 1st November 2003. He had already made a significant contribution to the music during his time as assistant to Kerry Beaumont and had gained a reputation as a fine organist and an excellent choir trainer. Since his appointment Andrew has continued to maintain the high standard of music at the cathedral.

Several recordings of both the organ and the choirs have been made, which are listed in the discography.

Chapter 13

THE ORGANS AT RIPON CATHEDRAL

Some Basics

A pipe organ is a 'box of whistles'; pipes of different lengths (hence sounding notes at different pitches), mounted in rows on a box of pressurised air. Each pipe is shut off from the air supply in the box by a valve (known as a pallet), and when this is opened, the air in the box flows into the base of the pipe and it 'speaks', sounding a note. When the pallet is closed the pipe stops speaking.

The valve to each pipe is controlled by a lever linked to a keyboard, with a lever (key) for each note (i.e. each pipe).

In the earliest instruments the levers that opened and closed the pallets were wide pieces of wood which the player of the organ operated with his fist. Hence the organist was often known as *pulsator organorum* or 'organ thumper'. When he pressed down (or in some cases pulled) on the lever the pipe made a sound, and when he lifted his fist (or pushed in the lever) a spring returned it to its original position and the pipe became silent. As the organ and its repertoire grew in complexity, the levers gradually reduced in size until they formed a 'console of levers' which became the modern keyboard.

It is not understood why the practice of organs being built with the larger (long) pipes on the left, and the smaller (short) pipes on the right, developed, but it was this that resulted in the convention of keyboards having low notes on the left and high notes on the right.

Brief History of the Organ

The earliest known organ was called a *hydraulus* and was invented in the third century BC by a Greek engineer, named Ktesibios, working in Alexandria. Surviving records indicate that he did not realise he was inventing a new instrument. As far as he was concerned, he was solving the problem of how one person could play more than one wind instrument at a time. His solution was to place several existing wind instruments of different sizes above a chamber containing air under pressure. This was created by simple hand-operated pumps, and was controlled by the weight of water (hence *hydraulus*) in a high-level container. The access of air to the wind instruments on the top of the chamber was controlled by a system of valves operated by levers. In later instruments of the second century AD the pumps and water regulators were replaced by bellows.

By 300 AD the Roman Empire had split into the Western Empire, centred in Rome, and the Eastern Empire, centred on Byzantium (later renamed Constantinople, and now Istanbul). While the Eastern Empire flourished, the Western Empire declined, and after 476 AD when the last Roman Emperor, Romulus Augustulus, was deposed, Greco-Roman culture, including knowledge of the organ, was gradually lost to the inhabitants of Western Europe. As a result, from about 500 to 750 AD the organ appears to have been virtually unknown in the West. The evolution of the organ continued in the East, however, and reports survive indicating that it was used for both secular and sacred purposes.

The probable reintroduction of the organ to Western Europe occurred in 757, when the Byzantine Emperor Constantine VI Copronymus presented an instrument as a gift to Pepin the Short, King of the Franks and father of Charlemagne.

At about the beginning of the second millennium, written musical notation started to develop, firstly for the voice and later for the organ and other instruments. It is thought that the earliest notation consisted of marks written above the Latin words as an aide-mémoire for the singers of plainsong. These marks developed into what became known as neumes (later notes) written on lines (later the stave).

During the Middle Ages the organ in Western Europe developed in three ways according to its use:

The Portative Organ

This was the smallest of the medieval organs, and was a single manual instrument with only one, or occasionally two, ranks of pipes and bellows at the back. The keyboard was normally less than two octaves in range, and the musician usually played it with one hand and operated the bellows with the other.

As its name implies, this was a fully portable instrument which was used for both sacred and secular purposes. The portative organ clearly became very popular, as many manuscript illustrations have survived showing courtly ladies or angels playing the instrument.

The Positive Organ

A larger instrument than the portative, this usually had a single manual of greater compass and several ranks of pipes. The keyboard was sufficient to allow the performer to use both hands so that chords and polyphonic music could be played. At first all the ranks sounded together, but later a mechanism was introduced to stop individual ranks from sounding; hence the term 'stop' for a rank of pipes. A second person was needed to pump the bellows, often using both hands. Positive organs were built either as free-standing or table-top instruments. They could be moved, but were heavy and certainly could not be considered portable.

These organs had two primary uses; the first was secular, in the home and at festive gatherings. The earliest preserved keyboard music, from about 1325, consists of three dances and three intabulations (arrangements of vocal pieces for keyboard). Scholars have concluded that the degree of sophistication in these pieces suggests a thriving keyboard practice was in existence in the early fourteenth century. The second was sacred, for use in churches to accompany, and alternate with, the singing of the choir. Descendents of these organs can still be found in some European churches today.

A positive organ.

The Church Organ

The early church authorities took a dim view of the organ. It was not used for worship until about the middle of the tenth century, and even then only to a limited extent in the Western, and hardly at all in the Eastern, Churches.

These organs were initially of limited compass and may have been used to provide a note for singers, as well as to alternate with, and later to accompany, the plainsong. It has been suggested that they may have provided the bass note of the mode in which and over which the plainsong was sung, rather like a drone. As the keys became narrower, the compass of the keyboard increased to up to four octaves and the musician played with both hands. In early medieval times the monks or priests from the choir (vicars choral) played the organ when necessary, and it was only from the fifteenth century onwards that a particular trained and skilled person was appointed to the role of organist.

Organs gradually grew in size and sophistication, and by the mid thirteenth century large permanent instruments were being installed in abbey churches and cathedrals. Such organs were most often referred to as *Blockwerk* instruments and most had multiple pipes for every note, including some that produced a note a fifth above the unison. The invention of the 'roller board mechanism', in the late fourteenth – early fifteenth century, obviated the need for the keyboard levers to be in line with the pipes that they controlled, and this was an important innovation.

By about the middle of the fifteenth century several organs in Northern Europe had more than one keyboard, and in a few cases also a pedal board. The 'console of levers' had become a keyboard incorporating sharps and flats, and the modern church organ was born between about 1475 and 1525, the most advanced instruments of that period being built in North Western Europe.

The earliest pedal boards were simply attached by ropes to the lower notes of the manual, but independent pedal pipes started to appear on the larger mainland European instruments from about 1550. England, however, lagged behind, and the pedal division did not appear on organs in this country until as late as 1790. Even then they remained a rarity for several decades, and there are instances of cathedral organists being reluctant to use the pedals, or to have them installed on their instruments, well into the nineteenth century. Following the establishment of the Church Commissioners in 1835 and the major reforms that ensued, many churches were built in and around highly populated urban centres, and this, coupled with the growing popularity of hymn singing, brought a need for more powerful organs, with a solid bass, to accompany large congregations. The other factor was the revival of interest in the organ music of Bach, with its independent pedal parts, which was stimulated by Mendelssohn when he came to England in 1840. By the beginning of the second half of the nineteenth century, the incorporation of pedal boards into English organs became quite widespread, but even so these were often of limited compass and invariably straight. In The Musical Times of Friday 1st April 1881, Alex Cooper, FCO made a plea for what he called *the absolute necessity of radiating and concave pedalboards,* and he went on to suggest that the College of Organists should settle what the degree of concavity and radiation should be. Nevertheless, the more user-friendly radiating and concave pedal boards were not fitted to English organs as a matter of standard practice until well into the first half of the twentieth century.

Modern technology during the nineteenth and twentieth centuries brought major changes to organs, especially in relation to organ actions (the means of linking the keyboards to the pipes) and registration aids (whereby the organist is able to change different combinations of stops). These facilities have been further developed as a result of pneumatic, later electric and more recently solid state circuitry and computer technology, but some new organs have reverted to the basic 'tracker action' whereby the player has regained the direct linkage between the keyboard and the pallets controlling the pipes.

Ripon Minster

The first reference to an organ at Ripon Minster is found in the fabric rolls of 1399:

> *Et in ij corriis equinis emp. pro iiij paribus bellows organorum de novo faciendis, 2s. 8d.*
> *Et in j corrio vituli et iij corriis ovinis emp. pro praed. organis, 18d.*
> *Et in di. mil. parvorum clavorum emp. pro praedictis organis, 8d.*
> *Et in pacthrede emp. pro praedictis organis, 3d.*
> *Et in s.j. hominis operantis et facientis de novo praedict. bellows ex convencione, 3s. 4d.*
> *Et in potu dato praedicto homini, 2d.*

The translation of this entry, which is peppered with some Latinised English words, reads:

> *And for two horse hides bought for four pairs of bellows made for the new organs, 2s. 8d.*
> *And for one calf skin and three sheep skins, bought for the aforesaid organs, 18d.*
> *And for *500 (2,000) small nails bought for the aforesaid organs, 8d.*
> *And for the packthread bought for the aforesaid organs, 3d.*
> *And for the service of one man working on and newly making the aforesaid bellows according to the agreement, 3s. 4d.*
> *And for drink given to the aforesaid man, 2d.*

* Scholars differ with regard to the translation of the abbreviation *di.*

This instrument was almost certainly a positive organ comprising a single keyboard of limited compass, with possibly one or two ranks of pipes and stops to control which rank sounded. There is no information concerning who played the instrument, nor its use, but it was probably one of the priests, with a second person operating the bellows. This organ would probably have been placed in the choir, but there is evidence that it might have been located on the choir screen.

An entry in the minster records of 1408 reads:

> *in j porcione merremii emp, de Will. Wryth pro j fundo in le purpytyl et pro hostio ibidem ad magnas organus 18d. ... in j sera emp. pro eodem 6d.*

This translates:

> *Item for the piece of timber bought from William Wryth for a chest in the pulpitum and for the entrance in the same place to the great organ 18d. ... for one saw bought for the same 6d.*

The 'purpytyl', 'purpetill', later called the 'pulpitum', was the name given to the screen between the choir (where the priests sang the services) and the nave (to which the laity were admitted).The original screen is thought to have dated from circa 1380 and it was so named because the pulpit was mounted upon it. This pulpit now stands on the floor of the crossing at the north end of the screen. The 1408 entry implies that the organ may also have been located on the screen.

In 1453 *Will the Organ Maker to be payde 20 shillings for mending ye organ* and later that year *4s. 2d. for work on ye purpetill be payde to Robert Wright.*

The minster archives of 1531 record that a new organ was installed: *James Dempsey be payde £4 8s. 4d. for making an organ.* There is no information regarding its specification but it was probably a single manual instrument with two or more stops.

Shortly after this, however, the Church in England was greatly changed by the upheavals of the Reformation, and the music at Ripon Minster suffered enormously (Ref. Chapter 3). We know that the organ was still in use in 1546, because the chapter records confirm *13s. 4d. payd yerlie to the organ player.* The collegiate church in Ripon was, however, dissolved by Edward VI in 1548, and at this time the choral foundation ceased to exist. William Solber, the organist, appears to have been dismissed, and it is fair to assume that the organ was little used during the next 56 years, until James I granted the charter reconstituting the collegiate church in 1604. He also reinstated the choral foundation and a new organist, John Wanlass, was appointed in 1613, implying full use of an organ once more (Ref. Chapters 4 and 12).

In 1642 the Civil War began, and over the following two years all choral establishments in England were closed down. Ripon Minster was extensively damaged by Parliamentary troops in 1643 when much of the organ was destroyed and it is said that some of the lead pipes were melted down and used to make pewter mugs and plates.

The Stuart monarchy was restored in 1660 and the whole country set about repairing the damage done during the Civil War. The choral foundations were reconstituted and organs rebuilt. Unfortunately, at Ripon the steeple on the central tower was blown down on 8th December 1660 causing widespread damage to the choir roof, the canopies of the choir stalls, and the screen. This, together with the parlous state of the minster's finances, undoubtedly caused delays in the replacement of the organ. A new organist, Henry Wanlass, was appointed in 1662 but the history of the instrument itself over the ensuing decades is not clear.

The minster accounts for October 1662 state that *Mr Wanlesse to be paide for going to view ye organs of the Lord Darcey; two shillings,* and it is thought that this visit may have been to make arrangements for the loan of the instrument. In 1663 *a payment of fifteen shillings to be made to William Preston, organ maker, for his journey to Ripon,* and later the records refer to *mending organs.* In 1667 reference is made to *a payment of 14s. 9d. for organ and bellows* and in 1674 *for the house organ bought from Mr Wilson the late organist for the use of the next organist, £7.* Evidently Mr Wilson had an organ at his home, and when he left Ripon, it seems that this was purchased by the Dean and Chapter, possibly for use in the minster. However, there are no defining references as to the status of the minster organ at this time.

In 1677 the chapter agreed *To give unto William Preston, Organ Maker the sum of Tenne Pounds for making an organ ... to have five stops ... such as shall be approved by Mr Brownhill and Mr Sorrell.* This implies that William Preston of York provided a new organ, and indeed some previous writings on the subject have assumed this to be the case. There are however grounds for caution in arriving at such a conclusion. Firstly, the Dean and Chapter were desperately short of money, and secondly, the amount paid to William Preston was only ten pounds (one source quotes £30, another £90), whereas a new organ installed at Durham Cathedral at about this time, albeit a much larger instrument, cost several hundred pounds. It is therefore probable that William Preston did not build a new organ, but undertook repairs to the existing instrument and increased the number of stops to five.

Regarding the reference to *Mr Brownhill and Mr Sorrell*, nothing is known of Brownhill, but William Sorrell was organist at Ripon Minster at the time (Ref. Chapter 12). Some two years later, in the minutes of a chapter meeting on Saturday 31st May 1679, it is recorded that out of the fabric money *an annual allowance of five shillings be paid to Mr Sorrell for wire and his pains in repairing the organ.*

The year 1695 marks the building and installation of a new organ at Ripon Minster. The chapter minutes of 25th May of that year state *Ordered and agreed that towards purchasing of a new organ for this Church the Deane shall contribute tenne pounds and each Prebendary five pounds and that it shall be left to ye Sub-deane to give what he shall thinke fitting to the same.*

This instrument was built by Gerhard Schmidt, the nephew of the renowned organ builder from Germany, Father (Bernhard) Schmidt (1630-1708). The musicologist Charles Burney (1726-1814) wrote that, soon after the Restoration, Bernhard Schmidt came from Germany to England with his two nephews, Gerhard and Christian, and several assistants. They knew that many instruments had been damaged or destroyed during the Civil War and consequently that there was a great demand in England for organ builders. Bernhard quickly built up a great reputation which incidentally included playing the organ (he was appointed organist of St Margaret's, Westminster and remained there until his death). He was responsible for new instruments at St Paul's Cathedral, the Temple Church and St Margaret's, Westminster. Schmidt (whose name was anglicised to Bernard Smith) was appointed 'Organ Maker in Ordinary to the King' in 1681, and had apartments in Whitehall allocated to him.

It appears that Gerhard Schmidt set up on his own account in about 1689 and moved north to live in Ripon. The Ripon parish register contains the following entry: *Gerard, son of Mr Gerhard Smith Organ Maker at Ripon was baptized May ye 10th 1695.*

The historian John Richard Walbran (in his 'Guide to Ripon', 1862) describes the Schmidt organ at Ripon as *one of the sweetest-toned in the kingdom. The diapasons of the Great organ were of a rich, full, inimitable melody; but there was no Swell and only eighteen stops.* While Walbran refers to the number of stops, which would suggest an instrument of two divisions, he says of the organ that *there was no Swell.* Early in the eighteenth century, mechanisms were gradually developed whereby a division of the organ could be enclosed in a box with shutters that could be manipulated by the organist to produce a smooth change in the volume. This device became known as a 'swell box', and the division (group of pipes) enclosed within it the 'swell organ'. Abraham Jordan claimed the invention as his own in his 1712 instrument for St Magnus Church, London Bridge. Swell organs did not become commonplace until the nineteenth century, and thus for Walbran, writing in about 1880, its absence would have been remarkable. It would have been even *more* remarkable, however, if there had been a Swell organ in the Ripon instrument, which had been built in 1695. The two divisions of the Schmidt instrument would probably have comprised a Great organ and either a Chair organ (this was usually behind the organist's chair and faced the choir – it later became known as the Choir organ) or, more likely in view of the number of stops, an Echo organ. In common with other English instruments of the late seventeenth and early eighteenth centuries, there would have been no pedal division.

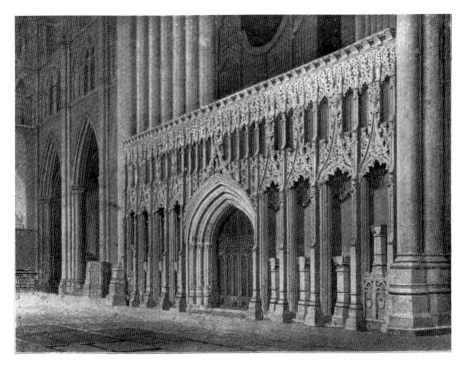

The 1695 Schmidt organ (shown above) is believed to have had its console in the oriel gallery on the east side of the choir screen. It was probably at this time that the curious carved wooden hand was made (see illustration on following page). This projected from the oriel gallery and was connected to a foot lever at the console (there was no pedal board) which enabled the organist to move it up and down to beat time for the choir. This was probably not very effective,

but it is an unusual feature which survives to this day and is possibly unique to Ripon. When the organ console was later moved to a different location on the choir screen, a system of rods and levers was installed to enable the organist to continue to operate the hand by a lever at the side of the console.

The chapter minutes of Saturday 29th May 1708 record *Whereas the organ hath been much damaged by the fall of the trumpet stop amongst the small pipes,* and they go on to state that the damage was repaired by Thomas Preston who was paid £10 for his work.

The organ was repaired again on two subsequent occasions (1719 and 1754) by a man named Dallam. One important organ builder in England during the second half of the seventeenth century was Thomas Dallam and he, together with his son Robert, provided new instruments at King's College, Cambridge, Westminster Abbey, and Durham Cathedral. It is possible therefore that the Dallam who repaired the organ at Ripon was related to Thomas. This later Dallam may have set up an organ building and repair practice in York, or alternatively he travelled from London to do the work on the Ripon organ. The minutes of the Ripon City Council record that in 1754 they *authorised the Mayor to subscribe ten guineas towards the repair of the Minster organ, the sum to be paid out of Corporation Stock.*

In 1789 repairs to the organ, and the addition of a new stop, were undertaken by Donaldsons of York. This new stop was paid for by Dr Edmund Ayrton, Master of the Children at the Chapel Royal, as a tribute to his brother William, who by then had been the organist at Ripon Minster for over forty years.

Brief mention is made, in one source, of the organ being re-modelled in 1833 by Booths of Leeds, but the situation is not clear, and as a firm called Booth was involved in making a new organ case a few years later, there may well have been some confusion. It is known, from a memorandum in 1834, however, that the Ripon Chapter was contemplating the provision of a new three manual organ with a new case.

Ripon Cathedral

Ripon Minster became a cathedral in 1836 when the new Diocese of Ripon was established. While it is impossible to be certain, it seems probable that between 1835 and 1837 Messrs Renn & Boston (sometimes mis-spelled Wrenn & Boston) of Manchester completely rebuilt and considerably enlarged the organ.

This instrument is quoted by Sperling (an organ antiquarian) in about 1838 as being:

Great: Thirteen stops
Swell: Seven stops (Enclosed)
Choir: Five stops
Pedal: One stop

Evidently four ranks of pipes from the 1695 Schmidt organ were incorporated into this instrument. Edwin Crow, in a letter to The Musical Times of 1st November 1881 quotes from 'Walbran's Guide to Ripon Cathedral' *the open and stopped diapason (really a rohr flute), principal, dulciana* (from the Schmidt organ) *are retained in the present instrument.*

This organ was provided with a new case designed by Sir Edward Blore (who undertook the major restoration work on Ripon Minster in 1830-1835)

West face of 1835-1837 organ.

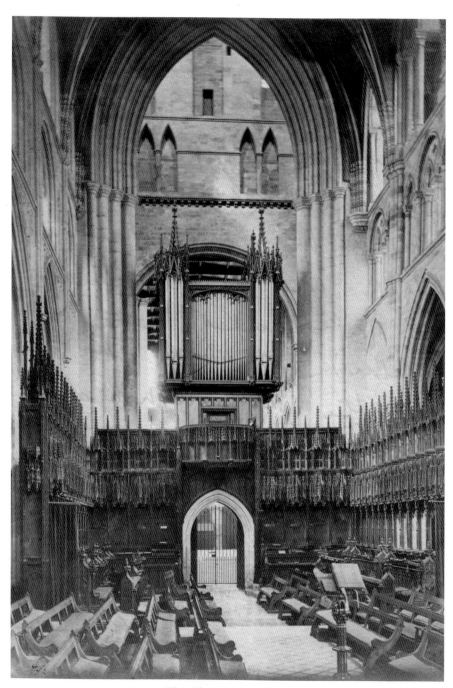

The Choir, circa 1865.

154

and made by Booth & Company of Wakefield. It was Gothic in design with crocketed finials (See illustration opposite). The west facing front pipes were ornately decorated (see illustration on previous page), and at the bottom of the case on both east and west faces were four carved angels which were copies of those on the old woodwork of the oriel gallery in which the console of this instrument was housed.

The new organ case did not meet with universal approval; Sperling wrote in one of his notebooks *when Renn enlarged the organ in about 1837, the fine old case of the original Schmidt instrument was taken away and a wretched gothic case of hideous detail, with the front pipes painted yellow, was installed in its place.* Fortunately the new case did not disturb the woodwork of the oriel gallery, nor the carved hand beneath it or any of the other fine old woodwork on the east side of the choir screen.

Hitherto, all the pipes, soundboards and mechanism of previous organs had been housed within the case on the choir screen. When the 1835-1837 organ was installed, however, the pipes of the Choir division were placed in the west arches of the north and south choir aisles, behind the canopies of the stalls. It is unlikely that either section of this Choir division was enclosed.

Like all organs in those days, the instrument was hand-blown, and it is recorded in the 1840s that one Robert Gill was employed to blow the organ (i.e. to pump the main bellows by means of a hand-operated lever) at a salary of £5 per year. It is interesting to note that some twenty years later, the then blower, Henry Lupton, was paid an annual salary of £7 12s. 0d.

Cathedral status brought a growing number of services, and from the late 1850s onwards several of these were held in the nave. This trend continued, and in 1862 the Dean and Chapter asked two organ builders, Mr Jardine of Manchester (who had taken over the tuning of the instrument from his fellow Mancunian, Mr Renn in about 1850) and Mr Joy of Leeds, to report on the feasibility of constructing another console on the west side of the organ. The estimated cost of this work was presumably prohibitive because the project came to naught. It was not until 138 years later that satisfactory facilities for playing the organ for nave services were finally provided by the installation of a new mobile console in the nave (Ref. 'The Nave Console' later in this chapter).

About 1875 the Dean and Chapter realised that a new and larger organ, worthy of Ripon's cathedral status and with a console suitable for accompanying services in both the choir and the nave, was required. They authorised the organist, Edwin Crow, to research the matter and to recommend a reputable organ builder and propose a suitable specification for the new instrument. Dr Crow visited numerous cathedrals and collegiate and abbey churches in various parts of the country, inspecting, playing and appraising the organs. He was particularly impressed by instruments built by the T.C. Lewis Partnership of London and recommended this firm to the Dean and Chapter, who agreed to entrust the building of the new organ to them.

Thomas Christopher Lewis, who started his career as an apprentice architect, went into organ building during the late 1850s, and in 1860 formed a partnership with John Tunstall and John Whittaker. He showed remarkable aptitude and skill, especially in voicing pipes, and his reputation grew. In 1884 the firm started trading as T.C. Lewis & Co. and they moved to a new factory in Brixton. However in 1900 Thomas Lewis left the firm, which changed its name to Lewis & Co., and in 1919 it merged with another London organ building company, Henry Willis & Sons.

The Dean and Chapter did not accept all aspects of Edwin Crow's advice however, and he became involved in a controversy regarding the position of the new organ in the cathedral. He later confirmed his opinion when he wrote in 'The Ripon Millenary Record' of 1886. *Unfortunately Sir Gilbert Scott refused ... to allow the organ to be divided and placed north and south and to remove the screen. I had, from the beginning, urged this course.* Doubtless the prospect of removing the choir screen was too much for the Dean and Chapter because Crow was excluded from the committee appointed to raise the money and supervise the whole undertaking.

Despite this trouble Edwin Crow was closely involved in drawing up the specification of the new organ, in consultation with Mr Walker Joy (was this the same Mr Joy who had been consulted about the possible new west console in 1862?) and T.C. Lewis.

The work commenced in 1877 and the new organ was completed and installed by late summer 1878, the total cost, excluding the case, being £4,000.

It is said that most of the old 1835-1837 organ went to Llandeilo Church in South Wales, but fortunately some of the pipes from the Schmidt organ of 1695 survived and were incorporated into the new instrument. These are thought to be the 8ft and the 4ft Rohr Flute pipes on the Swell organ, the 4ft Dulcet on the Choir, and the 8ft Pedal Flute.

The new 1878 organ comprised:

Great: Thirteen stops
Swell: Fourteen stops (Enclosed)
Choir: Nine stops
Pedal: Seven stops

Five couplers and seven composition pedals

A new case for the main section of the instrument, which like its predecessor was placed on the choir screen, was designed by Sir George Gilbert Scott and made in oak by Messrs Thompson of Peterborough. Scott had undertaken the major restoration work in Ripon Cathedral between 1862-1871, and this was the last organ case that he designed before his death in March 1878. It is not regarded as one of Scott's best designs and among its least successful features were the wings that protruded from either side of the west face of the case (See illustration).

The console of the new organ was placed on the south side of the

screen, within the case, and this went some way to solving the problem of accompanying services in both choir and nave. The organist now faced north into the instrument, and through the carved open grille-work at either side of the case, he could look to the right (east) into the choir, or to the left (west) into the nave.

Contrary to the normal convention, however, the Swell stop knobs were placed on the right hand side of the keyboards and those of the Great on the left. Even Crow thought that this was peculiar and later his successor, Charles Moody, said that *it was a source of bewilderment to the shortlisted candidates at the audition for the post of organist in January 1902.*

The soundboards and pipes of the Great, Swell and Choir divisions were all placed on the screen within the main case. Due to the size of the instrument and space restrictions, however, the Pedal organ was divided into two sections and the soundboards and pipes of this division were installed in the first bays of the north and south choir aisles.

This organ was undoubtedly one of the finest new instruments of its day and Edwin Crow was so delighted that he wrote to Messrs Lewis as follows:

Ripon Cathedral
30th September 1878
To:
Messrs T.C. Lewis & Company.

Gentlemen,

In a letter which I had the pleasure of addressing to you four years since, the following passages occur.

After an extensive examination of the work of our best organ builders (with a view to selecting a firm to build an organ for this cathedral) I have felt it my duty to recommend to the Dean and Chapter to entrust the work to you, and they have agreed to do so.

We have purposely avoided throwing the work open to competition because we wish to possess an organ which will really be a work of art.

Such an instrument I trust and believe you will give and thereby justify me recommending to the Dean and Chapter that they place the work in your hands.

I feel it is now due to you that I should express my entire satisfaction with the manner in which you have done the work.

The magnificent organ that you have placed in our beautifully restored cathedral has completely realised my hopes and may fairly challenge comparison with any other cathedral organ in England, whether considered in regard to tone, materials or workmanship.

I trust it may prove to be a lasting memorial to your skill and ability.

Believe me, yours very faithfully,
Edwin J. Crow, Mus Bac, FCO.

This letter contrasts somewhat with an article on the organ written by Crow in 'The Ripon Millenary Record' eight years later.

The present arrangement has many objectionable features. Placed on the screen, the organ is, for services in the choir, decidedly too loud, especially the pedal trombone, which, owing to a misunderstanding in the drawings, had to be raised twelve feet above where the builders intended it to go, and the pipes now project above the top of the case, with very ugly effect.

The pedal organ, divided and placed in the aisles, but without any case whatever, is decidedly more useful than beautiful; while that loud knock of the pallets (which were placed in a receptacle resembling an altar tomb instead of underground) is distinctly a nuisance, being audible through the softer music.

The blowing apparatus has been placed in the south aisle on a floor specially made some twenty feet from the ground. By this extraordinary arrangement, every noise made by the engines and bellows is heard all over the choir, to the great annoyance of the congregation, while the raised position, by reducing the water pressure, makes larger engines and increased costs unavoidable.

However the organ is certainly a most magnificent instrument. Its tone is probably unsurpassed by any other organ in the country, always excepting the old work which it was a pity to retain.

It is evident that although Crow was not entirely happy with certain aspects of the instrument, he was clearly very pleased with the overall result. In view of his concluding remarks, however, it seems that, if Crow had had his way, not only would the ancient choir screen have been removed, but so too would the old pipework by Gerhard Schmidt.

The new organ was blown by a water-powered engine that provided pressurised air to the bellows. The blowing apparatus was housed in a gallery chamber above the west end of the south choir aisle; the access door to this old chamber can still be seen on the left hand side at the top of the stairs to the cathedral library. As confirmed by Crow, however, this new blowing system was not a success because when the organ was in operation but not being played, or when it was being played softly, the noise was very distracting. Attempts to reduce the noise by further enclosing the blowing apparatus had little effect, and in 1890 two new patent blowing engines, presumably also water-powered, were installed at a cost of £117. The problem of noise from the organ blowers was not finally solved, however, until 1913 when all the blowing apparatus was housed in a sound-proof compartment outside the cathedral.

In 1902 Hill & Son replaced the Barker lever action of the organ with tubular pneumatic. They also installed a new console with the stops in the more usual places, revoiced the reeds and added an 8ft coupler and a tremulant to the Swell.

Charles Moody was appointed organist in 1902 in succession to Edwin Crow. He was an active recitalist and early in 1908 was invited to give a recital on the new organ at St Anne's Cathedral, Belfast, which had been built the year before by Messrs Harrison & Harrison of Durham. Moody was so impressed with this instrument that after the recital he wrote to Harrisons from his hotel room:

> *Midland Station Hotel*
> *Belfast.*
> *13th February 1908*

Dear Mr Harrison,

Your organ here is a triumph – a few more instruments like this and people will flock to hear them.

I never heard or played an organ which made so great an impression on me and I write with a vivid recollection of all the instruments – that is considerable instruments – I have played on.

I can only compare it to a first class orchestra, plus ideal diapasons. There was an immense congregation and the Precentor tells me he considers this the most appreciated recital so far. Don't misunderstand me – I don't say this egotistically because the organ was everything – but to show how warmly your noble instrument is appreciated.

The Dean has very kindly expressed a hope that I will come again and I hope that this may be made possible soon after Easter.

Your man here was most courteous and I should like to say how beautifully in tune everything was. What a tuba! If only they had one like it at York. And what would I not give to have such an organ at Ripon.

It is in every sense of the word, a masterpiece.

Ever sincerely yours
Ch. H. Moody.

It is not surprising therefore that in 1912, when it became evident that the Ripon Cathedral organ required extensive rebuilding, Charles Moody had no hesitation in recommending to the Dean and Chapter that the task should be entrusted to Harrison & Harrison. They were asked to give a full report on the instrument and they recommended :

New blowing apparatus.

The Lewis (1878) pipework to be preserved, but some stop changes and new stops; a soft Mixture to be added to the Swell and the 4ft Harmonic Flute transferred from Swell to the Great. In addition, a 32ft open wood rank to be added to the Pedal division.

Adding a Solo organ division (fourth manual) with all pipes, except the big tuba, to be enclosed in a swell box.

Relocation of the Choir and Pedal divisions in the western bays of the north and south choir aisles respectively.

Improving the console facilities and providing additional couplers.

Enlargement of the box to the Swell organ and raising the Great soundboards.

Extensive cleaning and revoicing.

All the above work involved considerable financial outlay and needed to be undertaken on a phased basis as time and available funds would allow. Harrison & Harrison were asked to submit separate quotations for each aspect of the proposed works, altogether totalling £1,070.

Meanwhile, the most pressing issue was to deal with the blowing apparatus. This continued to make an intolerable noise and moreover the blowing engines were by now obsolete and in need of replacement. Work started in 1912 and was completed by the next year. This was a considerable task because it was decided to install the two new high-capacity 'Discus' blowing fans, driven by a 9 hp gas engine, in a purpose-built compartment at the end of what at that time was the song school. This building was situated outside the cathedral some 45 yards from the south porch, and is now the former office adjoining the cathedral hall. An air duct was buried beneath the ground between the building and the cathedral and connected to the organ via trunking under the south transept floor. This new arrangement finally solved the problem of noise from the blowing apparatus.

The cleaning and revoicing of the organ followed, and then the tonal improvements and the provision of a Solo organ division. Several stops were changed and others added, but the Choir 4ft Dulcet rank of pipes, which was part of the old Schmidt organ, was removed. Fortunately, however, three of the Schmidt ranks were retained and survive to this day. They are:

> Complete rank of 8ft Flute pipes (now named 'Rohr Gedeckt' and incorporated in the Swell).

> Complete rank of 4ft Flute pipes (now named 'Rohr Flute' and incorporated in the Swell).

> Top end of 8ft Bass Flute pipes (now named Flute and incorporated in the Pedal division).

The box to the Swell division was enlarged and the pipes therein better distributed with improved access for tuning. The soundboard to the Great organ was raised, which enabled the pipes, particularly the Great reeds, to speak and be heard with greater clarity. The pipes of the 32ft open wood stop, added to the pedal division, were housed in the south choir aisle where it was necessary to excavate the floor to accommodate them.

The 1926 organ console.

All this work took place during 1913 and was completed by 1914, but due to the outbreak of the First World War the outstanding work on the console and renewal of the organ action had to be postponed.

By then, despite the initial estimate of just over £1,000, the total costs incurred had risen to over £3,000.

After the end of the war in 1918, the Dean and Chapter were so impecunious that the outstanding work to the organ, that had been considered necessary even in 1912, was not attended to. Emergency temporary repairs were undertaken in 1920 and 1921, but by 1923 the organ had become virtually unplayable and Harrison & Harrison were called in to assess the work required to restore it. The schedule of repairs and renewals was extensive and in particular Harrisons stressed that the entire mechanism of the organ should be replaced as a matter of urgency.

The crucial work was dealt with first, and all the recommendations, and more besides, were carried out over the next three years. These included a new action and console, and resiting the whole of the Pedal Division in the south choir aisle, and the Choir Division in the north choir aisle. This created more room within the main organ case on the screen, enabling the soundboards of the Great Division to be extended, the swell box to be enlarged, and the layout of the pipes to be reorganised so that they spoke more effectively.

By the end of 1926 the restored organ comprised:

Great:	13 stops (3 couplers)
Swell:	14 stops (enclosed – tremulant and 3 couplers)
Choir:	10 stops (enclosed – tremulant and 3 couplers)
Solo:	6 stops (tremulant and 3 couplers)
Pedal:	8 stops (4 couplers)

Swell, Choir and Solo (except tubas) enclosed
Numerous couplers, combination pistons and pedals

Those interested in the technical details and the final specification of the 1926 instrument are referred to Robert Marsh's book 'Ripon Cathedral – A Short History of the Organs' published in 1994.

The organ case, designed by Sir George Gilbert Scott in 1878, had been criticised over the years because the wings that protruded from the west face were considered by many to be intrusive, as they obscured the lower sections of the pillars of the eastern arch of the crossing and impaired the view from the nave looking east. Charles Moody considered that these side wings, which contained only non-speaking show pipes, should be removed, and he gained the support of Dean Mansfield Owen. In 1926 the Dean and Chapter agreed, and as part of the organ restoration, Harrison & Harrison arranged for Messrs Thompsons, Master Woodworkers, of Peterborough, to take down the wings and use the carved oak and the show pipes to front the sections of the organ in the north and south choir aisles. A donation of one hundred guineas from Tetley's Brewery, Leeds, greatly helped and also enabled the show pipes to be regilded.

The 1878 organ.

The original iron fixings, by which the wings had been attached to the pillars on either side of the screen, are still visible in the stonework of the two columns.

It seems that the removal of the wings was generally considered to have improved the appearance of the organ, and indeed of the whole prospect looking east down the nave. The Ripon Gazette of Thursday 4th November 1926 reported:

One of the predominant impressions at Wednesday's organ recital by Dr Moody (to mark the restoration of the organ) *was the absence of the wings that flanked the west side of the case. This Victorian excrescence had been obliterated with the cordial approval of the Dean and Chapter. The soaring columns of the great arch on the east side of the central tower, partially concealed since 1878, are again revealed. The elevation of this side of the organ case has been materially enhanced.*

The extensive organ restoration was completed in 1926, and a series of inaugural recitals was given by eminent organists of the day, including Dr Charles MacPherson of St Paul's Cathedral, and Professor Sir Walford Davies of St George's Chapel, Windsor. These drew sizeable audiences, but earlier, in 1925, shortly before the work was finished, Charles Moody had given a recital which was not well supported. The Ripon Gazette reported *the poor attendance was probably due to changes in public taste and the increased popularity of jazz.*

To mark the major 1912-1926 organ restoration work, Charles Moody wrote a book on the 'Ripon Cathedral Organ', published in 1926 by J. H. Taylor of Ripon, in which he stated *The beauty of Messrs Harrison's restoration work ... has won the highest encomiums from critics and music lovers generally. The work of this eminent firm in the present restoration has never been surpassed. ... The stops have been voiced and regulated by that supreme artist, Mr Arthur Harrison, and the tone is a delight to both player and hearer. ... No praise would be too fulsome.*

In 1930 the organ blowing apparatus (installed in 1912-1913 in the song school) was scrapped. The old gas engines, which previously drove the blowing fans, were replaced with electric motors, and these and the blower fans were housed in a compartment in part of the undercroft (crypt) beneath the chapter house.

Following the particularly severe winter of 1947, it was decided to install a new heating system in the cathedral. Unfortunately, this caused much of the woodwork and leatherwork of the organ soundboards and pedal pipes to dry out and crack. To combat this problem humidifiers were installed in the organ chambers by Watkins & Watson of London, but these were of limited success, and by late 1949 it was realised that major repairs were needed.

Charles Moody recommended that the contract be given to John Compton & Sons of London who at that time were at the forefront of the use of modern electric action in organ building. Comptons repaired the damaged woodwork, undertook electrification of much of the old pneumatic action and thoroughly cleaned and restored the instrument. The tonal scheme of the organ and its pipework remained unchanged. The total cost of this work was £4,900 and the money was raised by subscription, with Tetley's Brewery again being a major donor. Following completion of the work in the late spring of 1950, recitals were given in June and July by Lady Susi Jeans, Dr John Dykes Bower (St Paul's Cathedral) and Dr William Harris (St George's Chapel, Windsor).

It was not until 1957 that the blowing equipment, which had done its job satisfactorily for 27 years, needed to be replaced. Watkins & Watson of London installed more efficient fans, together with two new electric motors. All this apparatus was installed in a purpose-built soundproof pit that was constructed beneath the floor of the south choir aisle, where it remains to this day.

In 1963 a major rebuild of the organ, costing £12,000, was carried out at the instigation of the organist, Dr Philip Marshall, who planned the specification in close consultation with Cuthbert Harrison of Harrison & Harrison. In addition to a complete overhaul of the instrument, several major changes were made.

1. Three stops removed:

Choir:	Vox Angelica	8
	Viola da Gamba	8
Pedal:	Sub-bass	32

2. Seven stops added:

Choir:	Nazard $2^2/_3$
	Tierce $1^3/_5$
	Cimbal III rank mixture
Pedal:	Lieblich Bourdon 16 (extended from Choir)
	Viole 4
	Mixture III ranks
	Bombardon 32
	Tuba 16 from Solo
	Tuba 8 from Solo
	Tuba 4 from Solo

3. The box enclosing the pipes of the Choir division was removed.
4. More shutters were added to the north side of the Swell box to improve the egress of sound into the nave and increase the range of sound level control.
5. Provision of extra console control facilities.

Following the above, the specification of the organ consisted of :

Great:	13 stops (3 couplers)
Swell:	14 stops (enclosed – tremulant and 3 couplers)
Choir:	11 stops (3 couplers)
Solo:	6 stops (enclosed – tremulant and 3 couplers)
Pedal:	14 stops (4 couplers)

Swell and Solo (except Tubas) enclosed
Numerous couplers, combination pistons and pedals

Several alterations were carried out to the organ in 1972 by Harrison & Harrison in consultation with the organist Ronald Perrin. These involved replacing the 8ft Hohl Flute and the 4ft Harmonic Flute on the Great with a 4ft Coppel Flute and a $1^1/_3$ft Larigot. In addition, the IV rank Mixture on the Great was reconstituted and revoiced to enhance its brilliance.

A large Makin electronic organ was presented to Ripon Cathedral in 1981 and installed in the nave. The story of this is appended at the end of this chapter.

The years 1987-1988 saw a general overhaul undertaken by Harrison & Harrison who also installed a new stop. This was an Orchestral Trumpet 8ft, which was added to the Solo Organ (but not within the Solo swell box) and was given by a generous, though a little eccentric, local landowner. A plaque erected inside the organ loft reads:

HOC ORGANUM AD RESTITUENDUM

A.D. MCMLXXXVIII

TUBUM HISPANICAM DD DOMINUS PRAEDII VIR MORIBUS SINGULARIS

The master of a landed estate, a man who was unique in his character and ways, gave the Spanish Trumpet as a gift for the restoration of this organ.

AD 1988

This new reed stop is *en chamade,* that is the pipes (which are tapered) are mounted horizontally on the top of the swell box of the main organ, and speak

The organ, 2007.

westwards down into the nave. The Orchestral Trumpet makes a most exciting sound and it was specifically for this new stop that Ronald Perrin composed 'A Spanish Toccata' in 1987. Soon afterwards he recorded this and other pieces, which were issued on a tape cassette (Ref. Chapter 15 and the Discography in the Appendix).

During the 1990s only routine maintenance, cleaning and the regular tuning (about five times a year) were undertaken.

A chamber organ was jointly purchased by the Dean and Chapter and the Ripon Choral Society in November 1996. This is an instrument made by Harrison & Harrison of Durham, and cost £8,000 second-hand. It has three ranks, 8ft, 4ft and 2ft flute pipes, and is in a fine oak case with a built-in electric blower.

The chamber organ is on castors and has proved to be a very worthwhile acquisition. It is used regularly by the cathedral choir (especially for accompanying music of the Tudor era) and by the choral society, as a continuo with small instrumental groups and for accompanying arias.

In December 2000, after nearly eighteen months planning and seven months building, Harrison & Harrison installed a new mobile console in the nave. This was generously presented to the cathedral by a benefactor and used for the first time at the Service of Nine Lessons and Carols on Christmas Eve that year. The installation of this new console involved some work on the main organ, particularly the provision of solid state control mechanisms and electro-pneumatic machines to enable the shutters of the enclosed Swell and Solo organs to be operated remotely. Detailed information about the nave console is set out in a separate section (Ref. pages 170-172).

The next major overhaul of the Ripon Cathedral organ is due in 2009 and will involve extensive cleaning of the instrument with some renewals of the action and upgrading of control mechanisms. It is also proposed to re-enclose the Choir division to increase the expression capabilities.

The couplers and accessories shown in the following specification are those on the new nave console. These facilities, except the pedal divide, sequencer, and other modern specialist features, are also available on the console on the choir screen.

The Organ Specification 2008

Great

Double Stopped Diapson	16
Large Open Diapason	8
Small Open Diapason	8
Stopped Diapason	8
Octave	4
Coppel Flute	4
Octave Quint	$2^2/3$
Super Octave	2
Larigot	$1^1/3$
Mixture 19-22-26-29	IV
Contra Tromba	16
Tromba	8
Octave Tromba	4

Swell to Great	*Solo to Great*
Choir to Great	*Reeds on Choir*

Choir

Lieblich Bourdon	16
Lieblich Gedeckt	8
Flauto Traverso	8
Salicional	8
Lieblich Flute	4
Salicet	4
Nazard	$2^2/3$
Lieblich Piccolo	2
Tierce	$1^3/5$
Cimbel 22-26-29	III
Clarinet	8

Swell to Choir	*Solo to Choir*

Swell (enclosed)

Bourdon	16
Geigen	8
Rohr Gedeckt*	8
Echo Gamba	8
Voix Célestes (Ten C)	8
Geigen Principal	4
Rohr Flute*	4
Flautina	2
Sesquialtera 17-19-22	III
Mixture 12-15	II
Contra Fagotto	16
Oboe	8
Trumpet	8
Clarion	4

Octave	*Unison Off*
Sub Octave	*Tremulant*

Solo (enclosed)

Viole d'Orchestre	8
Concert Flute	4
Corno di Bassetto	16
Orchestral Hautboy	8
Contra Tuba	16
Tuba (unenclosed)	8
Orchestral Trumpet (unenclosed)	8

Octave	*Unison Off*
Sub Octave	*Tremulant*

Pedal

Double Open Wood	32
Open Wood	16
Violone	16
Sub Bass	16
Lieblich Bourdon (Ch)	16
Violoncello	8
Flute*	8
Viole	4
Mixture 15-19-22	III
Bombardon	32
Ophicleide	16
Tuba (Solo)	16
Octave Tuba (Solo)	8
Tuba Clarion (Solo)	4

Great to Pedal	*Choir to Pedal*
Swell to Pedal	*Solo to Pedal*

Accessories

Full complement of divisional/reversible pistons
8 General pistons
Balanced expression pedals for Swell & Solo Nave Console only
Pedal divide
Manual I & II exchange
Sequencer
General pistons stepper
Solid State Logic MIDI Interface (MIDI in & out)
*Three ranks of pipes retained from the Gerhard Schmidt organ of 1695

The Nave Console

In 1886 the organist of Ripon Cathedral, Edwin Crow, wrote in 'The Ripon Millenary Record' *The organist is placed inside the instrument where he can neither see nor hear, and a door in the organ case, intended to enable him to do so, will not open on account of the screen. A more absurd position could hardly have been devised.*

In early 1999, Canon Michael Glanville-Smith was approached by an old friend closely connected with Ripon Cathedral. He was a businessman who had sung in the choir as a supernumerary lay clerk at weekends for many years and he offered to present the cathedral with a mobile console which would enable the organ to be played from virtually any location in the nave. This was readily accepted and the new nave console was designed and built by Harrison & Harrison of Durham in consultation with Kerry Beaumont (the organist), the benefactor, and Patrick Crawford (the cathedral architect).

By computer-aided design and development and the use of the latest digital technology and miniaturised components, the size, particularly the height, of

the console was kept to a minimum. In terms of its functions, the nave console duplicated the console within the main instrument on the choir screen, but incorporated many additional features, providing the organist with greater control and flexibility.

Pedal Divide Stop. This enables the pedal board to be divided into two sections, so that the organist can play both a bass part with the left foot and counterpoint (using the manual-to-pedal couplers) with the right foot.

Manual I and II Exchange Stop. The operation of this stop allows the organist to play the Great division from the lowest manual (normally the Choir) and the Choir division from the second manual (normally the Great). This facility is particularly appropriate to French organ music.

Sequencer. This provides one thousand separate 'steps' of configurable stop changes to facilitate the registration of a complex and extensive programme of pieces for recitals, recordings and broadcasts. The sequencer is controlled by thumb and toe pistons and enables the organist to control 'Advance' (change to next registration in the sequence set up), 'Back' and 'Reinstate' (i.e. revert to the previously designated sequencer step before any stop changes made by hand).

In addition to, but entirely independent of, the sequencer, there are comprehensive Multi-level General and Divisional Pistons that enable organists to pre-set any desired combination of stops and couplers.

The Swell and Solo shutters are worked by direct mechanical connections from the screen console but when the remote nave console is in use, two Sixteen-stage electro-pneumatic 'wiffle tree' shutter machines are brought into play.

A MIDI Interface ('In' and 'Out'), with full configuration control facilities and interfaced with all five divisions of the organ is built into the console. This was designed and built by 'Solid State Logic' who also supplied the digital sequencer, and computerised communication systems.

There is also a facility for both the console on the screen and the nave console to be played simultaneously, with a Screen Cancel button on the nave console to withdraw all screen console stops.

The remote nave console is connected to the organ solely via a single cable, only 6mm in diameter, using computer-controlled multiplexing techniques. There are plug-in points at various locations in the nave, and the cable is long enough to allow the mobile console to be placed in almost any position in the nave, transepts or crossing .

The nave console enables the organist to hear the instrument properly and to accurately balance it with the choir and/or orchestra, and also to be in close proximity to, and have a full rapport with, the conductor and the performers.

The case of the console is built in natural oak to match the library staircase and complement the nave choir stalls and altar. It has non-reflecting glass doors which hinge through 270 degrees and, when opened, fit exactly down the sides of the console. They provide complete visual accessibility to cathedral visitors even when the nave console is not in use.

On Friday 20th January 2001 a Celebration Organ Recital was held to inaugurate the nave console:

Kerry Beaumont
Bridal Fanfare and March	Raymond Sunderland (1921-1977)
Scherzo	Eugène Gigout (1844-1925)
Prelude and Fugue in B major	Marcel Dupré (1886-1971)

Andrew Bryden
Tuba Tune	Norman Cocker (1889-1953)
Prelude & Fugue in D major	J. S. Bach (1686-1750)

Organ Duos
Organ Concerto No 4 in F major	G. F. Handel (1685-1759)
Concerto No 6 for two organs	Antonio Soler (1729-1783)

The above two items were duets, with Kerry playing the grand organ, via the new mobile console, and Andrew playing the chamber organ.

Grand Organ Duet from two consoles
Grand Choeur Dialogue	Eugène Gigout (1844-1925)

This final piece was played using all the resources of the organ, with Kerry playing the nave console and Andrew the console on the choir screen. This remarkable feat was achieved by virtue of the special switching device, referred to above, whereby the normal arrangement of the organ being controlled either by the nave console or by the screen console, can be overridden so that both consoles are working live and in parallel. The result was stunning and provided an appropriate conclusion to a memorable occasion.

The Makin electronic organ

In late 1980 an anonymous benefactor offered to present an electronic organ to Ripon Cathedral. The Dean and Chapter did not really require such an instrument as they already had the magnificent Lewis-Harrison pipe organ and would have preferred the gift of a mobile nave console from which to play it, but such a facility was not on offer. Bearing in mind, however, that the new electronic organ was a very comprehensive instrument costing over £40,000, and the donor was also paying for the installation, commissioning and maintenance charges, it was undoubtedly a very generous gift and the Dean and Chapter decided to accept it.

The cathedral organist, Ronald Perrin, drew up the specification of this four manual and pedal instrument, which had 78 speaking stops (more than the cathedral pipe organ!) and a host of couplers, pistons and three swell pedals. The organ, made by Makin Organs of Rochdale, was installed with a powerful high quality amplification system and a large bank of loudspeakers, in oak cabinets, mounted high up in the clerestory arches on either side of the nave. The Makin console was placed on the north side of the nave, adjacent to the choir stalls, and despite its weight of nearly half a ton, it could be moved – given two or three burly vergers – on its heavy castors to other positions around the north-east end of the nave.

Ronald Perrin gave an inaugural recital on the new instrument in May 1981 and, considering the sounds made by many of the electronic organs being produced at this time, the Makin instrument in Ripon Cathedral was in a class of its own. Many of its softer stops and flutes, a good deal of the diapasons and some of the solo stops, were very effective, but the louder stops and certain combinations with the mixtures served to remind the listener that it was not a genuine pipe organ. Nevertheless the Makin instrument was successfully used for large congregational services and concerts in the nave.

Whilst the organ 'purists' condemned the instrument, not so Ronald Perrin. He realised full well that the Makin offered no comparison with, and hence no serious threat to, the main pipe organ, but he enjoyed putting the electronic instrument through its paces. Several joint organ recitals were held which ended in a 'battle of the organs', when Ronald and the visiting recitalist would play a duet, pulling out most of the stops of each of the two organs. These events were very popular and greatly enjoyed by the audiences, Ronald Perrin, and visiting recitalists, alike.

During the early 1990s some technical problems developed and the instrument became very dated. Manufacturers of electronic organs, including Makin, began to use digital sampling technology which enabled the sounds (i.e. the timbre and overtone content in different frequency ranges, and the speaking characteristics) of actual organ pipes to be digitally captured and stored in solid state memory. This revolutionised the quality of electronic organs and the Makin instrument at Ripon became little used. When, in 1999, the prospect arose of a mobile nave console linked to the magnificent Lewis-Harrison pipe organ, the Makin was sold to All Saints Church, Braunston, Leicester where it has since been up-dated with the latest technology and is still giving good service.

Chapter 14

THE MUSIC

The monastery at Ripon was founded in 657AD, and for the next six hundred years the music in Ripon Minster was plainsong sung to Latin liturgical texts. During the very early years the liturgy was probably based on the Celtic rite, stemming from monastic establishments at Melrose, Lindisfarne, and Jarrow, but after the arrival of Wilfrid, and particularly following the Synod of Whitby in 664, the Roman rite prevailed.

The Mass was sung each day, usually in the morning. The seven Offices, or services (sometimes referred to as hours), were sung during the day at intervals of about three hours.

Matins	(later known as Lauds) at sunrise
Prime	during the first hour of daylight
Terce	the third hour
Sext	the sixth hour
None	the ninth hour
Vespers	at the end of the day (sunset)
Compline	prior to retiring to bed
Vigils	during the night (but not always performed)

The main psalms usually sung at matins were numbers 148,149 and 150, all of them psalms of praise involving use of the Latin word *Laudamus* – hence this service was often called Lauds.

Mass consisted of the Kyrie, Gloria, Creed, Sanctus, Benedictus and Agnus Dei, together with the Propers (the parts of the mass that varied according to the particular day or time and were 'proper' for the occasion). These included Antiphons (usually a verse from scripture sung before or after a canticle, psalm or part of the liturgy), Graduals (a pair of verses from the psalms sung or said after the epistle) and Responsories (sets of phrases and responses said or sung after a reading from the scriptures). On Sundays, festivals and saints' days, additional items were probably added for use in procession. The music of the Offices comprised the canticles, psalms and bible text appointed for the day.

There is little evidence of written musical notation during the first millennium; plainsong was learnt by rote and passed on from generation to generation. Some scholars believe that early notation began in the eleventh century with marks, written in above the Latin text, which served as an aide-mémoire for the singers. These imprecise marks developed into the neumes which were later placed on lines (initially no more than three or four) to give a more accurate indication of pitch. It was the combination of neumes and lines which later became the notes and stave of present day written music.

The plainsong melodies evolved into different modes (which later led to the concept of keys). Text underlay (the fitting of the words to the music) also developed with various inflections and melismata (the technique of slurring over several notes sung in quick succession to one syllable).

When Ripon monastery was converted into a collegiate church around the time of the Norman Conquest, the monks were replaced by clergy, who had responsibilities in the parishes and ceased to be predominantly dedicated to the singing of the services. Consequently, rather than adhering to the strict round of the Offices, it became the practice to merge services together and hold them at more convenient times. The Requiem Masses sung in the endowed chantry chapels, however, attracted additional income, and so were not similarly curtailed.

Polyphonic music emerged in the late thirteenth century and was in widespread use by the beginning of the sixteenth century. There is no record of the music sung at Ripon Minster during this period, but much of the repertoire was probably composed by the incumbent organist. Some music was obtained from other choral establishments but usually only when organists moved, taking their music with them.

The services and music at Ripon were interrupted for significant periods on several occasions. The north of England was invaded by the Danish Vikings in 860 and again in about 950. Services were severely disrupted once more by the collapse of the east end of the minster in 1280, which took many decades to rebuild. In 1450 the south-east section of the central tower collapsed, causing serious damage to a large part of the choir and the old choir stalls. As a result, new stalls were made by the Bromflet carvers, being completed in 1494. Nine years later work started on building new nave aisles, which were not completed until 1538. Consequently, much of the cathedral was a building site for some eighty years. In 1660 the steeple on the central tower was blown down, damaging the choir roof, the canopies of the choir stalls, the screen and what remained of the organ.

The music was all but eradicated on two occasions when the choral foundation was disbanded. Firstly in 1548 the collegiate church at Ripon was dissolved by Edward VI (Ref. Chapter 3), and secondly during the Commonwealth in the 1650s when all professional church musicians were dismissed (Ref. Chapter 5).

Sometime in the fourteenth century Ripon acquired an organ. Nearly all the main services, except processions and special masses in the chantry chapels, were held in the choir so the organ would almost certainly have been situated either in the choir itself, or on the screen between the choir and nave. We know from the fabric rolls of 1399 that an organ was constructed on the screen and this would probably have been used to alternate with and/or accompany the plainsong, and played by a priest. Indeed the first recorded organist at Ripon was Thomas Litster, priest, in 1447.

During the Reformation the first 'Book of Common Prayer' led to the composition of a whole new body of church music in English. In 1641 the Reverend John Barnard, a former lay clerk at Canterbury Cathedral and later a minor canon at St Paul's Cathedral, issued his 'First Book of Selected Church Music'. This was a ten volume set comprising individual part books for five voices; mean (boy trebles), two countertenors (male altos), tenor and bass, for both decani and cantoris. Barnard's book was a ground-breaking publication, being the first and only known printed anthology of English Church Music between 1565 and 1660. It is a unique and fine example of early printed music and was published by Edward Griffin of London, *to be sold at the signe of the three lutes in Pauls Alley* (See illustration).

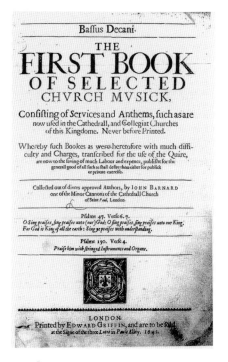

Several choral foundations, including Ripon Minster, acquired copies of Barnard's book. It seems probable, however, that because of the book's association with the King (*Sing praises unto our King* printed on the title page was enough to reveal Barnard's allegiances) and the political upheaval at the time, most of its distribution was held back until after the restoration of the monarchy in 1660.

John Barnard's selection shows his good judgement and no doubt he chose the best of the music being performed in London churches at the time. This 'First Book of Selected Church Music', as its name implies, was intended to be followed by a second book, but this never materialised and it is thought that Barnard fled the country in 1642 at the outbreak of the Civil War.

A considerable amount of music is included in Barnard's book, much of it published for the first time.

Services by Tallis, Byrd, Gibbons, Mundy, Morley, Parsons and Giles comprising 11 morning services (8 Venite, 11 Te Deum, 8 Benedictus and 2 Jubilate) plus 14 evening services (Magnificat and Nunc Dimittis), 9 Kyrie and Credo settings and a Gloria and Sanctus.

Responses by Tallis, Byrd and Gibbons.

Anthems by Byrd, Bull, Gibbons and Ward comprising 16 full anthems for four voices, 14 anthems for five voices and 5 anthems for six or more voices (including Byrd's 'Sing Joyfully') plus 12 verse anthems.

An enormous quantity of music was destroyed during the Commonwealth, and a vast amount was also lost in subsequent years through neglect and wear and tear. For example, of the 54 part books of music listed (soon after the Restoration) in the choir library of Lincoln Cathedral, all had been lost by 1900. However, while not one original set of Barnard's collection has survived intact, at least one copy of most of the ten individual voice parts has been unearthed at various locations. Hereford Cathedral possessed the lion's share and others were located by John Bumpus, one-time librarian of St Michael's College, Tenbury. As a result it was possible to reconstitute nearly all of the music that Barnard had collected, the primary source for many pieces later published. It is difficult to over-estimate the importance of this collection, which formed the basis of the church music repertoire for the next two hundred years. No trace could be found of the organ parts for any of the verse anthems, however, and indeed some scholars doubt that they were ever included in the original publication. Copies of Barnard's 'First Book of Selected Church Music' are now held in the libraries of Christchurch Cathedral, Oxford, the Royal College of Music and the British Library.

A bass decani copy of Barnard's collection came into the hands of Sir John Stainer, organist of St Paul's Cathedral from 1872 to 1888, and this is one of

Jubilate by Thomas Preston, bass part.

those now held in the British Library. On examination a remarkable discovery was made. Bound into the printed book were 49 folio pages of manuscript music, much of which was composed and handwritten by Thomas Preston, the Elder, who was organist at Ripon Minster from 1690 to 1730. Indeed some of the pages bore what appears to be his signature.

Were it not for the survival of these manuscripts, our knowledge of the music at Ripon Minster in the seventeenth century would be non-existent, as nothing from that period remains in the cathedral library.

There was also an anthem composed by Alexander Shaw, who had been a chorister at Durham and was organist at Ripon from 1674 to 1677. Records confirm that soon after his arrival at Ripon, the Dean and Chapter paid Shaw for copying some music and it is likely that this is the collection that he had brought with him from Durham. The chapter minutes of May 1696 verify that Thomas Preston was likewise paid for copying music, presumably much of it his own (Ref. Chapter 5).

Included in the manuscript sheets there was:

Music by Alexander Shaw

    Anthem: 'I will sing unto the Lord' – This was a verse anthem for bass solo

Music brought to Ripon from Durham by Shaw

    Anthems: 'Behold how good and joyful', Hutchinson (organist Durham 1614-1661)
                    'When the Lord turned again', Foster (organist Durham 1661-1677)
                    'Almighty and everlasting God', Foster
                    Several anthems possibly written by Durham lay clerks

Music by Thomas Preston, The Elder

Services:	in G minor	Te Deum, Jubilate, Magnificat and Nunc Dimittis
	in E minor	Te Deum and Jubilate
	in D	Te Deum, Jubilate, Magnificat and Nunc Dimittis
	Tripla in Bb	Te Deum (Tripla signifies triple time)
	Tripla in F	Te Deum and Jubilate
Anthems:	'It is a good thing'	
	'Rejoice in the Lord'	
	'O be joyful in the Lord'	

'O praise God in his holiness'
'I waited patiently for the Lord'

Unfortunately these manuscripts only contained a bass part, and reconstruction is not possible because, as far as is known, no other copies exist.

During the late sixteenth and early seventeenth centuries, composers such as Tye, Farrant, Tallis, Byrd, Morley, Tomkins, Weelkes and Gibbons produced a wealth of new church music, particularly for the Chapel Royal. Much of this was probably of greater complexity than could be managed by many of the provincial choral establishments. It is likely therefore that the repertoire at Ripon in the late seventeenth century was quite small, relying largely on the efforts of local composers, and that undemanding settings of the canticles were sung, together with simple anthems. Verse anthems were probably popular, as they frequently used the lower voices in the verse parts, and concluded with a simple chorus of Alleluia or Amen that was not too taxing for the boys. It seems that by the end of the seventeenth century Ripon had approximately 16 settings of both morning and evening canticles and about 70 anthems in its choir library. There is little evidence of additions to the repertoire, apart from some chants, until about 1760.

Early attempts at setting music to an English version of the psalms were undertaken by Thomas Tallis using harmonised melodies based on Gregorian tones, but from about 1565 onwards the more congregational metrical versions by Sternold and Hopkins began to gain a firm hold. With the introduction of the Book of Common Prayer in 1662, impetus was given to changing the way in which psalms were sung. The Gregorian psalm tones had been harmonised using the tenor line as the *cantus firmus* (as in Tallis's chants), but increasingly, after the Restoration, the tone (melody) was placed as a top line. A further natural development was to vary, and then abandon, the *cantus firmus* altogether in favour of a melody unrelated to the tone.

At Ripon Thomas Preston, the Elder wrote a chant which still survives (See below). This is a double chant in B minor, which was ahead of its time as most of the chants in the eighteenth century were single. It was discovered in the

Thomas Preston

British Library but was subsequently found to have been included in a Durham Cathedral chant book of about 1865.

An early version of the preces and responses for the English rite was harmonised by Tallis and, like the harmonised psalm tones, retained the tenor *cantus firmus*. These were included in Barnard's collection along with versions by Byrd and Gibbons. Jebb's 'Choral Responses and Litanies' of 1847 shows there was wide variation in the way in which responses were used, as well as a surprising number of different sets. It was, however, the very simple ferial (and sometimes the festal) responses, with basic harmonisation, that were the most widely sung. It seems that at Ripon the ferial responses were the only ones used until the 1940s.

William Boyce was a chorister at St Paul's Cathedral and studied music with Maurice Greene. He was appointed Master of the King's Musick in 1755 and became organist at the Chapel Royal three years later. Due to severe deafness, however, he retired and began work on compiling 'Boyce's Collection of Cathedral Music'. This included works by Tallis, Byrd and Gibbons, plus later music by Aldrich, Bevin, Blow, Child, Purcell and Rogers. There are 12 settings of the morning canticles, 14 evening canticles, 15 single chants, 4 double chants, 40 full anthems and 32 verse anthems (6 of the full anthems and 7 of the verse anthems are still in regular use).

Boyce published his three volume collection in 1760, 1768 and 1773, and, unlike Barnard, this was in full-score, all the different voice parts being printed together. Boyce was acutely aware that church music of the Renaissance and the Restoration periods was in danger of being lost, and his collection, like that of Barnard, was hugely influential. It was unfortunate that Boyce lost a considerable amount of money from his enterprise. Boyce's publication was later reprinted by Vincent Novello, who also made separate copies of the anthems and services available.

The Dean and Chapter of Ripon are listed as subscribers to all three volumes. William Ayrton was organist at Ripon during their publication, but what proportion of this fine church music was actually performed by the choir is not known.

Standards of music in cathedrals and collegiate churches fell dramatically during the eighteenth century and Ripon Minster was no exception (Ref. Chapter 6). It is unlikely that choral services were sung every day, and probably the settings of the canticles were only sung on Sundays, one or two weekdays and on Holy Days. The clergy were lax and indifferent and, but for any good influence from the organist, presumably the choir was too.

Some glimmer of progress evidently occurred in 1823, when the dean made an extra payment to John Bond, the organist, for *improvement of the choir.* Bond was also responsible for introducing services by Kelway, Kempton and Travers.

In the 1830s the Oxford Movement worked to improve the worship in the Anglican Church, with particular stress on restoring ancient church rituals and enhancing the standard of music. Although regarded with suspicion by many as being 'Popish', its wide-reaching influence made the church re-examine many of its practices.

George Bates, who became organist at Ripon in 1829, introduced much new music, including his own settings of the morning service. He was also a prolific

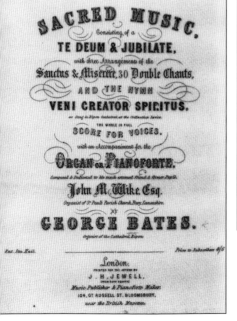

Title pages of 'Sacred Music' and 'Hymn' by George Bates.

composer of chants and it is believed that many were used for the canticles.

A magazine, 'The Monthly Remembrancer: A Guide and Companion to the Church for the Clergyman and Musician', was launched in London in 1856. This was short-lived, but Volume 1 set out a list of *The Choral Services in the Various Cathedrals in England on the Sundays in the Month of May 1857* which gives a fascinating insight into what was being sung at the time in Ripon Cathedral.

Sunday 3rd May 1857

<u>Morning Service</u>

Chants	Tallis and Bates No 19
Service	Dr Clarke Whitfield in F
Anthem	'I will remember thy name', Ebdon
Sanctus	Bates in C
Kyrie	Stopford

<u>Evening Service</u>

Chant	Jones in E sharp
Service	Dr Clarke Whitfield in F
Anthem	'Blessed be the Lord', Dr Nares

Sunday 10th May 1857

<u>Morning Service</u>

Chants	Tallis and Jones in D
Service	Porter in D
Psalm	100
Sanctus	Porter in D
Kyrie	Porter in D

<u>Evening Service</u>

Chant	Mornington in E
Service	Porter in D
Anthem	'O Lord our Governor', Kent

Sunday 17th May 1857

<u>Morning Service</u>

Chants	Tallis and Goodenough in Bb
Service	Matthew Camidge
Anthem	'God is our hope', Dr Green
Sanctus	Bates in Eb

Kyrie	Dr Elvey in A

<u>Evening Service</u>

Chant	Jackson in Bb
Service	Matthew Camidge
Anthem	'He maketh wars to cease', Callcott

Sunday 24th May 1857

<u>Morning Service</u>

Chants	Tallis and Bates No 1
Service	T.L. Fowle in Eb
Anthem	'Sing O Heavens', Kent
Sanctus	Clarke in E
Kyrie	Clarke in E

<u>Evening Service</u>

Chant	Dr Crotch in C
Service	T.L. Fowle in Eb
Anthem	'O give thanks', Purcell

Choral settings of the Sanctus and Kyrie were tacked on to the end of matins, as happened in most other cathedrals in England. Evidently it was widespread practice to follow matins with a service of ante-communion. The Sanctus was probably sung as a bridging motet between the two services, the whole finishing before the Prayer for the Church Militant. The remainder of the communion service, including the administration, did not take place.

Bill Forster's book on Ripon Cathedral (1993) notes that, *in the nineteenth century most people in England – including Queen Victoria – received Holy Communion only twice a year.* Communion services were indeed celebrated infrequently during this century, although generally about four times a year was usual, and therefore choral settings are few in number. It is recorded that weekly Sunday communion services at Ripon became a fixture in 1875, but it is not clear when they became choral. The 1662 prayer book does not provide for a Benedictus or Agnus Dei, and these were not included in musical settings until the end of the nineteenth century, possibly as a result of the Oxford Movement. Stanford was amongst the first to write communion settings which included these two movements.

John West in his book entitled 'Cathedral Organists' published in 1899, stated that when Edwin Crow was appointed to Ripon in 1874, Dr Edwin Monk, organist of York Minster, described the music at Ripon as *so bad that it*

185

could not by any possibility be worse ... There was no proper cathedral choral service, the canticles being merely chanted. In the light of what we know from the service lists of 1857 this was clearly not true on Sundays, but we do not know about weekday services nor the standard of singing.

While researching this book, a large bound volume of music came to light marked 'Services-Volume 2'. It is inscribed *Precentor 16th October 1875* (Samuel Joy was precentor), the same year that daily choral matins and evensong was established. The settings listed below give some insight into the repertoire of the day at Ripon Cathedral:

Evening Service in Bb, Felix B. Mendelssohn

Te Deum, Sanctus, Kyrie and Creed in F, Dr James Nares

Evening Service in F, Dr James Nares

Evening Service in A minor, Dr Benjamin Rogers

Te Deum, Jubilate, Kyrie, Creed, Sanctus, Gloria, Cantate Domino and Deus Misereatur *in the Key of A with the greater third*, Sir Frederick Gore Ouseley

Te Deum, Jubilate, Kyrie, Creed, Sanctus and Gloria *in the Key of E with the greater third,* Sir Frederick Gore Ouseley

Evening Service in E, Sir Frederick Gore Ouseley

Te Deum, Jubilate, Kyrie and Creed *in the Key of D with the greater third*, Dr Benjamin Rogers

Evening Service in D, Dr Benjamin Rogers

Te Deum and Jubilate in A, William Russell

Evening Service in A, William Russell

Six Double Chants, William Paten

Evening Service in Bb (written for the sons of clergy 1870), Henry Smart

Te Deum, Jubilate, Kyrie 1 & 2, Creed, Sursum Corda, Sanctus and Gloria in F, Henry Smart

Evening Service in F, Henry Smart

Evening Service in E, John Stainer

Te Deum, Jubilate and Kyrie in F, Dr Charles Steggall

Evening Service in F, Dr Charles Steggall

Te Deum, Jubilate , Sanctus, Kyrie and Creed in F, John Travers

Evening Service in F, John Travers

Te Deum, Jubilate, Kyrie 1 & 2, Sanctus and Creed in E, Samuel Sebastian Wesley

Evening Service in E, Samuel Sebastian Wesley

Chant Service in F, Te Deum, Jubilate, Samuel Sebastian Wesley

Te Deum, Jubilate, Kyrie, Sanctus and Creed in F, Samuel Sebastian Wesley

The communion settings listed would be mainly used for ante-communion. The selection included only two services from the seventeenth century (Rogers), two from the eighteenth (Nares and Travers), with the remaining items contemporary with its compilation. The inclusion of Wesley's evening service in E, possibly the finest setting of the nineteenth century (the only one on the list still in regular use) indicates that the standard of the choir had risen considerably under Dr Crow.

Advances in printing technology in the mid nineteenth century brought down the price of music and it became easier to have compositions published. Like several of his predecessors, Crow introduced his own settings of the canticles and also wrote pieces for special occasions, some of which were published and have survived.

In 1886 Ripon celebrated the millenium anniversary of the supposed granting of a Charter by King Alfred in 886 (Ref. Chapter 7). Extensive and lavish celebrations commenced on Wednesday 25th August with a service held at noon in the cathedral. The festival service *was intoned by the Rev H. Lunn, Precentor, and the Suffrages* (Preces and Responses) *were sung to Tallis's festal use. The Venite was Tallis's arrangement of the sixth tone and the two psalms were sung to chants by Flintoff, Ayrton and Nares.* There then followed the Te Deum and Jubilate sung to the setting by Attwood in D minor. The records go on to state that *The anthem was Purcell's 'O Sing unto the Lord', one of the finest compositions of the greatest musical genius England ever produced. The Old 100th psalm preceded the service and was not the least effective part of the service. Handel's Alleluia Chorus was sung after the sermon. This work, by a foreigner, had its special appropriateness, for it showed the period when English art was eclipsed by the genius of a German backed up by royal patronage.*

John West writing about Ripon Cathedral in 1899 records that *the* (bad) *state of things has since been entirely altered … Full Choral Services have been established, and on Sunday afternoons Oratorios, Cantatas etc. are frequently given either complete or in part. Perhaps the most notable achievement of the Cathedral Choir in its later days was the singing of Brahms's German Requiem by twelve boys and six men.* It is not certain how accurate this latter statement was, but it seems fair to say that Dr. Crow was the unsung hero of music at Ripon. This makes it all the more unfortunate that he was treated so badly at the end (Ref. Chapter 8).

A North Eastern Cathedral Choirs Association Festival was held at Ripon in the summer of 1901, when it is recorded that the choirs of York, Durham and Ripon sang the 'Dettinger Te Deum' by Handel. The following year, 1902, the festival was held at York Minster and Charles Moody wrote his Magnificat and Nunc Dimittis in A specially for this occasion. It was performed with a full orchestral accompaniment for which Moody wrote the score, and the original bound copy of this survives to this day.

Most of the records of the music sung at Ripon over the last two hundred years have been lost. However, the Precentor's Order Books for the years 1946-1951 and 1971-1978, in which the precentor and organist wrote down the music due to be sung, have survived. The first set of books was found by Dean Keith Jukes amongst old boxes of files in Minster House, and the second was made available by Robert Thompson (a tenor lay clerk for thirty years and latterly lay succentor).

The 1944 Education Act specified the minimum number of hours each week that children should receive education, and the Ripon choristers, engaged in singing matins almost every weekday, were clearly in breach of this. The Dean and Chapter did not act immediately, but evidently in early 1945, to comply with the new requirements, choral matins on Mondays and Fridays ceased.

There follows a list of the music sung at the services in early February 1946, just before the choir finally ceased the singing of weekly matins on Tuesday 18th June of that year.

February 1946

Sunday 3rd February
    Matins (10.30 am)   Te Deum, Stainer in Bb
                               'Lord we pray thee', Haydn
    Communion (11.45 am) Introit 'Jesu Word of God', Mozart

	Darke in F
Evensong (6.30 pm)	Magnificat and Nunc Dimittis to chants
	'Praise the Lord, my soul', Wesley
Monday 4th February	
Matins (9.30 am)	Said
Evensong (5 pm)	Noble in A minor
	'God with us still', Bach
Tuesday 5th February	
Matins	Somervell in F
	'How goodly are thy tents', Ouseley
Evensong	Dyson in F
	'From all that dwell', Walmisley
Wednesday 6th February	
Matins	Said
Evensong	Said
Thursday 7th February	
Matins	Garrett in D
	'Ponder my words', Colborne
Evensong	Garrett in D
	'Jesu, lead my footsteps', Bach
Friday 8th February	
Matins	Said
Evensong	Purcell in G minor
	'Thou knowest Lord', Purcell
Saturday 9th February	
Matins (9.30 am)	Bennett in Bb
	'Lead me Lord', Wesley
Evensong (5 pm)	Said
Sunday 10th February	
Matins	Te Deum, Martin in C
	'Saviour who in thine own image', Cornelius
Communion	Said
Evensong	Magnificat and Nunc Dimittis to chants
	'Deliver us, O Lord', Gibbons
Monday 11th February	
Matins	Said
Evensong	Morley, Faux Bourdon
	'Jesu Joy', Bach

Tuesday 12th February

Matins	Lloyd in Eb
	'O Lord, increase my faith', Gibbons
Evensong	Nicholson in Db
	'O thou the only true light', Mendelssohn
Wednesday 13th February	
Matins	Said
Evensong	Said
Thursday 14th February	
Matins	Nicholson in Db
	'Let thy merciful ears', Weelkes
Evensong	Elvey in A
	'We will rejoice', Croft (Part 1)
Friday 15th February	
Matins	Said
Evensong	Lloyd in Eb
Saturday 16th February	
Matins	Ireland in F
Evensong	Said

Dean	Precentor	Organist
Godwin Birchenough	Hugh R Williams	Charles Moody

Sunday evensong canticles were sung to chants, not to special settings, so the congregation could participate. This matter had been a source of dispute between Charles Moody and the Dean and Chapter (Ref. Chapter 8). An analysis of the entries in the Precentor's Order Book of 1946 indicates that, during this twelve month period, 56 different settings of the morning canticles were sung, 6 settings of choral Eucharist, 72 settings of the evening canticles and a total of 214 different anthems. Some were repeated, but rarely more than three or four times in the year.

The most repeated morning canticles were Stanford in A and Lloyd in Eb, and the most popular evening canticles were Stanford in C and Shaw in Eb. Apart from 'O Lord increase my faith' by Gibbons, 'God with us still' by Bach and Purcell's 'Thou knowest Lord', there were no obvious favourite anthems, but 36 of them were items, in whole or in part, from oratorios written by Mendelssohn, Bach, Handel, Haydn and Mozart.

In 1946 Moody had been organist at Ripon Cathedral for 44 years, but he was certainly not rooted in the past (although an evening service by his predecessor, Crow in D, was still sung twice a year). Amongst the music sung in that year were services by Howells, Gray and newly commissioned services including W. G. Alcock in G. Early anthems, many of which were just becoming available in new editions, were being performed, including works by Dowland, Orlando di Lassus, Palestrina, Vittoria, Weelkes; also anthems by Dvorak and Warlock.

On Saturday 28th June 1947 the Princess Royal visited Ripon Cathedral to unveil the new figures in the choir screen. The canticles sung were Sydney Nicholson in Db and the anthem was 'How lovely are thy dwellings fair' by Brahms.

Following a rebuild of the organ by John Compton & Sons of London in 1950, Dr Moody organised a Festival Evensong with the combined choirs of York Minster, Durham Cathedral and Ripon Cathedral. This took place on Wednesday 21st June with Charles Moody conducting and Francis Jackson playing the organ. The music sung was:

Magnificat and Nunc Dimittis   W. G. Alcock in Bb

Anthems:
    'O clap your hands', Gibbons
    'The Lord is my Shepherd', Stanford
    'Lord, Thou hast been our refuge', Vaughan Williams

No service sheets from 1954 to 1969 have been kept in the Ripon Cathedral archives, and therefore the authors have been unable to ascertain the music sung during the period in which Lionel Dakers and Philip Marshall were in office.

Below is a list of the music sung at the services during the first two weeks of May 1975:

May 1975
Responses Plainsong and Piccolo

Sunday 4th May
    Holy Communion (9.15 am) Hymns
    Matins (11 am)   Te Deum, Vaughan Williams in G
                         'Awake thou wintry earth', Bach
    Evensong (5 pm)   Harwood in Ab
                         'The strife is o'er', Ley

Monday 5th May
    Evensong (Boys' voices) Bairstow in Eb
                         'Adoramus te Christe', Di Lasso

Tuesday 6th May
> Evensong   Dyson in D
> 'O Lord look down', Battishill

Wednesday 7th May
> Evensong   Said

Thursday 8th May (Ascension Day)
> Evensong   Said
> Choral Communion   Darke in F
> 'Alleluia, ascendit Deus', Byrd

Friday 9th May
> Evensong   Wood in Eb
> 'Exultate Deo', Scarlatti

Saturday 10th May
> Evensong   Gray in F minor
> 'God is gone up', Croft
> Organ Recital (8 pm)   Jonathan Bielby, Wakefield Cathedral

Sunday 11th May
> Matins attended by the   Te Deum, Stanford in C
> Mayor and Councillors   'God is gone up', Finzi
> Evensong   Bairstow in D
> 'O clap your hands', Vaughan Williams

Monday 12th May
> Evensong (Boys' voices)   Vaughan Williams in C
> 'Pleni sunt coeli', Palestrina

Tuesday 13th May
> Evensong   Tomkins, Fifth Service
> 'Psallite Domino', Byrd

Wednesday 14th May
> Evensong   Said

Thursday 15th May
> Evensong   RSCM Choirs Festival

Friday 16th May
> Evensong   Holmes, Faux Bourdons
> 'Non vos relinquam orphanus', Byrd

Saturday 17th May
> Evensong   Collegium Regale, Howells
> 'O where shall wisdom be found?', Boyce

Sunday 18th May Whitsunday
  Confirmation and First
  Communion (10. 30 am)   'O Lord give thy holy spirit', Tallis
  Evensong   Blair in B minor
                           'God is a spirit', Sterndale Bennett

Dean	Precentor	Organist
Edwin Le Grice	Duncan Thomson	Ronald Perrin

On Thursday 4th April 1985 the Royal Maundy Service took place at the cathedral with the Queen and Prince Phillip in attendance. The choirs of Ripon Cathedral and Her Majesty's Chapels Royal combined, and the music they sang was:

'Lord for thy tender mercy's sake', 16th century, unknown composer
'Loving Shepherd of thy sheep', Arnold Cooke
'Wash me throughly', Samuel S. Wesley
'Locus iste', Anton Bruckner
'Zadok the priest', Handel

The singing of a short introit, usually in the south transept before Sunday services, was often a feature of the 1970s and 1980s, but this practice largely died out during the 1990s. However, the vestry responses by Francis Jackson, introduced in the late 1960s by Ronald Perrin, continue to be used, although alternated with others. Another noticeable change is that the old composite service and anthem books, and latterly chant books and psalters, are no longer used. They have been replaced with specific single copies of the music, and for the psalms, individual sheets for each day containing the words and chants.

Like previous organists, Ronald Perrin used the Northern Three Choirs Festival as an occasion to introduce new larger scale pieces to the repertoire:

Britten	'Rejoice in the Lamb'
Tomkins	Third Evening Service
Tomkins	'Almighty God the fountain of all wisdom'
Whyte	'O praise God in his holiness'
Schutz	'The heavens are telling'
Hawes	Evening Service in D

Mendelssohn wrote his anthem 'Hear my Prayer' in Berlin in 1844 only three years before his death. It became popular in England especially after it was recorded at the Temple Church, London, in March 1928, with George Thalben Ball at the organ and Ernest Lough the boy soloist. This was issued on a 78 rpm record by His Master's Voice and became a best seller.

Quite when 'Hear my Prayer' was first introduced into the repertoire at Ripon is not known, but in 1978 Duncan Thomson, the precentor, and Ronald Perrin, the organist, evidently mindful that this anthem was much loved by the ladies, decided to perform it on Mothering Sunday that year. On this occasion the solo was sung by Marcus Maguire, and it was so well received that 'Hear my Prayer' became the stock choice for evensong every Mothering Sunday thereafter. Thanks to former choir librarian Robert Thompson, the names of all the boy soloists who have sung this piece from 1978 to 2008 have been listed and these are reproduced in the appendix.

One of the few surviving service sheets from the 1990s reveals the music sung in mid April 1995:

April 1995
Responses Plainsong and Piccolo

Monday 10th April
    Evensong (boys' voices) Watson in F
    (5.30 pm)   'A song of hope', Stanford
Tuesday 11th April
    Evensong   Farrant (Short Service)
                           'Civitas sancti tui', Byrd
Wednesday 12th April
    Evensong   Said
Maundy Thursday 13th April
    Evensong   Said
    Eucharist (8 pm)   Wood in the Phrygian mode
                           'Ubi caritas', Duruflé
                           'Panis angelicus', Rebelo
                           'Miserere mei', Byrd
Good Friday 14th April
    Matins, Litany & Reproaches (9.30 am)
                           Litany, Tallis
                           Lamentations, Bairstow
                           'In the departure of the Lord', Bull
Saturday 15th April
    Evensong   Said

Easter Sunday 16th April

Eucharist of the Dawn (6.00 am)   Darke in C

'If we believe that Jesus died', Goss

Parish Eucharist (9.30 am) Introit. 'This joyful Eastertide'

Darke in E

'Dum Transisset Sabbatum', Taverner

Matins (11.30 am)   Te Deum, Vaughan Williams in G

Jubilate, Kelly in E

'Ye choirs of new Jerusalem', Stanford

Evensong & Introduction
of New Choristers   Dyson in D
(6.30 pm)   'T'is the day of resurrection', Wood

Christopher Campling, Dean.   Kerry Beaumont, Director of Music

David Ford, Peter Marshall, Michael   Robert Marsh, Assistant Organist

Glanville-Smith, Canons   Ronald Perrin, Organist Titulaire

David Murfet, Cathedral Chaplain   Robert Thompson, Lay Succentor

There follows an example of the music sung a year after Andrew Bryden was appointed director of music:

June 2004

Responses Leighton and Rose

Monday 7th June

Evensong (sung by the boy choristers)

Rose in E

'Sing we merrily', Symons

Tuesday 8th June

Evensong   Wise in F

'Jesu, grant me this, I pray', Bairstow

Wednesday 9th June

Evensong   Said

Thursday 10th June Corpus Christi

Evensong   Said

Choral Eucharist & Procession

(7.30 pm)   Missa Lauda Sion, Palestrina

'Lauda Sion', Palestrina

Friday 11th June
     Evensong   Cooper Fauxbourdons
                                 'Faire is the heaven', Harris

Saturday 12th June
     Evensong   Bryden in A
                                 'Cantique de Jean Racine', Fauré

Sunday 13th June
     Parish Eucharist   Jackson in G
     (9.30 am)   'O sacrum convivium', Messiaen
     Matins (11.30 am)   Boyce in A
                                 'My shepherd is the living Lord', Tomkins
     Evensong (sung by girl choristers and lay clerks)
                                 Walmisley in D minor
                                 'All wisdom cometh from the Lord', Moore

John Methuen, Dean   Andrew Bryden, Director of Music
Keith Punshon, Canon in residence

To conclude this chapter, details are given below of the music sung at the National Festival of the Federation of Cathedral Old Choristers' Associations in July 2008, which coincided with the publication of this book.

July 2008

Saturday 5th July
     Festival Evensong

                               Responses, Moore
                               Psalms 27, 28, 29
                               Hymn, Angel voices ever singing
                               Perrin in Ab
                               'Ascribe unto the Lord', Wesley

Chapter 15

WRITTEN FOR RIPON

PSALTERS AND CHANT BOOKS

The Ripon Psalter, circa 1418

Contains the Psalms of David, Antiphons, Te Deum, Benedicite, Magnificat, Benedictus, Litany, a Breviary, Missal and Offices for the Octave of St Wilfrid at Ripon Minster.

This ancient bound book was presented to the Dean and Chapter of Ripon Cathedral by the Marquess of Ripon, 21st July 1874.

Ripon Cathedral Chant Book, 1907

Compiled by Dr Charles Moody. Published Novello.

The Ripon Psalter, 1908

The Reverend Ernest Henry Swann was appointed succentor in 1887 and served at Ripon Cathedral for 30 years, becoming precentor in 1908. He was evidently a keen musician, having been organ scholar at Corpus Christi College, Cambridge, and he compiled and pointed The Ripon Psalter, which was printed and published by William Harrison of Ripon in 1908. The system of pointing uses bold type words, which, according to the 'Directions For Using The Psalter', are *to indicate where the strict time of the chant begins,* but this and the pointing indicate a very mannered way of singing. This Psalter was referred to in a printed booklet for choirs participating in the Ripon Diocesan Festivals at Ripon Cathedral and Richmond Parish Church in November 1933.

The Ripon Cathedral Chant Book, 1961

Compiled and beautifully handwritten by Dr Philip Marshall. *This Chant Book was compiled by the Organist to mark the Foundation of the Choir School: Ad usum Scholae Cantoris Riponiensis.*

CHANTS

Thomas Preston, the Elder
Double in B minor. This is in the Durham Chant Book of about 1865 compiled by the organist Philip Armes

George Bates
Thirty double chants. Published J.H. Jewell & Co., London, circa 1850

Rev Joseph Jameson (Precentor 1821- c.1840)
Double in G

Edwin Crow
Single in Eb
Doubles in G, G minor, A, A minor, C minor (In regular use at Norwich Cathedral and recorded by them)

Rev G.E. Alvis (Succentor 1905-1909)
Single in Eb
Doubles in C, Bb

Rev Ernest Swann (Precentor 1907-1917)
Singles in Ab, Db
Doubles 2 in F, A, Eb

Charles Moody
Singles 2 in C
Doubles in D, E, F#minor, Eb minor, B minor, G, Eb

Lionel Dakers
Single in F minor
Double in Ab

Philip Marshall
Singles in D minor, G
Doubles in A, Bb, D, F

Ronald Perrin
Doubles in A minor, E minor, D minor, D

Kerry Beaumont
Single in A minor
Doubles in C minor, E, D, D minor, G minor, Eb minor, A

Andrew Bryden
Doubles 2 in A, C# minor, F# minor

PRECES AND RESPONSES

The Ripon Amen by Charles Moody, 1902. Published by Banks, York.
Republished Novello, London 1920, in versions for full choir, men
only and boys only
The Special Suffrages for the Funeral of King Edward VII composed
by Charles Moody for the Memorial Service in Ripon Cathedral on
18th May 1910
Preces and Responses, Ronald Perrin, 1979
Preces and Responses (Trebles) SSA, Kerry Beaumont, 1997
Lord's Prayer for Ripon, Humphrey Clucas, 1998
His responses were originally written in 1962 but did not include
a setting of the Lord's Prayer. Clucas wrote a setting of the Lord's
Prayer for Kerry Beaumont to go with his responses, which were first
broadcast by the cathedral choir on 7th June 2000
A Litany for Deacons, Kerry Beaumont, 2001
Closing Responses for trebles, Kerry Beaumont, 2001
Preces and Responses for men's voices, Thomas Leech, 2008

CANTICLES

Thomas Preston, the Elder
Te Deum, Jubilate, Magnificat and Nunc Dimittis in G minor
Te Deum and Jubilate in E minor
Te Deum, Jubilate, Magnificat and Nunc Dimittis in D
Tripla Service Te Deum in Bb
Tripla Service Te Deum and Jubilate in F

George Bates
Te Deum and Jubilate in C
Published J.H. Jewell & Co. circa 1850

Edwin Crow
Cantate Domino and Deus Misereatur in G
Published Novello, London, 1879
Te Deum and Jubilate in C
Published Novello, Ewer & Co. circa 1881

Magnificat and Nunc Dimittis in A
Composed for the North Eastern Cathedral Choirs' Festival at Ripon
in July 1883. Published Novello, 1883. A copy of this is in the British
Library, London.

Magnificat and Nunc Dimittis in G, 1884

Te Deum and Jubilate in C. Composed for the official opening of the
new cathedral organ on Sunday 24th April 1878

Magnificat and Nunc Dimittis in D
Published Novello Ewer & Co, 1891

Benedicite
For unison singing. Published 'The Organist', London, 1896

Charles Moody
Te Deum and Jubilate in F
Published Banks & Son, York

Festival Service in A (with full orchestral score)
Composed for the North Eastern Cathedral Choirs' Festival,
York Minster 3rd July 1902

Magnificat and Nunc Dimittis in F
circa 1930

Magnificat and Nunc Dimittis in D minor
Composed for the Fountains Abbey 800 years Commemoration
Service, 14th August 1932. Published Oxford University Press, 1932

Philip Marshall
Benedicite in D minor (shortened form)
Published Novello, circa 1960

Ronald Perrin
Benedicite in C, 1971

Te Deum in C, 1969
Published Ripon Publications, 1991
(R. Thompson) (Recorded on LP 'Sing Joyfully' 1987)

Magnificat and Nunc Dimittis in Ab
(*Dedicated to the memory of Tricia*)
Published Ripon Publications, 1990

Magnificat and Nunc Dimittis in D for boys' voices
Published Ripon Publications, 1994

Magnificat and Nunc Dimittis in A for boys' voices
Published Ripon Publications

Third Trebles Service in D
Published Ripon Publications, 1997

Te Deum for boys' voices. Manuscript

Kerry Beaumont
The Ripon Service, Magnificat and Nunc Dimittis, 1999

Andrew Bryden
Magnificat and Nunc Dimittis in A, 2000

Te Deum for men's voices, 2002

Benedicite for men's voices, 2003

First Trebles Service, 2004

Second Trebles Service, 2007

Other composers

Magnificat and Nunc Dimittis in G
by Sir Walter G. Alcock. Published Novello, 1936
Written for and first performed at a Festival Service on 1st July 1936
sung by the choirs of Ripon, York, Durham and Newcastle Cathedrals,
and broadcast live by the BBC

Magnificat and Nunc Dimittis in E
by Robin Beaumont (Kerry Beaumont's father), 1969

Magnificat and Nunc Dimittis for boys' voices by Marcus Huxley,
using Alternative Service Book words, 1983

Te Deum in C for boys' voices by Christopher Campling, 1992

The Ripon Service, Magnificat and Nunc Dimittis, by Stanley Vann,
1996, commissioned by Alan Duffield (former Ripon lay clerk) in
memory of his mother

The Ripon Service, Te Deum, for choir, organ, brass and timpani
by Philip Wilby, 1999

The Ripon Service, Magnificat and Nunc Dimittis by Humphrey
Clucas, 2000

Jubilate (*In memoriam LW*) by Philip Wilby, 2000

Te Deum and Jubilate, for the girls' choir, by Alasdair Jamieson
Written for their tour to St David's Cathedral, Wales, August 2006

COMMUNION SERVICE SETTINGS

Sanctus in C by George Bates. On the music list for Sunday 3rd May
1857. Published J. H. Jewell, London, circa 1850

Sanctus in Eb by George Bates. On the music list for Sunday 17th May
1857. Published J. H. Jewell, London, circa 1841

Miserere (Responses to the Commandments) by George Bates.

Published Leoni, Lee & Coxhead, London, circa 1841

Communion Service in F by Edwin Crow. Won a College of Organists prize in 1872. Reviewed in The Musical Times of 1st March 1873

Communion Service in A by Edwin Crow, date unknown

Communion Service in Bb by Charles Moody. Published Oxford University Press, 1943

Missa Riponiensis (Sanctus, Benedictus and Agnus Dei) by Ronald Perrin, 1973

The St Wilfrid Mass by Ronald Perrin, 1979. Published Ripon Publications, 1991

St Augustine Eucharist, Rite A by Christopher Campling, 1985

Missa Sancti Petri by Ronald Perrin. Published Ripon Publications, 1995. First performed on 29th October 1995

Gloria by Ronald Perrin. Published Ripon Publications, 1995 to complete the Missa Riponiensis and the St Wilfrid Mass above, neither of which had a Gloria, because when these works were written in the 1970s the Gloria was always sung to Merbeck

Missa Brevis for trebles, SSA by Kerry Beaumont, 1997

Mass For Our Time by Philip Wilby. Published Maecenas Music, Kealey, Surrey, 1997

ANTHEMS, MOTETS AND CANTATAS

Alexander Shaw
I will sing unto the Lord

Thomas Preston, the Elder
It is a good thing
Rejoice in the Lord

O be joyful in the Lord
O praise God in his holiness
I waited patiently for the Lord

Edwin Crow
Praise ye the Lord, a cantata for chorus and soloists written in 1874 for his Bachelor of Music degree and reported upon in 1st December issue of The Musical Times of that year

Lord we pray thee. Performed at the 1899 North Eastern Cathedral Choirs' Festival at York Minster

Charles Moody
Giver of Peace words by W. G. Hocking. Published Novello & Co. London, 1903

Before the ending of the day. Published Vincent Music, London, 1927 First sung by St Paul's Cathedral Choir, London on 18th June 1906

Choral Elegy – Give rest O Christ
Words translated from the Russian by W. J. Birkbeck
Published Novello & Co, London, 1916

In Terra Pax
Published R. Ackrill Ltd, Harrogate, 1928

Except the Lord build the house
Published Banks & Son, York, 1936

Philip Marshall
When morning gilds the skies
Published Kevin Mayhew, 1959. Dedicated to Fr Charles Kemp Buck (Precentor Ripon Cathedral 1957-1960)

When the Lord turned again the captivity of Zion
Published by Banks, circa 1964. First performance by Durham, Ripon and York at the Northern Three Choirs' Festival, York

Ronald Perrin
O be joyful
Published Anglo-American, 1974

Alleluia, sing to Jesus
Published Anglo-American, 1974

Let God be gracious
Published Ripon Publications, 1994
Written for visit of HM the Queen Mother 1st June 1986

Except the Lord
Published Ripon Publications 1994

O Sing to God
Sung at the Northern Three Choirs' Festival 22nd July 1990

Angelic Chorus
Published Ripon Publications, 1994

Before the ending of the day
1994, boys' voices

Angel voices, boys' voices
Published Ripon Publications

O Praise the Lord

Spirit of Mercy, Truth and Love

This new Christmas Carol

We give Immortal Praise

Kerry Beaumont
Christ is all in all, SATB Unacc., 1999
Encore Music Publications, 2000

Come Holy Ghost, SATB Unacc., 1999
Encore Music Publications, 2002

Jesu my Lord, Unison and organ, 1999

Rorate coeli desuper, SSAATTBB, 1999

Andrew Bryden
God be in my head, 2001
Seek him out, 2004

Other composers
My soul truly waiteth still upon God by Gerard Cobb. Written for the
North Eastern Cathedral Choirs' Festival at Ripon 1893.
Published Novello 1894. Reprint 1922

My beloved spake
by Patrick Hadley. Published Curwen, 1938
Written for the wedding of one of his students (dedicated to Ursula and
Martin Watson) at Ripon Cathedral, Saturday 2nd May 1936

O thou the central orb
by P.R. Pfaff (Ripon lay clerk and music master at Ripon Grammar
School). Published James Rawes, Birmingham, 1939

The Wakeman – Except the Lord keep the house
by Robin Beaumont, circa 1968

Hear my Crying O God
by Roger Hemingway (First sung in the cathedral in 1971)

Love Unknown, a cantata on the Passion and Resurrection of Jesus by
Malcolm Arnold, words by Edwin Le Grice (Dean of Ripon
1968 - 1984). Published Kevin Mayhew

Sing we merrily by Adrian Carpenter
First performed in BBC broadcast Choral Evensong
on 12th October 1983

Glory and Honour by Christopher Campling
(Dean of Ripon 1984-1994)

Jesu, saviour of the world by Christopher Campling 1992

Praise the Lord in his sanctuary by Christopher Campling 1992

Caedmon's Dream by Philip Wilby, first performed in July 1995
at Dean Christopher Campling's leaving service

Praise his name in the dance by Brian Kelly. Dedicated *To Kerry
Beaumont and the Choir of Ripon Cathedral*. First performed at
evensong at Ripon Cathedral on Saturday 15th May 1999

The Spirit of the Lord God is upon us by Delyth Cresswell written for
the 25th anniversary of the ordination of John Methuen, Dean.
First performed on Sunday 24th January 1999

Except the Lord by Stanley Vann, 2004. To commemorate the 400th
anniversary of the granting of the Charter by James I in 1604

Behold thy servant by Christopher Rathbone, 2006

ORGAN MUSIC

Five Short Voluntaries for Organ
Edwin Crow. Published Donajowski, London 1890

March in G
Edwin Crow. Published Donojowski, London 1894. (Taken from the
Short Organ Voluntaries above, the March, No 5, proved so popular it
was published separately)

Prelude and Chaconne
Philip Marshall. Published Banks & The Finzi Trust
Written for the recital, given by Francis Jackson, to inaugurate the
organ following the major rebuild undertaken by Harrison & Harrison
in autumn 1963

A Spanish Toccata
Ronald Perrin. Published Anglo-American
Written for the new Orchestral Trumpet added to the organ in 1988

Fileuse
Ronald Perrin. Recorded on an E.P. by Ryemuse in 1967

HYMNS

Veni Creator Spiritus (Come Holy Ghost our souls inspire)
George Bates. Published Leoni, Lee & Coxhead, London,
circa 1841

Vesper or Dismissal Hymn
Edwin Crow. Published Vincent Music Co. London, 1897

Sing to the Lord, Hymn by Edwin Crow. Sung at the North Eastern
Cathedral Choirs' Festival, York, 1889

Descant to Praise my soul the King of Heaven by Charles Moody.
circa 1920. This magnificent setting was sung by the choir of St Paul's
Cathedral at the Silver Jubilee service for H. M. Queen Elizabeth in
1977 and it is in their choir library. Recorded on an LP entitled 'Royal
Music from St Paul's issued by Guild Records in 1977

O Spirit of our God (Confirmation Hymn)
Charles Moody, words by H.G. Shaddick.
Published Novello & Co., London, 1933

Descant to The King of Love my shepherd is, Charles Moody, 1937

O gladsome light, Christopher Campling, 1986

Christ who has sent us Celtic Saints, based on words by Edwin
Le Grice. Tune 'St Wilfrid of Ripon' by Christopher Campling,
harmonised Robert Marsh. Published in the 'New English Praise'
hymn book

CAROLS

In Bethlehem, a fifteenth century carol, Charles Moody,
Published Novello, London, 1907

The King's Nativity, Alan Dance, 1974

Of a rose, a lovely rose
Marcus Huxley, 1981. *For Alan Duffield*
Published Banks, York

The King's Glory, Christopher Campling, 1986

I saw three shepherds, SSA
Noel, Jesus is born (version 1) SATB
Silent Night
The Holly and the Ivy
Arrangements by Kerry Beaumont, 1988

Mary and Joseph, Christopher Campling, 1988,
harmonised Neil Richardson

Here with us, boys' voices and flute
Christopher Campling

There's a star in the east, SATB accomp.
Sweet dreams, SATB unacc.
Kerry Beaumont, 1998

The First Noel, descant Andrew Bryden, 1998

Noel, Jesus is born (version 2). SATB accomp., Kerry Beaumont, 1999

O come all ye faithful, descant Andrew Bryden, 2000

This is the truth sent from above, arrangement Andrew Bryden, 2002

Hark the herald Angels Sing, descant Andrew Bryden, 2003

Once in Royal David's city, descant Andrew Bryden, 2003

Now the green blade riseth, arrangement Andrew Bryden, 2003

In the bleak mid winter, arrangements for SATB and trebles Andrew Bryden, 2007

ORCHESTRAL MUSIC

Concerto for Organ, Piano and Percussion
Ronald Perrin, 1973. Originally played by Ronald Perrin (organ), Mary Perrin (piano) and Richard Pancheff (percussion)

Ye Choirs of New Jerusalem, by C.V. Stanford orchestrated by Kerry Beaumont, 2000

Suite for Young Players by Eric Goodhill (a pseudonym used by Kerry Beaumont), 1998, for the Ripon Choir School Orchestra

Eucharista, for symphony orchestra and double choir by Peter Dodson, 2002. First performed as integral part of Eucharist Service on 29th June 2000 for Ripon Cathedral Patronal Festival by St Cecilia Orchestra under Xenophon Kelsey with Cleveland Philharmonic Choir and Ripon Cathedral Girls' Choir

Patchwork for Ripon by Peter Dodson, 2004. First performed on Saturday 8th May in Ripon Cathedral for the 400th anniversary of the granting of the charter by James I in 1604. St Cecilia Orchestra under Xenophon Kelsey

Song of the Sea God, for solo bassoon and string orchestra by Peter Dodson, 2005

SECULAR

Circa 1418, Fifteenth Century Ballads, scored by Edwin Crow and sung by the Ripon Cathedral Choir on 21st July 1874 (Ref. Chapter 12)

When springtime flowers sweetly bloom and Come unto me, two songs composed by Edwin Crow. Published Ashdown & Parry, 1869. Reviewed in The Musical Times of 1st May 1869

The Final Toast, by Edwin Crow
A Masonic Lyric, beginning 'Are your glasses charged?' words by D.L. Richardson. Published London, 1871

Blow, blow thou winter wind, a part song for three voices by Edwin Crow, 1906. Published Novello & Co., 1906

The Prelude to the Day, words and music by Charles Moody. Written under the pseudonym 'Coulthart Brayton'. Published by Houghton & Co., London, circa 1910

Chapter 16

THE BELLS AND BELL RINGERS
Written by Martin Davies

The Bells

The current peal of 13 bells hung in the south-west tower of the cathedral form a magnificent musical instrument of which we are very proud. While they are relatively young, 10 being cast in 1932, 2 in 2007 and 1 in 2008, it is possible that bells have hung in the west towers of the minster since their completion in about 1224.

The earliest reference to bells in Ripon dates from 1354 when records show that Laurence Wright mended the clappers. Major work was carried out in 1379 when *Diverse expenses* were incurred conveying a bell from York to Ripon. This bell was obtained from Fountains Abbey and transferred from Ripon to Boroughbridge by sledge, then from Boroughbridge to York via the rivers Ure and Ouse. It was recast in York using additional metal and returned to Ripon to be hung in the north-west tower. The accounts of the time refer to payments for buying poles for the bell frame, paying men to work the windlass and the smith to make the clapper. The final cost was £11 10s. 0d. with an additional 12d. paid to Will Fallan for supplying a bell wheel. The bell was dedicated to the Virgin Mary and is believed to have survived intact in the north-west tower until 1762.

In 1391 *a new hearth was made in the hall of the prebend of Thorpe, in compensation for one which had been broken up for the purpose of casting a bell in the said hall.* By 1396 there were at least 3 bells in the towers. William Wright hung 2 bells and *repaired the defects in those of others* at a cost of 27s. 9d. New *brass bolsters* and *pypes were fitted,* presumably to carry the ropes through the ceilings. In 1448 Thomas Morton, Canon of York, left 40s. in his will for *repairing of the great bell-tower of Ripon.* The third bell was recast by George Heathcott of Chesterfield in 1540 at a cost of £8. An initial payment was made by the *President and Chapter of the collegiate church of Ripon* on 2nd July 1540 followed by a final payment on 15th August that year.

By 1663 the number of bells had increased to 6, believed to be 5 hung in the south-west tower and the 'Mary Bell' in the north-west tower. James Smith of York was commissioned to recast the fourth and fifth bells and Matthew Townley rehung all the bells on new frames in November 1663. The treble was recast in 1673 but the name of the founder is not known.

Thomas Gent, in his 'History of Ripon' of 1733 noted that the number of bells had increased to 7, stating that 5 bells were hung in the south-west tower for service ringing, 1 in the north-west tower and 1 in the turret on top of the central tower. He confirms that the bell in the north-west tower was reputed to have come from Fountains Abbey and was referred to as the 'Mary Bell'.

The Lester & Pack Peal of 8 - 1762

The 5 bells in the south-west tower and the 'Mary Bell' in the north-west tower were sold in 1762 for £355, used as part payment for a new ring of 8 bells. These, cast by Lester & Pack of London, were installed in the south-west tower in the same year and hung in a new wooden frame by James Harrison of Raisen, Lincolnshire, at a cost of £557 11s. 11d. They were tuned to the key of E and the tenor (largest) bell weighed 19-3-8 (19 cwt - 3 quarters - 8 pounds).

The north-west tower was now empty of bells and remains so today.

During work to the tower roof in 1865 the second and fifth bells were cracked by falling scaffolding, and

The Arms of the City (A hunting horn, with the letters 'Rippon') Reproduced on the 11th from the original 1762 Lester & Pack 7th.

were recast in 1866 by John Warner and Sons of London. The replacement bells weighed 6-1-9 and 10-1-16 respectively.

In 1868 the remaining Lester & Pack bells were quarter turned and re-hung in the 1762 wooden frame by Thomas Mallaby of Masham. The frame was later replaced but a portion of it is preserved in the ringing room and is inscribed:

Francis Wanley D.D., Dean; James Harrison of Raisen in Lincolnshire, Bell Hanger; John Hutchinson, Matthew Beckwith, and Thos Fothergill, Agitators. 1762.

214

Augmentation to 10 Bells - 1891

By 1890 the framework installed in 1762 had become unsafe. The Dean and Chapter instructed J. Shaw & Co. of Bradford to rehang the existing 8 bells in a new iron frame, which was designed to hold 10 bells. Two new bells were added, comprising a treble, donated by Messrs R. Kearsley & Co. to the memory of John Kearsley, and a second bell given in memory of Miss Anne Cross of Coney Garth by her brother and sisters. Both these bells were cast by Shaw's of Bradford.

Shaw's were also commissioned to supply a chiming mechanism for the clock set to sound the Cambridge Chimes (the clock chime at the Houses of Parliament and better known as the Westminster Chimes). The clock chime mechanism was paid for by public subscription, and the restored bells, clock and chimes were dedicated at a special service on Tuesday 14th April 1891.

The Taylor 10 - 1932

It seems the 1891 augmentation was not a great success; whilst a report in 'Bell News' described the bells as *splendid*, other reports in this journal were less kind:

the bells came in for a good deal of adverse criticism. The tone is poor and one cannot hear the trebles in the ringing chamber ... sound of that clanging peal ... the ring was of very mediocre tone.

Canon George Garrod, in a report believed to date from the late 1920s, highlighted a number of defects. He had consulted Mr Fred Tingle, President of the Ripon Cathedral Bell Ringers, and Rev C. Marshall, Vicar of St Chad's, Far Headingly and President of the Yorkshire Association of Change Ringers. The report revealed that Shaw's iron frame of 1891 had been built on oak foundation beams, possibly those installed to support the 1762 frame, and these had become infested and weakened by death watch beetle. Consequently the bell frame dipped considerably making the bells difficult and unpredictable to ring. He reported that the fittings were very worn, and suggested the sound of the ring would be much improved by recasting the 2 Shaw treble bells and retuning the older 8. In the event, in 1932, the oak foundation beams were replaced with steel girders, and the entire ring was recast and hung in a new metal frame by the John Taylor Bell Foundry of Loughborough.

During recasting all the inscriptions and decorations on the previous 1762 and 1891 bells were copied and reproduced on the new bells, with the exception of the 4 and 7 which had been recast by Warners in 1866. These reproductions included a fine set of seals, coats of arms and other decorative features on the ninth (now the eleventh) and tenor.

The first public performance on the bells was whilst they were still at Taylor's foundry. On 1st March 1933 they featured in a radio broadcast on church bells, given by E. Dennison Taylor, to illustrate the art of change ringing.

All the bells were returned to Ripon on 14th March 1933 and were officially rung for the first time following a dedication service on Saturday 8th April that year. Julia White of Ripon covered the cost as a memorial to her family as a tablet in the ringing room and inscription on the tenor records:

To the glory of God and in memory of her parents, brothers and sisters, the bells of this Cathedral were re-cast and the belfry restored by Julia White of Highfield, Ripon. 1932 -1933.

This generous gift laid the foundations for the fine ring of 13 bells we have today.

The new bells, 1932.
Back: Canon Tuckey, Canon Harford, Mr Fred Tingle, Canon Garrod, Mr Edward Winser, Dean Owen. Front: Miss B Collings, Miss P Collings.

The 1932 Taylor 10 in the south-west tower.

Augmentation to 12 - 2008

In recent years the number of ringers at the cathedral has increased and 10 bell ringing for Sunday services has become established. For the first time in many years the cathedral band was strong enough to consider ringing on a full peal of 12 bells, and the provision of two additional bells at Ripon was frequently discussed. The number of youngsters and trainee ringers also increased and it became apparent that improvements to the bell installation were required to facilitate teaching them.

In January 2005 the 'Ring out Ripon Bells' appeal was launched to raise £42,000 to install 3 new bells, thus augmenting the existing 10 to a full peal of 12 plus 1. To provide a diatonic ring of 12 in the key of Eb major, 2 smaller treble bells were to be added. The thirteenth was to be a flat 6th semitone bell to furnish a lightweight ring of 8 in Ab major, when used in conjunction with bells 2 - 5 and 7 - 9 of the 12. The light ring would be easier to handle than the alternative heavy 8 (bells 5 - 12) previously used. This modification would help in teaching new ringers and ease the progress of those more experienced.

Details of the Current Peal of 12 (+1)

Bell		Inscription	Year Cast	Diameter (inches)	Weight (cwt.)	Note
Treble (1)	Waist (a)	TO THE HEAVENS AND OVER THE SEA, WE RING FOR THEE, THOSE WE LOVE AND THOSE WE LOST, IN RESOUNDING MEMORY.	2007	25	4-2-10	Bb
	Waist (b)	FOR, NAOMI W. BROOKS, 1937 – 1999 & WILLIAM E. KIKER, 1931 - 2002				
2	Waist (a)	IN MEMORIAM JOAN PITTS- TUCKER QUAESTORIS	2007	26	4-2-26	Ab
	Waist (b)	...PER VITAS CONIUNCTAS SIMUL LAETE SONENT" SUI FILII FECERUNT MMVII				
3	Inscription Band	JOHN KERSEY. CIV : RIPON : AMABILIS OB : 1890 R KEARSLEY. H.C. BICKERSTETH AND K KEARSLEY D:D: IN MEMORIAM	1932	26.5	4-3-19	G
	Waist	CAST 1890 RECAST 1932				
4	Waist (a)	+ TO THE GLORY OF GOD AND IN MEMORY OF ANNE CROSS WHO DIED 1890	1932	27.5	5-0-19	F
	Waist (b)	CAST 1891 RECAST 1932				
5	Inscription Band	LESTER AND PACK OF LONDON FECIT 1761	1932	29	5-2-6	Eb
	Waist	RECAST 1932				
6	Inscription Band	CAST 1866	1932	30	5-2 -20	D
	Waist	RECAST 1932				
6b	Waist (a)	IN MEMORIAM JIM PITTS- TUCKER PRAECEPTORIS	2008	31	6-1-18	Db
	Waist (b)	"ILLAE CAMPANAE DUAE SICUT VIR ET UXOR... SUI FILII FECERUNT MMVII				

No.	Part	Inscription	Year	Diameter	Weight	Note
7	Inscription Band / Waist	LESTER AND PACK OF LONDON FECIT 1761 / RECAST 1932	1932	32	6-2-3	C
8	Inscription Band / Waist	LESTER AND PACK OF LONDON FECIT 1761 / RECAST 1932	1932	34.5	7-3-21	Bb
9	Inscription Band / Waist	CAST 1866 / RECAST 1932	1932	37.5	9-2-15	Ab
10	Upper Waist / Waist	LESTER AND PACK OF LONDON FECIT 1761 / RECAST 1932	1932	40	12-0-16	G
11	Inscription Band	THE RITE REVᴰ. ROBᵀ. DRUMMING ARCHBISHOP LESTER AND PACK OF LONDON FECIT 1761 RECAST 1932	1932	44	15-3-1	F
	Waist (a)	A boar's head (Dean Wanley's crest), with the inscription- "F. WANLEY . DD. DEAN . OF . RIPPON" The Archbishops mitre.				
	Waist (b)	A hunting horn, with the letters " RIPPON " interspersed (the arms of the city), with the inscription-"IOHN . TERRY . ESQ . MAYOR"				
Tenor (12)	Inscription Band	THE REVD INO DERING SUB DEACON GULᵁˢ. LAMPLUGH HENRY GOODRICKE HUGH THOMAS INᴼ. FOGG CHRIS. DRIFFIELD AND JAS: WILKINSON PREBENDS LESTER AND PACK OF LONDON FECIT 1761	1932	50	23-0-24	Eb
	Waist (a)	TO THE GLORY OF GOD AND IN MEMORY OF HER PARENTS, BROTHERS AND SISTERS THE BELLS OF THIS CATHEDRAL WERE RE-CAST AND THE BELFRY WAS RESTORED BY JULIA WHITE OF HIGHFIELD, RIPON 1932 -1933 *				
	Waist (b)	CHARLES MANSFIED OWEN. DEAN GEORGE WATTS GARROD JOHN BATTERSBY HARFORD CANONS ARTHUR HERBERT WATSON RESIDENTIARY JAMES GROVE WHITE TUCKEY EDWARD WALLACE WINSER SECRETARY TO THE CHAPTER * The seal of the Minter (an Angus Dei). The arms of Aislabie of Studley. The arms of Lawrence of Kirkby Fleetham				

It was also planned to install a new rope guide in the high-ceilinged ringing room to make the bells more predictable to handle and straightforward to ring. The appeal aimed to secure the future of traditional change ringing at Ripon and the surrounding area, by increasing the flexibility of the existing ring to benefit both trainee and experienced ringers, and make the cathedral better equipped for attracting new recruits.

By early 2007 the necessary funds were raised thanks to the generosity of the local community, and especially the Kiker and Pitts-Tucker families who gave the new bells. The late Dr David Bowen donated new bell frames, and generous financial support was forthcoming from the Foundation for Sports and the Arts, the Yorkshire Association of Change Ringers and the Ripon Cathedral Development Campaign. In August 2007 Hayward Mills Associates, Bell Hangers of Nottingham, were engaged as the main contractor to redesign the existing 10 bell framework to accommodate 13 bells, and carry out all the work required in the tower. The casting and tuning of the three new bells was entrusted to Taylors, Eayre & Smith Bell Foundry of Loughborough (formerly the John Taylors Bell Foundry which cast the 10 bells in 1932), and David Town of Northallerton supplied the new bell wheels. The cathedral ringers, donors and members of the chapter and congregation visited Loughborough on 15th November 2007 to observe the casting of the two new treble bells and view the flat 6th semitone bell cast on 8th November. Unfortunately

The new flat 6th bell arriving at the cathedral on 19th March 2008 with Andrew Mills and Paul Mason of Hayward Mills Associates.
Mike Cowling/Yorkshire Post

these castings were unsuccessful; the trebles were successfully cast on 13th December 2007 and the flat 6th on 6th March 2008 following another failed casting on 3rd January 2008.

The framework was adapted to hold the 13 bells during February, and the new bells were installed and rung for the first time on the evening of Wednesday 9th April 2008.

Bells 3 to 12 bear the stamp and name of John Taylor and Co., Loughborough on the waist. Bells 1 and 2 bear the stamp of Taylors, Eayre and Smith of Loughborough 2007 on the inscription band. The flat 6th bears the stamp of Taylors, Eayre and Smith of Loughborough 2008 on the inscription band.

The inscriptions of bells 3 and 4 are facsimiles of the 1891 bells from which they were recast.

The inscriptions of bells 5,7,8,10,11 and tenor are facsimiles of the 1762 bells from which they were recast. The reproduction includes seals, coats of arms, and decorative patterns on the 11th and tenor. Some additional text was added to the original inscriptions in 1932.

Central Tower (also known as St Wilfrid's Steeple)

In 1733 Gent reported that the turret on top of the central tower contained a single bell. Later, probably in 1768, this bell was removed and broken up to provide metal for the new ring of 8 being cast for the south-west tower. A fragment of this bell is known to have remained in the cathedral until the late 19th century and bore the date (1)710.

Prior to the Second World War the bell turret had fallen into disrepair and was removed. In June 1964 the turret was replaced and a bell, purchased from John Taylor & Co., Loughborough, was hung in it. The bell was fitted with a trigger action clapper and is in regular use as a service bell. It was refurbished in 2006 by David Town of Northallerton as part of the major restoration of the central tower roof.

The Cathedral Bell Ringers

Early documents concerning the bell ringers at Ripon have been hard to trace, but it is probably safe to assume that a band was trained to ring the Lester & Pack ring of 8 following its installation in 1762. Records for 1764, however, confirm that a band had been formed and the members were :

Thomas Hunter (Verger), Thomas Dowson, Thomas Fothergill, John Gilbertson, Thomas White, Robert Askwith, Jos Turkington, John Orton, Edward Harrison and Matthew Thirlwall.

A set of ringers' rules was drawn up in 1764 and mounted on the north wall of the ringing chamber. These rules, still in situ, read:

> *Orders made and agreed upon the second day of February, in the year of our Lord 1764, by the Society of Ringers, and to be observed by strangers and others that enter this belfry.*
>
> *Every person refusing to keep his hat off after having been requested by any member so to do, shall forfeit sixpence.*
>
> *Every person making a bell sound with hat or spur on shall forfeit sixpence.*
>
> *Every person swearing, giving the lie, offering to lay wagers, guilty of any other abusive or indecent language, or behaving himself in any disorderly manner, shall forfeit sixpence.*
>
> *Every person guilty of the malicious and unwarrantable practice of spoiling or besmearing the painting, cutting or marking the wood or plastering of this belfry, or otherwise obliterating or defacing any part thereof, shall forfeit two shillings and sixpence.*
>
> *And lastly, all the above forfeitures for every time such respective offence may be committed shall be immediately paid to the President or Treasurer for the time being of the said Society, or in his absence to such member thereof here present then to be appointed to receive the same, and it is earnestly requested by the said Society that all persons here assembled would be very still and keep strict silence whilst they are ringing.*

In January 1863 the ringers resigned because they were prohibited from ringing when they wished without the prior approval of the Dean and Chapter. Consequently a chiming apparatus was installed in the tower so the bells could be sounded by a single person. The stand off between the ringers and the Dean and Chapter continued until October 1864 when the ringers apologised and accepted the new conditions for ringing, and they were duly re-instated.

The 1762 bells required rehanging in 1868. It is unlikely that this would have been necessary if the bells were not being regularly rung, and this provides evidence of an active band of bell ringers between these years.

The Ripon Millenary in 1886 was celebrated by a peal on the bells of 5056 Kent Treble Bob Major. This peal is recorded on a stained glass peal board mounted in the south window of the ringing room, donated by Mr Thomas Clark, the conductor of the peal and President of the Cathedral Society of Change Ringers.

On January 22nd 1890 the Ripon and District Campanological Society was formed to promote hand bell ringing and improve change ringing at local churches. The society membership was drawn from bell towers around Ripon including the cathedral, Boroughbridge, Harrogate and Sharow. The cathedral ringers were influential in forming and supporting this society, Thomas Clark, a Ripon ringer, holding the position of secretary throughout the early 1890s. Reports of performances by the Society taken from 'Bell News' revealed a talented team of ringers at Ripon, with members from the cathedral regularly ringing Stedman and Treble Bob methods at society meetings.

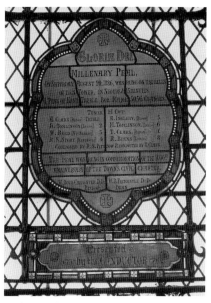

The 1886 stained glass Peal Board.

The cathedral bell ringers were very active throughout the 1890's with method ringing on 8 and 10 bells firmly established under the leadership of Thomas Metcalfe. Kent Treble Bob Royal, Stedman Triples and Grandsire Triples were evidently rung regularly as were quarter peals on 8 and 10 bells. The bell ringers also held outings to Pateley Bridge in 1894 and Tadcaster in 1896. A major triumph was achieved on May 20th 1893 when five local ringers (James Metcalfe, Thomas Clark, Walter Pick, Anthony Ingleby and Thomas Metcalfe), together with members from Durham and Newcastle, took part in the first peal on 10 bells to be rung in the tower. This was 5040 Kent Treble Bob Royal, conducted by Charles Routledge and took 3 hours and 25 minutes to complete.

In August 1893 it appears there was some unsettled behaviour within the tower. John Shodden (Senior) was dismissed from the band despite having been a ringer at Ripon for over 22 years and a previous president of the society. Shodden subsequently wrote to the dean demanding an explanation and criticising the behaviour of Thomas Clark whom, he said, often attended ringing on *Royal Days in such an intoxicated state that he cannot ring.* This disagreement may have had its roots in 1886 when Shodden, who had returned to ringing from ill health, was proposed for a second term as president to replace Clark, on the basis that this position should go to the longest serving member rather than the most appropriate to lead the team. Clark subsequently wrote to the dean suggesting some amendments to the ringers' rules and regulations, particularly with regard to the appointment of president, but it was not until 1903 that the new rules appeared.

Rules and Regulations for the Bell-ringers of Ripon Cathedral - 1903

1. *The Bell-ringers are to consider themselves as engaged by the Dean and Chapter to ring the Bells only upon such occasions and under such authority and regulations as stated in the following rules.*

2. *The number of Bell-ringers to be eight (now 10).*

3. *If a vacancy occurs in the body, the remaining members may propose a suitable person to succeed to the vacancy, to be appointed by the Dean or Canon in Residence.*

4. *The Ringers shall elect one of their members annually as President. The Dean shall be informed of this and his consent asked to the appointment.*

5. *Whenever the Bells are required or allowed to be rung, the key of the Bell chamber is to be fetched for the purpose from the Deanery or Residence, at whichever place it may be, and carried back again to the same place by the president of the Bell-ringers.*

6. *No beer or spirituous liquors shall at any time be brought into the Belfry or any part of the Church on pain of instant dismissal.*

7. *Any member absenting himself without leave from the majority of the Ringers present during the specified time of ringing shall be fined 8d.*

8.	Any member neglecting to attend at any time appointed in these Rules, for the Bells to be rung shall be fined 2d and after the first quarter of an hour 4d, and should such member fail to attend altogether or not send a satisfactory substitute he shall forfeit all claim to any benefit arising from such ringing.

9.	Whenever a peal is required to be rung, other than the stated times mentioned in the rules and permission is given to do so, the President shall give notice to each member who, in case of absence at the appointed time, shall be fined 6d, and after the expiration of the first quarter of an hour he shall be fined 4d. If, and should such member fail to attend altogether and not send a satisfactory substitute, he shall forfeit all claim to any benefit arising from such ringing, but if through any mistake the summons fail to reach him, such member shall be entitled to a chance peal at the rate of 1s in the £.

10.	The President is to keep an account of the fines incurred, such fines to be deducted from the member's salary when due, and such fines shall be equally divided amongst those members who have not incurred any fines. Before payment the sheet to be submitted to the Dean or Canon in Residence.

11.	The Ringers shall receive from the Dean and Chapter a salary of £4 per annum each, and one probationer at £2 a year to be paid by the Chapter Clerk half yearly on the 21st December and 21st June in each year, subject to the provision of Rule 10.

12.	The Bells are to be rung every Sunday and Christmas Day from a quarter before 10 a.m till Service time and a quarter before 6 till the time of Evening Service.

13.	The Bells shall be rung for half an hour between 8 and 9 am or between 7 and 8 pm on the occasion of a Coronation, the anniversary of the Accession of the Sovereign, the Birthday of the King, Queen, or Prince of Wales, also the Birthday of the Princess of Wales. Any further peals on other days such as any anniversary or event connected with any member of the Royal Family, or any occasion of National rejoicing, for

225

which they may be ordered to be rung by the Dean, or in his absence by the Canon in Residence or at other times of the day than those specified, to be paid for by the Chapter.

14. The Bells are also to be rung for half an hour on the Installation of a Bishop, Dean or Canon Residentiary of the Cathedral (a gratuity of 2 Guineas being given by the Dignitary installed) at the time appointed by the Dean, or in his absence or Installation, by the Canon in Residence and also on New Year's night for half an hour beginning at midnight.

15. The Bells are never to be rung on any other occasion than those mentioned, but with the express permission first obtained by the Dean, or in his absence, of the Canon in Residence, or, in the absence of them both of the Senior Minor Canon.

16. If it is desired by parties to be married in the Cathedral or other Church within the Parish that the Bells should be rung on the occasion, the sum charged shall be 2½ Guineas.

17. On the occasion of the election of the Mayor or new Alderman or a Member of Parliament, or the arrival of any inhabitant or visitor of distinction, the Bells may be rung with the permission of the Dean, or in his absence of the Canon in Residence and the ringers shall be allowed to receive any gratuity that may be given by the parties for whom they ring.

18. There shall be a practice of the Ringers one night in the week from 7 to half past 8 commencing from the first week in October and concluding the last week of February, and any member failing to attend (after due notice has been given) at the time appointed, shall be fined 2d. and after the expiration of the first quarter of an hour, such member shall be fined 4d. and for non attendance 6d.

Mem: Until the strength is made up to 10 the probationers (now 3) to have £2 a year.

From the attendance book it appears that the payments and ringing times specified in these rules were adhered to until regular ringing stopped in 1963.

It is known that there were at least 11 ringers in 1908 as recorded in a picture of the band (see illustration).

In 1912 an article appeared in 'Bell News':

Stowed away in the little hamlet of Hutton Conyers, near Ripon, is a venerable old man who holds the proud distinction of being the oldest bellringer in the British Isles. Mr Joseph Baines, now in his ninety-first year, has performed many notable bellringing feats in his seventy years connection with Ripon Cathedral and the neighbouring church at Sharow.

The Ripon Ringers, 1908.

During the 1920s and 1930s bell ringing at Ripon flourished. In April 1927, Edward (Ted) Hudson, a newly trained young ringer from Sharow, made his first visit to Ripon when he accepted an invitation from two of his work colleagues, who were ringers at the cathedral, to ring for a wedding. Ted reports that:

The cathedral band raised the bells in peal and rang touches of Grandsire and Stedman Triples. I was then permitted to ring 3 plain courses of Grandsire Triples on the treble.

As a result of this meeting Ted decided to attend the Tuesday night practice, and so began a long association with the cathedral.

At the enthronement of Geoffrey Lunt as Bishop of Ripon on 13th February 1925, Grandsire and Stedman Triples were rung. On 23rd June 1932 the team rang the old 10 bells for the last time before their removal to Loughborough for recasting. The band joined the ringers at Sharow while the cathedral bells were out of commission. The first official ringing on the new bells was on the 8th April 1933 following the Service of Dedication.

In 1939 the band was awarded the First Certificate under the Sunday service ringing scheme of the Cleveland and North Yorkshire Association. To celebrate, Dean Mansfield Owen entertained the ringers to supper at the Black Bull. Amongst those attending were the following Ripon veterans with a total of 375 years ringing experience between them: J. Metcalfe (52 years), J.

Rumbold (50), T. Ingleby (50), G. Langshaw (50), C. Howroyd (40), F. Tingle (37), W. Dixon (35), R. Duffield (25), Mr Pearson (14) and E. Hudson (14).

On June 9th 1940 the bells were rung for the last time before being silenced in accordance with the 'Control of Noise Defence Order' issued by the Ministry of Home Security, which stated that church bells should only be rung to warn of an imminent invasion. This was lifted in April 1943, but during the war a number of bell ringers were lost. Although ringing was re-established on cessation of hostilities, it failed to engender the enthusiasm of the pre-war years. There was a resurgence of interest in the late 1950s when Thomas Gardiner was president, but this was short-lived, and ringer numbers fell again during the early 1960s. In 1963 regular ringing ceased, the last ringing recorded in the attendance book being on Sunday 23rd June when 6 members attended including Ted Hudson. This date is exactly two days after the half-yearly wages would have been paid.

In accordance with the rules and regulations, the bell ringers were paid a salary by the Dean and Chapter:

	Annual Salaries (1931-1963)	**Wartime Retaining Fees**
President	£7 10s. 0d.	£6 10s. 0d.
9 Ringers	£6 10s. 0d.	£5 10s. 0d.
	(payable to 10 ringers from 1955)	
Probationers	£2 0s. 0d.	£2 0s. 0d.
Oiling of Bells	£1 0s. 0d.	

The ringers were paid an extra one third of one shilling for ringing on Crown Days, such as Coronation Day, Empire Day, and New Years Eve. They were also fined for unauthorised absence, 1s. 4d. for non-attendance on Sundays, 1s. 3d. for Crown Days, 6d. for practice nights and 2d. for being late.

From 1963 onwards there was no regular Sunday ringing, but Friday evening practices for an area band were arranged by Ted Hudson. The attendees included Geoffrey Dalton from Bedale, Arthur Bashforth from Kirby Wiske, Elsdon Metcalfe from Thirsk, William (Bill) Johnson from West Tanfield with his son Geoffrey, John Brown from Ripon, Marion, David and Peter Town plus Jennifer Dunning (later Town) from Northallerton, Leonard Bean and Alan Winter from Knaresborough, and Harry Osbourne from Winksley.

These practices moved from tower to tower, usually held at places associated with the various ringers, and some of these were held at the cathedral. The band could ring Plain Bob and sometimes Grandsire Caters, not to a very high standard of striking, but generally brought to a successful conclusion. Ted conducted from the 9th bell, which in those days used to shout down the clock case. He always enjoyed explaining about the curfew bell to visitors and frequently lowered the back bells to allow it to strike at 9pm and then carried on ringing the front six until quarter past the hour. During the 1970s a few quarter peals were rung on the cathedral bells by bands drawn from these practices. They also rang occasionally for special services and events such as weddings, the Nine Lessons and Carols, and the St Wilfrid's Day procession.

Clearly not having a band of bell ringers to ring for Sunday services was far from satisfactory. In 1977 the Dean and Chapter tried to remedy the situation; they contracted the Whitechapel Bell Foundry to overhaul the bells and fittings, and asked David and Jennifer Town to organise and train a new cathedral band. Advertisements were placed in the Ripon Gazette and Yorkshire Post which resulted in over forty people attending an inaugural meeting of potential bell ringers in May 1978. This included a tour of the bell tower and a talk on bell ringing by David Town. Practices, held on Tuesday evenings, started at the end of May with members of the Northallerton band assisting. The majority were new to bell ringing, but a few had previous experience including Kenneth Lancaster, who learnt at Kirklington, and Geoffrey Johnson, who was taught at West Tanfield. By the autumn the new ringers were sufficiently competent to ring for Sunday services, and on Sunday 1st October 1978 the new band rang for the 9.15 am Eucharist for the first time in 15 years. Service ringing has continued every Sunday since.

David and Jennifer Town continued in charge of the practices and training the local band until November 1979, with Geoffrey Johnson organising the Sunday service and wedding ringing. On 6th November 1979 the Ripon Cathedral Society of Change Ringers held its first AGM and appointed the following officers:

Tower Captain and Ringing Master:	Geoffrey Johnson
Assistant Ringing Master:	Christine Burnett
Secretary:	Margaret Haywood
Treasurer:	Peter Teasdale
Steeple Keeper:	John Ramsey
Chairman:	Dean Edwin le Grice

Since its inception the society has seen many changes of membership but Geoffrey Johnson and Kenneth Lancaster are still active in the cathedral band, currently holding the positions of Tower Captain and Steeple Keeper respectively.

During the 1980s an annual dinner and regular ringing tours were established. The team also benefited from experienced ringers joining whilst studying teacher training at the College of Ripon and York St John. The band regularly competed in local striking competitions with a good deal of success, frequently gaining top three positions. Under successive leaderships of Harry and Wendy Winter it gained experience and confidence, ringing a number of quarter peals in more advanced methods.

On 30th August 1986 five members of the cathedral band took part in a peal of 5185 Plain Bob Caters to celebrate the 1100th anniversary of Ripon's apocryphal Civic Charter of 886 and the 100th anniversary of the 1886 Millenary peal. This was recorded on a stained glass tablet, designed to match the one for the 1886 peal, which was mounted in the east window of the ringing chamber. It was painted and fired by Septimus Waugh, a stained glass artist from York, with the bell ringers raising £3,000 to fund the work. These stained glass peal boards are two of only four known in England, the others being at St John's Church, Sharow and St Peter's Church, St Albans.

On 5th December 1992 the band rang a full peal of 5040 Grandsire Triples. This is the only local band peal rung on the current bells since they were installed in 1933 and probably the only peal rung by a local band at the cathedral. It is recorded on a peal board mounted on the north wall of the ringing chamber.

Ripon Cathedral Society of Change Ringers
On Saturday December 5th 1992 in 3 hours and 12 minutes
5040 Grandsire Triples
(Burton's 12 Part)

1. Gerald M Brady	5. Harry Winter (Conductor)
2. Maureen Lowe	6. Wendy Winter
3. Janet M Wadsworth	7. Christopher S Dodds
4. Geoffrey W Johnson	8. Kenneth C Lancaster

The band lost some of its more experienced ringers in 1995 but a nucleus remained which has become the core of the current team. Under the leadership of Janet Wadsworth, and then Martin Davies, the band has slowly re-established and now numbers more than twenty. Methods such as Grandsire and Stedman are once again practised at the cathedral, with 10 bells normally rung for service and on Wednesday evening practice nights. Like their predecessors the current band has enjoyed success in local striking competitions and continues the traditions of an annual dinner and ringing tours.

In 2005 the band set up the 'Ring Out Ripon Bells' appeal to augment the bells to 12 plus an additional semitone bell, and a committee was created to co-ordinate the fundraising activities:

Chairman:	Martin Davies	
Secretary:	Jo Mitchell	
Treasurer:	Dean Chapman	
Members:	David Edwards	Mike Kiker
	Geoffrey Johnson	Maureen Lowe

The appeal was launched in the cathedral by James Bell, Bishop of Knaresborough, on 22nd January 2005, following which the bell tower was opened to the public. The committee arranged many events including further tower open days, teddy bear parachute jumps from the top of the south-west tower, and a mini ring day in Huby's Tower at Fountains Abbey. A display explaining the appeal's objectives was erected in the nave of the cathedral. The committee applied to local businesses and fundraising bodies to secure finance for the project which came to a successful conclusion in January 2007 when the target of £42,000 was reached.

The Ringing Chamber, 2008.

The new bells were cast between December 2007 and March 2008, and installed in April. Work included refurbishment of the ringing room to expand the floor area to accommodate the new 12 bell rope circle, provision of a new carpet, and the restoration of the magnificent view from the east window.

The enthusiasm and commitment of the current band, coupled with the recent work in the bell tower, places traditional bell ringing at Ripon Cathedral on a strong footing and bodes well for the future.

The Cathedral Ringers 2008

Tower Captain: Geoffrey Johnson
Ringing Master: Martin Davies
Assistant Ringing Master: Janet Wadsworth
Secretary: Maureen Lowe
Treasurer: Ian Mcdonald
Steeple Keeper: Kenneth Lancaster
Ringers' Chaplain: Canon Keith Punshon
Members: Andrew Aspland

- Gerald Brady
- Bethany Edwards
- David Edwards
- Margaret Harrison
- Alexander Kiker
- Angela Kiker
- Charlotte Kiker
- Michael Kiker
- Kathleen Kiker
- John Mitchell
- Jo Mitchell
- Barbara Packer
- Alison Scott
- Ruraigh Wadsworth
- John Welsh
- Wendy Winter

The authors are extremely grateful to Martin Davies, Ringing Master, who wrote this chapter. Thanks are also due to Andrew Aspland, Andrew Bull, the late Nick Davies, Geoffrey Johnson and Jennifer Town for providing information.

Chapter 17

RIPON CATHEDRAL OLD CHORISTERS' ASSOCIATION

The idea of a reunion for old choristers of Ripon Cathedral originated from the Dean and Chapter who, in October 1910, decided to organise a meal for the old choirboys, the precentor, succentor and organist. This was the same year that the Federation of Cathedral Old Choristers' Associations, the national body, was founded.

A year later the Ripon Cathedral Choir Old Boys' Association was established on the initiative of the Reverend Ernest Henry Swann, the precentor, and Charles Moody, the organist. The first meeting was presided over by T. Benson, the oldest member, and was attended by ninety-eight old choristers. Also present was the dean, the Hon William Fremantle, who was elected president, together with various members of the chapter who were appointed to the committee. E.H. Ingram was made honorary treasurer, J.T. Ambler honorary secretary, and W. Render assistant secretary. It was decided that the minimum subscription would be one shilling per year, and the annual reunion would be held in August.

It was said at the first meeting that *though the railway strike and lack of trains has prevented many from a distance attending, it has also prevented some local members from being absent.* Following the meeting, members attended evensong at the cathedral and heard an address by the Bishop of Ripon, who described music as being *a message far beyond the message which it conveys to the ear; it is a message to the heart, and it is a message of hope to the human mind.* An excellent rendition of the anthem 'Ascribe unto the Lord' by John Travers was given. Following evensong, what was described in the newspaper report as *a fine tea* was provided at Wrights Assembly Rooms, culminating in a concert of twelve light-hearted items and 'Auld Lang Syne'.

Norman Benn was a chorister who left the choir in 1920. To mark his time at Ripon, a head chorister's badge was donated (See illustration over). This was made of silver and had on its face a fine relief of the minster, with a Hebrew inscription *Jehovah* above. On the reverse is engraved *Norman Temple Benn, Monitor 1919-1920.* The responsibilities attached to being a monitor are not known, but this was probably a different position from that of head chorister.

This and a similar badge are still worn by the head chorister and his deputy.

During the 1930s and 1940s the choristers went on annual summer outings to places such as Carlisle, Blackpool and Scarborough. They travelled in a charabanc, and the costs were met out of an 'outing fund' which was accumulated from donations from the old choristers, various clergy and members of the cathedral community.

A reunion was held at the Victoria Café in 1943 when a record number of old choristers attended. An informal

Head Chorister's Badge, 1920.

photograph, taken at the cathedral before evensong, showed many of them in uniforms of the Army, Royal Navy, Royal Air Force, and the Civil Defence Services. During evensong a memorial chaplet was placed to the memory of fallen old choristers, and this act of remembrance at the reunion continues to this day.

At the annual general meeting that year it was unanimously agreed, after animated discussion, that a letter of protest be sent to the Dean and Chapter about the changes they had imposed on the music sung at Sunday services in the cathedral. These changes meant that *the canticles were sung to chants and the services, not being fully choral, were only equal to those of a parish church*. The meeting maintained that this decision was in total contravention of the statutes of the cathedral which laid down that *There shall be full choral services every Sunday morning and evening*; this was the beginning of a long running battle (Ref. Chapter 8).

Soon after the formation of the Ripon Association it became customary for the music sung at evensong on the day of the reunion to be chosen by the chairman of the association for that year. This practice continued through the incumbencies of organists Moody, Dakers and Marshall, but apparently Ronald Perrin, appointed in 1966, discouraged it and the tradition died out.

Unfortunately records of the annual reunions prior to 1951 have not survived, although some old photographs are available (See illustrations).

The first national meeting of the Federation of Cathedral Old Choristers'

Associations hosted by Ripon Cathedral was held in 1922, but little information is available. However, the second FCOCA national festival at Ripon was in September 1934 and on this occasion, following a light lunch, Dr Moody conducted delegates round Fountains Abbey. At the dinner, held that evening at the Unicorn, formal dress was the order of the day. A handwritten letter dated August 1934 from the Unicorn Hotel & Posting House to the precentor, Reverend H. R. Williams, has survived giving proposed menus. There are two options, both offering a meal of eight courses, one at four shillings a head and the other five shillings.

Cathedral Choir Old Boys' Reunion, 1920.

Cathedral Choir Old Boys' Reunion, circa 1937.

Two other national FCOCA festivals have been held at Ripon, one in 1957 and the other in 1990. Both were based at the Ripon Diocesan Training College, which provided accommodation and banqueting facilities.

In 1951 the association was given a badge of office for the chairman, donated by Maurice Geary who was chairman at the time. Each year a bar, engraved with the name of the chairman, has been added to the ribbon (Ref. Appendix).

In 1996 the director of music, Kerry Beaumont, with the support of the Dean and Chapter, formed a girls' choir (Ref. Chapter 11). As a result, the Ripon Cathedral Choir Old Boys' Association was renamed the Ripon Cathedral Old Choristers' Association, and old girl choristers are now members and attend the annual reunions.

The Association continues to support the music foundation, and maintains contact between the Ripon Cathedral old choristers, the recent establishment of an internet web site proving invaluable.

Cathedral Choir Old Boys' Reunion, circa 1956.

Chapter 18

CONCERTS IN THE CATHEDRAL

Cathedral Choir Concerts

Following the creation of the new diocese in 1836, Charles Longley, the first Bishop of Ripon regularly invited the cathedral choir to his palace to sing for his guests, especially at Christmas. These were the first records of concerts given by the choir. By 1860 the dean was inviting the choir to the deanery each Advent to sing Christmas music to his guests. These concerts were so well attended that, in 1867, they were moved to the public rooms which accommodated a larger audience.

Throughout Crow and Moody's eras the choir regularly gave concerts in the cathedral, sometimes joining with the Ripon Cathedral Oratorio Choir. John West wrote of Ripon in 1899 *on Sunday afternoons Oratorios, Cantatas etc are frequently given either complete or in part.* Large scale choral works, such as Handel's 'Messiah', Bach's Passions, Mozart's Requiem Mass, Mendelssohn's 'Elijah', Haydn's 'Creation' and Dvorak's 'Stabat Mater', were performed with professional soloists, and these were always accompanied by the organ rather than an orchestra. The cathedral choir, combining with the oratorio choir, gave one of the earliest performances of Brahms' Requiem in the north of England in about 1885, and perhaps the first performance in England of Schumann's Requiem.

Between the mid 1980s and 1995 the Northern Three Choirs' Festival gatherings were expanded to include choral and organ concerts. During these festivals held at Ripon quite ambitious works were performed including Tallis's 'Spem in Alium' and Walton's Coronation Te Deum. More recently concerts have been held in Leeds and other venues for the Ripon Cathedral Development Campaign, and now the choir provides musical entertainment at RCDC functions such as 'The Angel Dinner'.

Once a term the choir travels to different churches in the diocese, giving concerts as part of the cathedral outreach programme. Until 2007, they also sang two concerts each year in the cathedral on St Cecilia's Day (22nd November) and Palm Sunday, sometimes combining with the St Cecilia Orchestra. On these occasions, amongst the works performed were Fauré's

Requiem, Stainer's 'Crucifixion', Langlais' Messe Solennelle, and Duruflé's Messe Cum Jubilo.

The Wakeman Singers

In 1966 Alan Dance, assistant organist at Ripon Cathedral and teacher at the choir school, collected together a group of cathedral lay clerks and fellow teachers to form the Wakeman Singers, named after the ancient Wakeman of Ripon, whose successors still blow the horn to set the watch each evening in the market place.

Alan directed the group and sang tenor, Mollie Deller sang soprano, Robin Davidson alto, Simon Deller bass and Kelvin Gott whatever was required. They met from time to time, to plan their singing, at the Old Deanery Restaurant, run by an eccentric proprietor named Louis, who was a highly regarded chef and who had an extensive wine cellar. These visits usually occurred on exeat weekends, when the choristers were taken out by their parents.

The Wakeman singers began as a group of musicians singing for their own pleasure, but soon they were invited to give concerts at various venues including Ripon Cathedral, St Wilfrid's Church, Harrogate, St Mark's Church, Harrogate, Acomb Parish Church, York, Bradford Cathedral and Truro Cathedral. On one occasion, before the cathedral choir was expected to do so, the Wakemen sang for the Christmas Midnight Mass at Ripon Cathedral. Occasionally fees were paid, but in most cases concerts were given for charity.

The repertoire tended towards the madrigalian tradition together with Tudor church music. The Tallis 'Lamentations' and the Byrd Four and Five Part Masses were regulars. Occasionally accompanied items were included, such as Gibbons' 'Cries of London' and Purcell's 'Strike the Viol' for alto solo (Robin) with cello (Kelvin), recorder duet (Mollie and Simon) and spinet (Alan) from 'Come ye Sons of Art'. More adventurous pieces followed such as E. J. Moeran's 'Songs of Springtime', Vaughan Williams's 'Five Folk Songs' and Debussy's 'Trois Chansons de Charles D'Orleans'. Light fare was provided by such items as Seiber's 'Yugoslav Folk Songs' and Haydn's 'Maiden Fair', where an irate father (bass) is heard berating two lovesick suitors (tenors) for his daughter's hand.

In 1968 a piece was composed specially for the Wakeman Singers by Robin Beaumont, for a short time alto lay clerk at the cathedral, and father of chorister Kerry (who twenty-six years later became director of music at Ripon). He based this on the first two verses of Psalm 127, *Except the Lord build the house, the watchman* (wakeman) *waketh but in vain*, which are the words inscribed over Ripon Town Hall.

Simon and Mollie Deller left Ripon after Christmas 1969, but the Wakemen continued for a while with other singers, notably Angela Willoughby-Meade (soprano) and Richard Suart (bass). However, when Alan Dance left in 1974, the group finally broke up.

The name 'Wakeman Singers' was temporarily resurrected by Ripon lay clerk and organ scholar Adrian Roberts, when he formed a group of Ripon Cathedral based singers in the late 1990s, but this choir only lasted a short time.

The Moody Choir

In 1965 Alan Dance, assistant organist at Ripon Cathedral and resident teacher at the choir school, brought together some of his pupils to form a group of singers. He wrote *I began this choir because a significant number of boarders (practically all pupils were boarders then) asked "Why can't we sing too?" So with about twenty volunteers (after gentle voice trials) I began weekly rehearsals using both secular and church music.*

Initially this group was called 'The Choir School Choir', but Duncan Thomson, the headmaster, was unhappy with the name and held a competition to find a new one. Alan won the prize, a bottle of wine, by suggesting 'The Moody Choir' after Charles Moody, who had retired six years earlier after 52 years as cathedral organist.

Alan Dance wrote in the choir school magazine of 1972-1973; *The Moody Choir is formed from boys in the school who are non-choristers but like to sing. They rehearse once a week and have a small repertoire of easy anthems and some cheerful songs and rounds.*

It is always a pleasure for the Moody Choir to be invited to sing in nearby parish churches. In particular they have enjoyed singing at Harvest Festival Thanksgivings at West Tanfield and Baldersby – joining in the ensuing supper with as much gusto as they demonstrated when singing.

I hope that further opportunities to sing at outside locations will occur as there is no better way to encourage and reward the boys' enthusiasm.

During the 1970s and 1980s the Moody Choir continued making visits to harvest festivals, and the venues were extended to include Copt Hewick, and Pateley Bridge. The choir also augmented local church choirs at RSCM

Festivals, mainly at St Wilfrid's Church, Harrogate, which challenged the boys to learn new music, broadening their repertoire considerably.

When Alan Dance left in 1974, Marcus Huxley, his successor at the cathedral and choir school, took over the Moody Choir with help initially from Simon Gaunt and later Robert Thompson, both teachers and cathedral lay clerks.

The school became co-educational in 1978, and so girls joined the choir, which continued through the 1980s and 1990s.

By the start of the millennium, the Moody Choir performed mainly at the Ripon Men's Forum meetings and Markington Church Christmas carol concerts.

Andrew Bryden directed the Moody Choir after his arrival in 1998, and it flourished for a few more years. The number of non-chorister boarders at the school decreased in the early 2000s however, and the choir became more difficult to sustain, finally ceasing to exist in 2005.

Ripon International Festival

Ripon International Festival was founded in 1997 by the renowned pianist and conductor, Janusz Piotrowicz, and classical music promoter Susan Goldsbrough, who, with the encouragement of local and national sponsors and a team of dedicated volunteers, brought to fruition plans they had nurtured for some time to create an annual arts festival of the highest standard in the City of Ripon. Its founder-patrons were the Marquess of Zetland, the Bishop of Ripon, Baroness Masham of Ilton, and Sir David Willcocks.

The inaugural festival took place in 1998, opening at Ripon Cathedral on 12th September with a gala concert by Manchester Camerata, conducted by Janusz, of Mozart's Prague Symphony, Bach's Double Violin Concerto, and Mozart's Jupiter Symphony. The concert was praised by Donald Webster of the Yorkshire Post for its *sweet-toned … classical poise … spiritual aura … imperial splendour.* The cathedral also hosted concerts by the Lindsay Quartet, the Yorkshire Building Society Brass Band (reigning European champions) and a piano recital by Janusz. There were recitals, poetry, puppetry, film shows and theatre workshops at other locations.

The Festival made an immediate impact on the city and surrounding area, and drew unanimous appreciation for its quality, variety and welcoming atmosphere, generating eager expectation of further festivals to come.

Ripon Cathedral remains its focal point, providing a magnificent setting, warm ambience and a kind acoustic loved by performers and audiences. Its cornerstones are the symphony concerts conducted by Janusz Piotrowicz, whose profound musical insight and energy generate powerful performances. These concerts attract sell-out attendances with demand for tickets growing each year.

Janusz has invited some of the finest orchestras in the country to Ripon to perform the symphonic repertoire of Beethoven, Brahms, Dvorak, Mahler, Mendelssohn, Mozart, Schubert, Sibelius, Shostakovich and Tchaikovsky as well as other works from Bach to Arvo Pärt, with choral contributions from The Leeds Philharmonic Chorus. The London Bach Orchestra, Goldberg Chamber Orchestra, Orchestra of Opera North, Northern Sinfonia and Royal Liverpool Philharmonic Orchestra have all graced the festival with their fine musicianship. Performances of particular note include Miklos Perenyi in the Dvorak cello concerto with Northern Sinfonia; Tchaikovsky 6th and Sibelius 1st with the orchestra of Opera North; Mahler 1st and Shostakovich 5th with the RLPO (Shostakovich 5th *was given a superb performance ... though our lasting memory will be of the sheer power Janusz unleashed,* Yorkshire Post 2005).

Another major achievement was to secure one of the finest choirs in Europe for the 2004 festival. The thirty-eight members of the St Nikolai Church Choir of the State Tretyakov Gallery, Moscow – *astonishingly young, but their voices are as old as time* (The Times) – gave a breathtaking performance of the Rachmaninov Vespers in the year which marked the 400th anniversary of the city's Royal Charter granted by King James I.

A stream of stage and literary celebrities has also graced the programme; Sir Derek Jacobi (the Festival's president), Geraldine McEwan, Michael Pennington, Richard Pasco, Barbara Jefford, Rohan McCullough, Liverpool poet Adrian Henri, and writer Michael Holroyd have all appeared in Ripon. Other popular events have included Spanish flamenco, Japanese Taiko drummers, puppet theatre, Zulu dance, song and drums, jazz and folk concerts, and outstanding young musicians.

The Festival reaches out into rural areas, staging events in ancient village churches and great houses up to twenty miles distant, such as Aske near Richmond, home of the Marquess of Zetland, St Mary's, Nun Monkton, near York, one of Yorkshire's architectural jewels, and Markenfield Hall, a fortified medieval manor.

Over the years the Festival has steadily enlarged the scope of its programme and built a strong following from the northern region and as far afield as London, the south of England and the north of Scotland. Spring concerts were added in 2005 and 2006; Opera North in a Mozart Gala and the RLPO in Mendelssohn's Scottish Symphony and Dvorak's New World Symphony. These concerts proved enormously popular and one is planned for 2008.

Local companies and individuals continue to contribute to the success of the Festival: ten years on, many of its founder sponsors are still involved, more have come forward and many people have joined the team of volunteers.

The Festival celebrated its tenth anniversary in 2007 with the first visit to Ripon of a famous London orchestra, the Royal Philharmonic. Under the baton of Janusz Piotrowicz, the orchestra gave a gripping performance of the fifth symphonies of Beethoven and Tchaikovsky. This was an experience etched into the memory of all present and the Festival looks forward to many more such occasions in this wonderful cathedral church.

The Cathedral Concert Society

On Monday 4th October 1993 about ninety music lovers assembled in the choir of the cathedral in a spirit of curiosity. What was this concert society which had suddenly appeared? Who had started it? Would it work? They heard two quintets by Mozart and a new piano quartet by cathedral organist titulaire Ronald Perrin, with Christina Thomson-Jones on horn and other members of the Mowbray Ensemble. That they were there at all was entirely due to the imagination and foresight of Christina, Kelvin Gott and Xenophon Kelsey.

Previously there had been a flourishing concert series at Ripon College, but this had gradually faded away, and there was no longer an outlet for talented local amateurs, nor opportunities for professional musicians to perform. Grantley Hall held concerts, but these were not available to the general public, and the three founders wanted the proposed concerts to be accessible to all. The new society was to be a trust, and as the founders would be performing, they could not be trustees. Others, however, were cajoled into being trustees and forming a management committee, most of whom are still in place, older and stiffer, but still enthusiastically planning for future seasons. The founders stayed on as consultants and remained deeply involved as both performers and providers of inspiration. Until he died, Kelvin was our indefatigable page-turner, without whom no concert with piano accompaniment could succeed. He was replaced by Christina with similar quiet competence and distinction.

The Choir on the eve of a Cathedral Concert Society recital.

The original idea was to hold most of the concerts in the cathedral library, but the response for membership was more than had been anticipated, totalling over eighty. Consequently the first series of concerts was held in the choir and they have remained there ever since. Performers sometimes shiver, but love the cathedral and its atmosphere. The audience loyally turns out for the famous and the not so famous, the up-and-coming and the arrived, and from the start has been adventurous and interested in the unfamiliar. We have heard established artists like Ian Bostridge, Raphael Wallfisch, Julius Drake, Nicholas Daniel and Noriko Ogawa, as well as numerous young performers. Members have their favourites, but it is difficult to accommodate all the exciting performers that the society would like to invite, still less to have them back.

The Cathedral Concert Society is now in its fifteenth season, and under the dynamic chairmanship of Brian Kealy, confidently expects to hold its hundredth concert on 1st February 2010. It has around one hundred members who continue to enjoy the concerts and appreciate the quality of performers.

Lunchtime Concerts

Informal concerts at 1.15pm each Thursday during term time were initiated by Andrew Bryden in February 2004, and Thomas Leech took over their organisation that September.

Admission is free, and members of the audience are encouraged to come and go as they please. Many partake of the sandwiches and drinks provided, and some bring their own lunch.

Organ recitals make up approximately fifty percent of the concerts and, of these, about half are given by visiting organists, the remainder by the three organists of the cathedral.

Music students from Leeds University and pupils from the Ripon Cathedral Choir School and Queen Mary's School, Topcliffe, all perform regularly and musicians from elsewhere are invited.

When the concerts started in 2004 audiences numbered between ten and twenty people. They are now very popular, with sixty or so attending in the winter months and up to one hundred and fifty in the summer.

Ripon Choral Society

Ripon Choral Society was founded as 'The Ripon Cathedral Oratorio Choir' in 1884 by Dr Edwin Crow and flourished for many years, regularly performing in the cathedral. Dr Charles Moody, the organist from 1902 to 1953, became conductor in the early 1900s, and for a few years the Society moved steadily forward under his leadership and with the firm hand of Herbert Bower, Mayor and Society Chairman.

However, by 1907 things began to fall apart. Dr Moody stood down because of ill health, then resigned in 1908 citing the apathy of the membership, with typically only 30 of 70 members turning up at rehearsals. He was cajoled back on the understanding that the programme would diversify, Moody saying *Messiah was getting threadbare and was never taken up with enthusiasm either by members or by the audience.*

Things went from bad to worse. Finances were disastrous, attendances poor, and there was a feeling that the Society should be for the whole city (of whatever denomination). Dr Moody resigned again in 1912, as did the Mayor.

Nevertheless the Society, conducted by Mr P. R. Pfaff (a lay clerk at the cathedral and music master at the Grammar School), struggled on until 1931, largely performing secular works at other venues, such as the Victoria Opera House, with summer concerts in the Ripon Spa Gardens.

The Choral Society was re-established in 1954 by the Rev Harry Graham, Frank Orton, Jim Hall, Elvet English and the newly-appointed cathedral

Ripon Choral Society concert, 1956.

organist, Lionel Dakers, whose wife, Elizabeth, became the accompanist. After that the Society went from strength to strength. The first concert, 'Messiah' was given to a full cathedral and was followed by a gala occasion in May 1956 when the Society's patron, HRH Mary Princess Royal, attended a performance of Haydn's 'Creation', with Isobel Baillie, the renowned Scottish soprano, at the height of her powers.

Since then, the Society has flourished under a succession of conductors, Dr Philip Marshall, Ronald Perrin, Philip Miles and now John Dunford. Most performances have been held in the cathedral and works performed have ranged from Monteverdi's 'Vespers' to Jonathan Willcocks' 'Lux Perpetua', with a major oratorio repertoire in between. There have been numerous highlights; two that stand out are Ian Bostridge as the evangelist in Bach's 'St Matthew

Passion' in 1994 and John Mitchinson as Gerontius in 2000. The Society has enjoyed working with a range of orchestras from local professional groups to the students of the Royal Northern College of Music, and performing with the Ripon Harrison organ.

The singing of Bach's 'Christmas Oratorio' in December 1970 was enhanced by being held by candlelight due to power cuts caused by industrial action.

Alice Dyson, daughter of Yorkshire-born composer George Dyson (1883-1964), attended the November 1995 performance of his 'Nebuchadnezzar' (see illustration).

Alice Dyson, 1995.

The initial cohort of 60 singers in 1954 grew to 85 by 1964, including a number of students from Ripon Teacher Training College. The Choral Society continued to expand and now, with 170 singers, is one of the largest and most successful in Yorkshire.

Solvency has always been a challenge. In 1884 the total subscriptions amounted to £5 12s. 6d. and by 2006 this had increased to £11,950. In 1954 the nave ticket price was 4s, which had risen to £13 by 2006. The 1954 'Messiah' cost £15 to stage whereas a major concert in 2006 costs £9,500.

The press has been complimentary about performances over the years, even if the style of comment has changed somewhat. Thus *Mr Dakers did occasionally take a risk with the Cathedral's unpredictable acoustics by setting a brisk pace in a number of passages – but the gamble came off* (Ripon Gazette, 1956), compares with *Certainly expect plenty of musical fireworks when John Dunford lets the Ripon Choral Society loose on Walton's Belshazzar's Feast in the resplendent acoustic of the Cathedral* (Yorkshire Post, 2006).

The Society feels it is a central part of the life of the cathedral, bringing in members and audiences from every background to share in the spiritual atmosphere and acoustic glories of the magnificent building.

St Cecilia Orchestra

During the late 1980s there happened to be a number of useful string players amongst the cathedral community. Kelvin Gott, the prime mover, enlisted the help of fellow lay clerks Robin Browning and Harry Winter, and a few other friends and the St Cecilia Orchestra was formed. Its function was to accompany the cathedral choir at its annual St Cecilia's Day concert on 22nd November.

Two years later Xenophon Kelsey, conductor and double bassist, moved back to Ripon and Kelvin asked him to play with the orchestra. It didn't take long for Xen to see the potential, asking *Why do we only give one concert a year?*

Around this time Kelvin, Xen and Christina Thomson-Jones were laying the foundations of the Cathedral Concert Society, and a quintet of St Cecilia players, together with Ron Perrin, gave the inaugural concert. Xen was already developing the Mowbray Ensemble, a chamber group of local professional musicians, who also played in early Concert Society performances. The expansion of the St Cecilia Orchestra was an obvious move.

The Orchestra began giving additional concerts in the early 1990s and, helped by a number of local supporters, became a company limited by guarantee and a registered charity in 1993. The standard of performance was already well above that of other amateur groups in the region, and a considerable number of professional and semi-professional players, teachers, gifted amateurs, students and talented schoolchildren were eager to join.

The first major concert was a performance of Holst's 'Planets Suite' and Elgar's cello concerto, with former Ripon chorister Stephen Orton (principal cellist with the Academy of St Martins in the Fields) as soloist. An orchestra of nearly 100 players produced an inspired performance and a packed audience at the cathedral secured the future. This established the tradition of the orchestra's annual Gala Concert in September each year, an event which has produced many stunning performances of demanding and challenging pieces. Donald Webster, then Yorkshire Post music critic, wrote: *That a rural community can provide a capacity audience is praiseworthy, that it can also provide most of an orchestra of this size and quality is little short of miraculous.*

Since then the orchestra has gone from strength to strength. Over the last 14 years or so the St Cecilia Orchestra, and its professional offshoot, the Mowbray Orchestra (in demand for accompanying choral societies across the north of England) have given 193 performances in 48 different venues, playing 292 works by 90 different composers. The list of soloists who have appeared with the orchestra contains such illustrious names as Sir Thomas Allen, Sophie Barber, Leland Chen, Lynne Dawson, Peter Donohoe, Chloë Hanslip, Richard Harwood, Grace Huang, Karina Lucas, Stephen Orton, Artur Pizaro, Martin Roscoe, Matthew Trusler, and the renowned percussion group, 4-Mality.

The repertoire has been extremely varied, spanning four centuries and ranging from small chamber works to demanding works for large symphony orchestra, such as Bartok's 'Concerto for Orchestra', Elgar's Symphony No 1, Hindemith's 'Symphonic Metamorphoses', Janacek's 'Sinfonietta', Mahler's Symphony No 5, Rachmaninov's Symphony No 2, Shostakovich's Symphony No 5, Richard Strauss's 'Ein Heldenleben' and Stravinsky's 'Firebird Suite'. Local retired Anglican priest and musician, Peter Dodson, has composed several orchestral pieces for Ripon Cathedral (Ref. Chapter 15), which have been first performed by the St Cecilia Orchestra. In 2002 he wrote his 'Strings for Xenophon' for full orchestra, and this received its premiére in the cathedral on Saturday 16th March 2002.

In addition to promoting three or four of its own concerts each year, the St Cecilia Orchestra plays for the annual Palm Sunday and St Cecilia's Day concerts, and for two or three cathedral services. It also accompanies the choir on other occasions and recently performed at a major fundraising event in support of the Choir School Development Appeal.

The St Cecilia Orchestra sees the cathedral as its home and cherishes its close relationship with this inspiring building.

A P P E N D I X

BROADCASTS FROM RIPON CATHEDRAL

BBC RADIO PROGRAMMES

The authors are greatly indebted to Alan Duffield, a former tenor lay clerk at Ripon Cathedral who now sings with the Royal Opera, Covent Garden. Over a period of many months he has meticulously researched and examined documents at the British Library and BBC records at the Caversham Radio Sound Archives. In the course of this work a number of interesting comments in BBC notes came to light, and some of these are quoted in the following list below the broadcasts to which they relate. Information on particularly significant early broadcasting events are however dealt with more fully in Chapter 8.

The very first broadcast of choral evensong took place in October 1926 from Westminster Abbey: subsequent Thursday evensongs all came from there and were broadcast nationally. In the early thirties, the BBC added an additional weekly broadcast for the Northern Region and these all came from York Minster on a Tuesday.

By 1937 St Paul's had replaced Westminster Abbey on the National Service, now broadcasting on a Wednesday. The Northern Region broadcasts from York also continued every week until they, as well as St Paul's national broadcasts, were suspended at the outbreak of war in September 1939.

When the broadcasts were resumed on Tuesday 5th March 1940, they were only once a week and were all transmitted on the Home Service (formerly the National Service) but by now the BBC's outside broadcasting facilities had been developed and they travelled to different cathedral locations. After visiting Carlisle, York, Bristol and New College, Oxford, Ripon Cathedral was given its first broadcast choral evensong in 1940, although by then it already had a good deal of broadcasting experience.

As a national security measure during the war years the names of the cathedrals or colleges broadcasting choral evensong were not listed in the Radio Times, but were announced after the service had finished. Ripon was one of the first not to be mentioned in the Radio Times, in early August 1940, but by including his own setting of the canticles Dr Moody left few in doubt as to where the broadcast was coming from.

Remarkably, no complete list exists of choral evensongs broadcast by the BBC, either in their own archive or elsewhere. The only means of compiling a list of Ripon broadcasts was to read through the Radio Times kept at the British Library and to examine BBC files held at Caversham, covering a period of over 80 years. In view of the enormity of this task it is quite possible that some omissions or inaccuracies have occurred, for which the authors apologise.

One of the great disappointments has been the discovery of how few recordings of these old choral evensong broadcasts still exist. Sadly the BBC destroyed hundreds of recordings in order to re-use the tapes. Generally speaking, it is unusual to find any recordings dating from before 1970, but a note has been included in the details below of those broadcasts which are still held in the National Sound Archive at the British Library, and those of which the BBC have copies.

1932. Sunday 18th September
A Religious Service for Cyclists & Wayfarers
> Hymn: All before us lies the Way, Emerson
> Versicles and Psalm121
> Lesson read by the Mayor
> Hymn: He who would valiant be
> Prayers by the Dean
> Hymn: Father hear the prayer we offer
> Address by the Lord Bishop of Ripon
> Hymn: Abide with me
> Hymn: Jerusalem
> Prayers & Blessing

Dr C.H. Moody and the Cathedral Choir

1933. Wednesday 1st March
Broadcast from Taylor's Foundry, Loughborough, where the new set of 8 bells for Ripon Cathedral were rung for the first time prior to installation.

1934. Wednesday 31st January
> 'What the North owes to the early Cistercians'

Talk by Dr Charles H. Moody

1934.   Monday 26th March
The Music of the Church
Organ: Choral Prelude on 'Rockingham', Parry
Magnificat in D minor, Moody
Let my prayer come up, Purcell
All ye that pass by, Vittoria
Jesu, joy of man's desiring, Bach
Organ: Chorale in A minor, Cesar Franck
O Lord look down from heaven, Battishill
Deliver us O Lord, Gibbons
The surrender of the Soul to the everlasting love, Cornelius (8-parts)
Dr C.H. Moody and the Cathedral Choir

1934.   Sunday 20th May 7.55-8.45pm
A Religious Service
Hymn: O spirit of the living God (Winchester New)
Versicles & Responses
Psalm 138
Deus Misereatur: Hopkins in C
Prayers
God is a spirit, Sterndale Bennett
Address by the Lord Bishop of Ripon
Hymn: Breathe on me breath of God, Carlisle
Blessing
Dr C.H. Moody and the Cathedral Choir

and then straight into:

1934.   Sunday 20th May 8.45-9.02pm (Live to America)
Broadcast for the Columbia Broadcasting System, America
Bells from the Cathedral
The Town Crier from outside the Town Hall
The Mayor from inside the Town Hall
Address from the Cathedral by the Lord Bishop
Singing by the Choir (No details of what was sung)
Benediction
Fade back to the Town Hall for the Hornblower
Fade back to the Cathedral for Curfew
Dr C.H. Moody and the Cathedral Choir

1936.   Palm Sunday 5th April 7.55-8.45pm
Evening Service
> Hymn: There is a green hill
> Psalm 85 (Martin)
> Anthem: O Saviour of the World, Goss
> Address: The Lord Bishop, Dr Lunt
> Hymn: It is a thing most wonderful

Dr C.H. Moody and the Cathedral Choir

Note. *The payments made for this broadcast totalled £13 2s. 0d.*
> *Organist   £2 2s. 0d.*
> *Lay Clerks   £6 6s. 0d.*
> *Choristers   £1 4s. 0d.*
> *Vergers   15s. 0d.*
> *Bell Ringers   £1 5s. 0d.*
> *Printing   £1 10s. 0d.*

A very large congregation and not enough hymn books to go round.
Following the service the Lord Bishop wrote to the BBC:
I write to thank you with all my heart for the service last night.
Except for the horrible scream of a descant at the end of the first hymn it was almost my ideal of what a broadcast should be.
Later in his letter to the head of religious broadcasting (Dr Iremonger) the Bishop of Ripon commented *I entirely agree with what you say about our descant verse. It took some doing to keep our organist under control so that he did not perpetrate any worse horrors! It will strengthen my hand in dealing with him next time.*

1936.   Wednesday 1st July 3-4.45pm
A Festival Service from Ripon Cathedral sung by the choirs of Ripon, York, Durham & Newcastle
> Processional Hymn: Thy hand O God has guided, Basil Harwood
> Versicles and Responses
> Alcock in G, specially written for this festival
> Blessed City Heavenly Salem, Bairstow
> Hymn: Praise my Soul the King of heaven, William Ellis
> In exitu Israel, Samuel Wesley
> Fugue in Eb, Bach

Conducted by Dr C.H. Moody

1936. Wednesday 11th November 3.30-4.45pm

A Centenary thanksgiving commemorating the re-creation of the See of Ripon

> The Lord Bishop's Greeting
> Hymn: Thy hand O God has guided
> Anthem: The God of our fathers give thee favour, Parry
> Hymn: For all the Saints

Dr C.H. Moody and the Cathedral Choir

1936. Tuesday 17th November

Organ Recital from Ripon

> Absoute, Vivet
> A Little Tune, William Felton
> Festspiel, Noble
> Psalm Prelude No 2, Howells
> Lento Espessivo (from Schemelli song book), Bach
> Phantasie in A, Op.188, Rheinberger

Dr C.H. Moody

1937. Easter Sunday 28th March 7.55-8.45pm

A Religious Service

> The Bells
> Hymn: A brighter dawn is breaking
> The Easter Anthems
> Anthem: Ye choirs of new Jerusalem, Stanford
> Hymn: Jesus lives
> Hymn: Ye watchers & ye holy ones

Dr C.H. Moody and the Cathedral Choir

Note. Following the above Dr Moody wrote to the BBC requesting that they pay each of the Ripon musicians an additional fee of £1 1s. 0d. for the extra time rehearsing. The BBC were however concerned that if this was paid, other cathedrals would require payments. The cost of the Easter Day broadcast rose to £17 3s. 0d. The BBC suggested *a fee of 10/6 or 15s. at the most, without prejudice* and added that *the additional cost must be borne in mind when planning other broadcasts from Ripon.*

1937. Saturday 30th October
Massed Singing of Diocesan Festival Choirs
> Hymn: The King of Love, St Columba, descant by Moody
> Psalm 148, Moody
> Nunc Dimittis: King Hall in Eb
> Anthem: The Lord is my shepherd, Stanford
> Hymn: The God of Abraham praise

Conductor Dr Charles H. Moody, Organ, Conrad Eden

1938. Saturday 15th October
Massed Singing of Diocesan Choirs
> Psalm 97, Boyce (Ripon Psalter)
> Hymn: Blessed City, Urba beata
> O what their joy, Harris
> Nunc Dimittis, C.H. Lloyd in Eb
> Anthem: Giver of Peace, Moody
> Hymn: Immortal invisible

Conductor, Dr C.H. Moody, Organ, Dr H.K. Andrews

1938. Sunday 20th November 7.55-8.45pm
A Religious Service
> Hymn: When all thy mercies
> Psalm 147
> Nunc Dimittis
> Responses
> Anthem: Judge me O God, Mendelssohn
> Hymn: For the beauty of the earth
> Hymn: Ye servants of God

Dr C.H. Moody and the Cathedral Choir

1938. Wednesday 30th November
Music in Ripon Cathedral
> Turn thee O Lord, Orlando di Lasso
> Glorious in heaven, Vittoria
> Jesu dulcis memoria, Dering
> Bow thine ear, Byrd
> We laud and praise, Palestrina
> Organ: Adagio & Allegro – Concerto in D minor, Handel
> Sing we merrily, Batten

O Lord, look down, Battishill
Lift thine eyes, Mendelssohn
Saviour who in thine own image, Cornelius
Dr C.H. Moody and the Cathedral Choir

1939.   Wednesday 25th January
A Recital of Hymns from Ripon Cathedral
The Radio Times announced *This programme is presented by the Very Rev.*
Charles Mansfield Owen DD. Dean of Ripon and is the second of the North
Regions new series of specially presented hymn recitals by church choirs
whose singing is of a notably high standard.
The Ripon Cathedral Choir, Organist and Master of the Choir
Dr C.H. Moody CBE

1939.   Tuesday 4th April
An Organ Recital
        Choral Prelude on Rockingham, Parry
        Harmonies du Soir, Karg Elert
        Canzona – Sonata in C minor, Whitlock
        Pavanne, Byrd
        Ayre, Stanley
        Trumpet Tune, Purcell
        Tambourin, Handel
Dr C.H. Moody

1939.   Wednesday 17th May 7.30pm
A Recital of Hymns from Ripon Cathedral
Presented by The Ven C.C. Thornton, Archdeacon of Richmond
The Ripon Cathedral Choir, Organist and Master of the Choir
Dr C.H. Moody

1940.   Tuesday 6th August
Choral Evensong
        Psalm 32
        Moody in D minor
        Thee Lord before the close of day, Balfour Gardiner
        Hymn: 'Tis good Lord to be here
Dr C.H. Moody and the Cathedral Choir
Note. This is the first broadcast of Choral Evensong from Ripon Cathedral.

1940. Tuesday 13th August
Choral Evensong
> Martin Shaw in Eb
> Justorum Animae, Byrd
> Hymn: Crossing the bar

Dr C.H. Moody and the Cathedral Choir

BBC Note. *Musically the service was up to standard and well planned & rehearsed. For us the weak spot was minor canon Williams – getting a little too old for precentor work. His enunciation was 'mouthy'.*

1941. Thursday 27th March
Organ Recital BBC Home Service
> Sonata No 2 in F minor, Mendelssohn
> Adagio & Fugue (2nd Concerto), Handel
> Requiem Aeternam, Harwood
> Fugue in C, Bach

Dr C. H. Moody

1942. Tuesday 6th January
Choral Evensong
> Psalm 96 (Moody)
> Alcock in G
> Thee Lord before the close of day, Balfour Gardiner
> Hymn: Earth has many a noble city

Dr C.H. Moody and the Cathedral Choir

BBC Note. *Musically the service was up to standard. It was of special interest because Dr Moody has persistently criticised the singing of the psalms by the BBC singers.*

1942. Tuesday 13th January
Choral Evensong
> Psalm 8 (Graham)
> Cooke in G
> Jesu the very thought is sweet, Martin Shaw

Dr C.H. Moody and the Cathedral Choir

1942. Wednesday 21st January 1.15-1.50pm
Organ Recital
　　　　Air and Variations, Mendelssohn
　　　　Chorale in A minor, Franck
　　　　Meditation, B. Jackson
　　　　Fugue in Eb (St. Anne), Bach
　　　　Toccata in A major, Purcell
Dr C.H.Moody

1942. 24th May (Whit Sunday)
Empire Broadcast for Pacific Transmission
　　　　Hymn: When God of old came down from heaven
　　　　Anthem: Come Holy Ghost, Attwood
　　　　Address: The Lord Bishop of Ripon
　　　　Hymn: Come Holy Ghost, thy people bless
Dr C.H. Moody and the Cathedral Choir

1942. Wednesday 23rd December
A talk given by Dr C.H. Moody, an authority on Campanology
'The Church Bells of England'. This was included in the programme 'The World goes by'.

BBC note dated 21st January 1944. *We have four cathedrals who have not broadcast for many months – Ripon, Chester, Durham and Lincoln. I am particularly embarrassed that the doyen of cathedral organists, Dr Moody, has only been used as a stop gap these past few years. Professionally and spiritually Dr Moody is still a young man and he has broached the subject several times.*

Further note dated 3rd March 1944. *At present Ripon Cathedral has 16 boys and 6 men. We certainly found the work at Ripon is of the very highest standard on the last few occasions we have been there.*

1944. Tuesday 11th April
Choral Evensong
　　　　Psalm 61
　　　　Blair in B minor
　　　　Expectans Expectavi, Wood
Dr C.H. Moody and the Cathedral Choir

1944. Tuesday 18th April
Choral Evensong
>   Psalm 93
>   Stanford in C
>   Come O creator spirit come, Noble
Dr C.H. Moody and the Cathedral Choir

1944. Monday 30th October
Organ Recital for Overseas Service
>   Canon in D minor, Buxtehude
>   Choral Song and Fugue, Wesley
Dr C.H.Moody

1955. Sunday 15th May 9.15-9.45am
Organ Recital (Recorded)
>   Entrée Pontificale, Bossi
>   Saraband Processional, W.H. Harris
>   Sonata in A minor, Rheinberger
Lionel Dakers

1956. Sunday 18th November
Organ Recital
>   Fugue on a subject of Corelli, Bach
>   Partita on Veni Creator Spiritus, Peeters
>   Prelude on Rhosymedre, Vaughan-Williams
>   Introduction and theme, Sumsion
Lionel Dakers

1957. Friday 5th April
Short Organ Recital (Recorded)
>   Prelude and Fugue in C minor, Mendelssohn
Lionel Dakers

1957. Friday 24th May
Short Organ Recital (Recorded)
>   Prelude in Eb, Stanford
>   Postlude in D minor, Stanford
Lionel Dakers

1969. February (Date unknown)
Choral Matins (Recorded) for broadcast later on the BBC Overseas Service

1969. Wednesday 13th August
Choral Evensong
        Responses: Rose
        Psalms 69, 70 (Barnby, Smart, Hine)
        Jackson in G
        Blessed City, Bairstow
Sung by members of the RSCM

1969. Wednesday 8th October
Choral Evensong
        Responses: Smith
        Psalms 41,42,43 (Pattern, Crotch)
        Weelkes: Service for five voices
        Like as the hart, Howells
Conductor, R.E. Perrin, Organ, A. Dance

1969. Wednesday 15th October
Choral Evensong (Recorded)
        Responses: Leighton
        Psalm 78 (Crotch, Smart, Flintoft, Havergal, Dakers)
        Patrick Short Service
        O Lord the maker of al thing, Joubert
Conductor, R.E. Perrin, Organ A. Dance

1979. Saturday 23rd June
Organ Recital (Recorded)
        Fantasia and Toccata in D minor, Stanford
        Chorale and Prelude on *Schmucke dich, O liebe,* Bach
        Passacaglia and Fugue No 2 in E minor, Healey-Willan
Ronald Perrin

1979. Wednesday 12th December
Choral Evensong
        Responses: Byrd
        Psalms 65, 66, 67 (Walmisley, Wesley, Perrin, Noble)
        Noble in B minor

Hosanna to the Son of David, Gibbons
Conductor, R.E. Perrin, Organ, M.R. Huxley

1980. Thursday 25th December
Christmas morning service BBC Radio 4
Missa Riponiensis, Perrin
On this day earth shall ring, Stewart
Nativity carol, Rutter
Conductor, R.E. Perrin, Organ, M.R. Huxley

1983. Wednesday 12th October
Choral Evensong
Exultate Deo, Scarlatti
Responses: Jackson
Psalms 65-67 (Walmisley, S. Wesley, Perrin, Noble)
Dyson in D
Sing we merrily, Adrian Carpenter
Finale from 2nd Symphony, Widor
Conductor, R.E. Perrin, Organ, M.R. Huxley

1984. Friday 20th January
Choral Evensong
From the rising of the sun, Ouseley
Psalm 104 (Hopkins, Barnaby)
Weelkes Service for trebles
Hail Gladdening Light, Charles Wood
Choral Song and Fugue, S.S.Wesley
Conductor, R.E. Perrin, Organ, M.R. Huxley

1985. Wednesday 13th February
Choral Evensong (Recorded)
Oculi omnium, Charles Wood
Psalms 69, 70 (Defell,Wesley, Noble,Walford Davies)
Weelkes Short Service
Oh pray for the peace of Jerusalem, Howells
Prelude and Fugue in A, Bach
Conductor, M.R. Huxley, Organ, R.E. Perrin

1985. Friday 19th July
Choral Evensong (Recorded)
        O Praise God, White
        Bairstow in D
        Behold now praise the Lord, Wilson
Conductor, M.R. Huxley, Organ, R.E. Perrin

1986. Monday 7th July +++
Choral Evensong (Recorded)
        Almighty & Everlasting God, Gibbons
        Responses: Reading
        Psalms 93, 94 (Boyce, Turle, Perrin)
        Gray in G
        O Lord arise into thy resting place, Weelkes
        Lied to the sun, Peeters
Conductor, R.E. Perrin, Organ, M.R. Huxley
+++Recording held by BBC

1987. Wednesday 1st July*
Choral Evensong
        O come ye servants of the Lord, Tye
        Responses: Piccolo
        Psalms 6,7,8 (Monk, Cooke, Corfe)
        Harwood in Ab
        Faire is the Heaven, Harris
        Finale from 6th Symphony, Widor
Conductor, R.E. Perrin, Organ, R. Marsh
*****Recording held in National Sound Archives, London**

1988. Sunday 24th April+++
Choral Evensong (Recorded 30th June 1987)
        God liveth still, Bach
        Responses: Morley
        Psalms 108, 109 (Hanforth, Goss, Hylton-Stewart)
        Amner, Cesar's Service
        Blessed be the God and Father, Wesley
        Carillon, Murrill
Conductor, R.E. Perrin, Organ, R. Marsh

1988.   Wednesday 7th December***
Choral Evensong
> Hosanna to the Son of David, Gibbons
> Responses: Perrin
> Psalm 37 (Goss, Jones)
> Statham in E minor
> When Israel came out of Egypt, M. East
> Toccata & Fugue in D minor, Bach

Conductor, R.E.Perrin, Organ, R. Marsh

1990.   Wednesday 24th October***
Choral Evensong
> Behold how good and joyful, Vann
> Responses: Reading
> Psalm 119 vv1-32 (Marshall, Jones, Matthews, Coward)
> St John's Service, Howells
> Let all the world, Leighton
> Prelude and Fugue in G, Bach

Conductor, R.E. Perrin, Organ, R. Marsh

1991.   Sunday 24th March
Sequence of Music for Lent & Holy Week (Recorded)
Led by Christopher Campling, Dean
> Hosanna to the Son of David, Gibbons
> Love one another, Wesley
> Love bade me welcome, Vaughan Williams
> Loving Shepherd of thy Sheep, Cooke
> And the Peace of God, Purcell
> I wrestle and pray, C.P.E. Bach
> How beautiful are the feet, Handel
> Thy word is a lantern, Purcell
> It is a thing most wonderful, Moore
> Jesus Christ the Apple Tree, Holman
> God so loved the world, Stainer
> But thanks be to God, Handel

Conductor, R.E. Perrin, Organ, R. Marsh

1992.   Wednesday 26th February***
Choral Evensong
> Comfort O Lord, Crotch
> Responses: Leighton
> Psalm 119 vv145-176 (Robinson, Crotch, Gauntlett, Marsh)
> Darke in F
> Almighty God, the fountain of all wisdom, Tomkins
> Prelude and Bell Allegro, Stanley

Conductor, R.E.Perrin, Organ, R. Marsh

1993.   Wednesday 16th June ***
Choral Evensong
> Locus iste, Bruckner
> Responses: Jackson
> Psalms 82-85 (Parisian Tone, Pring, Bairstow, Carter)
> Jesus College Service, Matthias
> The Heavens are telling, Schutz
> Dankpsalm, Reger

Conductor, R.E. Perrin, Organ, R. Marsh

1996.   Wednesday 8th May***
Choral Evensong
> Os Justi, Bruckner
> Responses: Tunnard
> Psalms 41, 42, 43
> Dyson in D
> Laudibus in Sanctis, Byrd
> Vox Dei, Wilby
> Thema met varies, Andriessen

Conductor, K. Beaumont, Organ, R. Marsh

1996.   October. Girls' Choir broadcast on BBC Radio 4 Daily Service
During the course of 1996, the Girls' Choir's first year, there was much interest from the local radio and television stations, as well as the local and national press. All this was a tremendous boost to the girls' morale.

1997. Wednesday 5th November***
Choral Evensong
>The Windows, Lloyd
>Responses: Lloyd
>Psalms 26, 27 (Spicer, R Moore)
>Bairstow in D
>When the Lord turned again, P. Marshall
>Prelude and Fugue on a theme of Vittoria, Britten

Conductor, K. Beaumont, Organ, R. Green

1998. Wednesday 4th November ***
Choral Evensong
>Justorum Animae, Stanford
>Responses: Byrd
>Psalms 26, 27 (Spicer, R. Moore)
>Gray in F minor
>Seek Him that maketh the seven stars, Dove
>Allegro maestoso, Symphony No 3, Vierne

Conductor, K. Beaumont, Organ, A. Bryden

2000. Wednesday 16th February
Choral Evensong – Transmission failure, not broadcast
>Gaudete omnes, Sweelinck
>Responses: Millington
>Psalm 108 (Allcock, Hurford)
>Tomkins, 3rd Service
>Vox Dicentis Clama, Naylor
>Allegro maestoso, Sonata Celtica, Stanford

Conductor, K. Beaumont, Organ, A. Bryden

2000. Wednesday 7th June
Choral Evensong
>Non vos relinquam, Byrd
>Responses: Clucas
>Psalm 37 (Archer, Coulson, Attwood)
>Tomkins, 3rd Service
>O clap your hands, Gibbons
>Fugue sur le thème du Carillon de la Cathédrale de Soissons, Dupré

Conductor, K. Beaumont, Organ, A. Bryden

2002. Wednesday 16th January
Choral Evensong
>O pray for the peace of Jerusalem, Nicholson
>Responses: Lloyd
>Healey Willan in A
>If the Lord had not helped me, Bairstow

Conductor, K. Beaumont, Organ, A. Bryden

2007. Sunday 6th May
Choral Evensong
>Behold, my servant, Christopher Rathbone
>Responses: Clucas
>Office Hymn: Walking in a garden (Dun Aluinn) – omitted from
>broadcast
>Psalms 32, 33, 34 (Perrin, Eden, Mitchell, Maw, How)
>The Ripon Service, Stanley Vann
>My beloved spake, Hadley
>Final Hymn: Ye choirs of new Jerusalem (St Fulbert)
>Rhapsody No 4, Howells

Conductor, A. Bryden, Organ, T. Leech

TELEVISION PROGRAMMES

To ascertain what television broadcasts have been made from Ripon Cathedral was a considerable problem, and the information has largely been collected from old choristers and members of the cathedral congregation. Several old video recordings came to light, but sadly the details of some of the broadcasts, particularly the earlier ones, are sketchy. The authors apologise for this, but what follows is the best that they have been able to achieve and is, they hope, reasonably comprehensive.

1955. BBC TV. Sunday matins

1962. BBC TV. Morning service – live broadcast

1968. Yorkshire Television 'Choirs on Sundays' series
>(Dates of recordings)
>**13th September** Cathedral.
>**26th September** Lounge Hall, Harrogate

	Rejoice in the Lord. Redford
	O taste and see, Vaughan Williams
13th November Cathedral	Turn back O man, Holst
	Thou wilt keep him, Wesley

1968. **13th November** (Recording) **14th November** (Broadcast)
Yorkshire Television Christmas Spectacular from Ripon Cathedral

1969. **Yorkshire Television Film 'Against the Tide'**
2nd-3rd April & 7th May (Filmed). **13th July** (Broadcast)
A film on the life of Ripon Cathedral Choir School

1970. **Sunday 18th January. BBC TV broadcast Choral Eucharist live**
Darke in F
Ave Verum Corpus
Here is the little door, Howells
O worship the Lord
Come down O love divine
O thou who at thy Eucharist did'st pray
Forth in thy name
Conductor, R.E. Perrin, Organ, A. Dance

1970. **20th January** (Recording) **Sunday 15th February** (Broadcast)
'Songs of Praise', BBC
Immortal invisible
All creatures of our God and King
O come, O come Emmanuel
My song is love unknown, solo Charles Bielby
Gracious Spirit, Holy Ghost
Jubilate Deo, accompanied by Mary Perrin, piano
Guide me O thou great Jehovah
Glorious things of thee are spoken
Conductor, R.E. Perrin, Organ, A. Dance

1979. **Christmas Music from Ripon Cathedral:** Choirs of Ripon
Cathedral, Leeds Parish Church, and Halifax Choral Society

1981. Tyne Tees Television. Just before Christmas 1981 the choirboys and lay clerks went to Newcastle with Marcus Huxley and recorded a series of pieces (unaccompanied or with piano) which were later used individually as part of a series of Epilogues, broadcast in the early part of 1982 each evening just before midnight.
God be in my head, Walford Davies
Give us the wings of faith, Ernest Bullock
Litany to the Holy Spirit, Peter Hurford
Hail gladdening light, Charles Wood
Round me falls the night, Drese
Peace perfect peace, Orlando Gibbons
Jesu the very thought of thee, Edward Bairstow
Evening Hymn, Henry Purcell

1982. Yorkshire Television. 'Hundred Best Hymns'
Choirs of Ripon Cathedral and Leeds Parish Church.
Conductor, Simon Lindley, Organ, Ronald Perrin.

1984. Yorkshire Television. 'Merrily on High', Music for Christmas from Ripon Cathedral, presented by James Mason.
Choir of Ripon Cathedral
The Royal Philharmonic Orchestra
The Halifax Choral Society and the Halifax Taverner Choir
Conductor, Peter Knight, Organ, R.E. Perrin (at the Makin organ)

1985. Thursday 4th April. Royal Maundy Service held at Ripon:
The Ripon Choir were joined by the Gentlemen and Children of Her Majesty's Chapel Royal

1985. Wednesday 24th December. BBC Television. Eucharist from Ripon Cathedral
Broadcast live at 11 pm. Introduced by Canon David Ford with sermon and celebration by Dean Christopher Campling, assisted by Canons Ronald McFadden and Peter Marshall.
The Ripon Cathedral Choir. The communion setting was 'Missa Riponiensis' by R. Perrin
Conductor, R.E. Perrin, Organ, M. Huxley

1986. 'Highway' with Harry Secombe, ITV

1986. **21st December. BBC 'Carols by Candlelight'**
The service began with the hornblower, it being the 1100th
anniversary of the apocryphal Ripon City Charter
O little town of Bethlehem
Adam lay y bounden
It came upon a midnight clear
The donkey carol
Silent night
While shepherds watched
For unto us a child is born
Zither carol
Torches
Hark the herald angels sing
Myn Lyking
We wish you a merry Christmas
O come all ye faithful
Conductor, R. E. Perrin, Organ, R. Marsh.

1987. **December. ITV broadcast a live Christmas Spectacular entitled
'Rejoice'** with the Ripon Cathedral Choir, the Black Dyke Mills
Band, and guest stars Robert Hardy and Janet Baker. Simon Lindley
played the organ, and Ronald Perrin and the Black Dyke Mills
director shared the conducting.
See illustration page 102

1996. **11th September. First rehearsal of newly formed Girls' Choir
BBC and ITV cameras present** – Broadcast on local news
programmes

2001 **13th-14th March. BBC Recordings for 'Songs of Praise'.** There
were two programmes; one was broadcast on Easter Day, the other in
the Autumn.

DISCOGRAPHY

Abbey Recording Co. Ltd., Oxford: Alpha Collection

1987. The White Doe; An Opera for children based on the Rising of the
Northern Earls in 1569. Commissioned by the Ripon Cathedral Choir
School. Music by Alan Ridout. Libretto by Allan Wicks.
Musical Director, Robert Marsh.
Makin Organ, Ronald Perrin, Organist and Master of the Choristers.
Harp, David Watkins (Principal London Philharmonic Orchestra).
Orchestra, including members of the English Northern Philharmonic,
led by David Greed. Cello, Stephana Thomson;
Flute, Christine Butterworth; Percussion, Robert Thompson.
First performed Ripon Cathedral 3rd December 1986
Recorded January 1986

1987. Sing Joyfully

Let all the world	Leighton
Magnificat and Nunc Dimittis	
for treble voices	Perrin
Sing Joyfully	Byrd
By the waters of Babylon	Sumsion
Insanae et vanae curae	Haydn
Though I speak with the tongues	Bairstow
Jesus Christ the apple tree	Holman
Psalm 32 chant by	Perrin
Lift up your heads	Mathias
Ex Ore Innocentium	Ireland
Te Deum in C	Perrin

Ripon Cathedral Choir directed by Ronald Perrin
Organ; Robert Marsh
Recorded 23rd-26th March 1987   **LP   NA**

Cantoris Records, Lincoln
(Paul Pinchbeck)

1998. Two Hundred Hymns; Music for Worship Series.
The Boy Choristers and Lay Clerks
Directed by Kerry Beaumont; Andrew Bryden, Organ   CD   CA

1998. Christmas Music

Adagio in E major	Frank Bridge
The First Nowell	Traditional
O magnum mysterium	Victoria
Tomorrow shall be my dancing day	Traditional
People look east	Basançon Melody
Jesus Christ the apple tree	Poston
Ukrainian Bell Carol	arr. Clover
Resonet in laudibus. Organ	Karg-Elert
I saw three ships	Traditional
A Hymn to the Virgin	Britten
Of the Father's Heart Begotten	Piae Cantiones
Hodie Christus natus est	Sweelinck
Good King Wenceslas	Piae Cantiones
Suo Gan	Trad. Welsh
In Dulci Jubilo	Trad. German
In Dulci Jubilo. Organ	Bach
Away in a manger	Kirkpatrick
The holly and the ivy	Traditional
Past three a clock	Traditional
Silent night	Grüber
Master in this hall	Trad. French

The Boy Choristers and Lay Clerks
Directed by Kerry Beaumont; Andrew Bryden, Organ   CD   CA

1999. Organ Kaleidoscope
played by Andrew Bryden   CD   NA

1999. Organ Classics from Ripon Cathedral

Rondeau from Abdelazar	Purcell
Trumpet Voluntary	Stanley
Ich ruf zu dir, herr Jesu Christ	Bach
Toccata and Fugue in D minor	Bach
Berceuse	Vierne
Carillon de Westminster	Vierne
Nun freut euch, leiben	
Christen g'mein	Bach
Crown Imperial	Walton

Vesper Voluntary No 3	Elgar
Nimrod	Elgar
Toccata in F	Pachelbel
Toccata from Symphonie V	Widor
Chant de Paix	Langlais
Nun danket alle Gott	Karg-Elert
Trumpet tune (the Cebell)	Purcell
Final from Symphonie I	Vierne

Played by Kerry Beaumont   CD   CA

1999. Favourite Anthems

Ye choirs of new Jersualem	Stanford
Hymn to the Trinity	Tchaikovsky
O Quam Gloriosum	Victoria
Zion hear the watchmen's voices	Bach
Jesu, the very thought of thee	Bairstow
Day by day	How
Here O my Lord	Whitlock
Locus iste	Bruckner
Ave Maria von Arcadelt. Organ	Liszt
Like as the hart	Howells
Set me as a seal	Walton
Litany to the Holy Spirit	Hurford
O Lord thou hast searched me out	Sumsion
Arabesque. Organ	Vierne
Ex ore innocentium	Ireland
Laudamus Te (from Gloria)	Vivaldi
Give us the wings of faith	Bullock

The Girl Choristers and Lay Clerks
Directed by Kerry Beaumont; Andrew Bryden, Organ   CD   CA

June 1999. The cathedral girl choristers and the lay clerks made their
first recording, comprising mostly well-loved anthems. This was
released on CD in December 1999 and Andrew Bryden, writing in the
1998-99 Choir School Magazine, said that *the cathedral shop staff
reported the sales of this CD in the period leading up to Christmas
broke a new record – so to speak!*

2003. The Organ of Ripon Cathedral
 Great Organs of Europe, Series No 66
 Played by Graham Barber CD CA

<u>**Foxglove Records, Leeds**</u>
  (Don Atkinson)

1992. Cathedral Music from the Twentieth Century

God is gone up	Finzi
Responses (First part)	Piccolo
Psalm 114	Bairstow
Magnificat and Nunc Dimittis in A flat	Perrin
Angel voices ever singing	Perrin
Te Deum in C	Perrin
Jesus Christ the apple tree	Holman
Let saints on earth	Ridout
O clap your hands	Rutter
For the beauty of the earth	Rutter
Like as the hart	Howells
Jubilate	Kelly
Loving shepherd of thy sheep	Cooke
Communion Service in F major	Darke

 The Choir of Ripon Cathedral
 Directed by Ronald Perrin; Organ, Robert Marsh

<u>**Herald AV, London**</u>

2002. Organ of Ripon Cathedral
  The Planets Suite, Gustav Holst
  Transcription for organ by Arthur Wills
  Played by Joseph Nolan

<u>**Hyperion Records Ltd., London**</u>
  <u>(Paul Spicer, Simon Eadon and Simon Perry)</u>

2000. Organ Dreams 2, Ripon Cathedral
  In Paradisum Theodore Dubois

Adagio in E major	Frank Bridge
Rieve	Alexandre Guilmont
Vesper Voluntaries	Edward Elgar
Siciliano for a High Ceremony	Herbert Howells
Study in A flat major	Robert Schumann
Adagio for Strings	Samuel Barber
Evocation a la Chapelle Sistine	Franz Liszt
Four pieces	Samuel Wesley

Played by Christopher Herrick   **CD   CA**

Meridian (Duo-Meridian)

1995. Recorded in June and released Oct-Nov 1995. **Portrait of an Orchestra**. Orchestra de Camera with Ripon Cathedral Choir

CD   CA

Priory Records Ltd., Leighton Buzzard

1996. Magnificat and Nunc Dimittis: Volume 12

Magnificat and Nunc Dimittis in G	Wood
Magnificat and Nunc Dimittis (Cesar Service)	Amner
Magnificat and Nunc Dimittis (Short Service in the Dorian mode)	Tallis
Magnificat and Nunc Dimittis (Third Service)	Tomkins
Magnificat and Nunc Dimittis (For Five voices)	Weelkes
Magnificat and Nunc Dimittis in Bb	Day
Magnificat and Nunc Dimittis in A	Harris
Magnificat and Nunc Dimittis in D	Dyson
Magnificat and Nunc Dimittis in F	Ireland

Choir of Ripon Cathedral directed by Kerry Beaumont   CD   CA

2001. Great European Cathedral Organs
Graham Barber plays the organ of Ripon Cathedral   CD   CA

2002. Te Deum and Jubilate: Volume 4

Te Deum in G	Sumsion
Canterbury Te Deum	Ives
Jubilate Deo in Bb	Walton
Jubilate Deo in Eb	Britten
Te Deum and Jubilate in B minor	Noble
Te Deum (St Cecilia)	Leighton
Jubilate Deo	Leighton
Te Deum and Jubilate in D	Dyson
Te Deum and Jubilate	Wilby

Choir of Ripon Cathedral
Directed by Kerry Beaumont; Organ, Andrew Bryden   CD   CA

Radio Tees; 257 Records
(Toby Horton)

1980   Christmas Carols .
circa   Choir of Ripon Cathedral directed by Ronald Perrin
Organ and piano, Marcus Huxley

RCA Ltd., London

1972. The Organ of Ripon Cathedral; 1,300th Anniversary

Paean	Howells
Three choral preludes	Peeters
L'Ange a la trompette	Charpentier
Allegro; Symphony No VI	Widor
Concerto in A Minor	Vivaldi arr. Perrin
Tu es Petrus	Mulet

Played by Ronald Perrin

Regent Records, Wolverhampton
(Gary Cole)

2005. The Ripon Cathedral Organ; English Cathedral
Series Vol. XII

Concert Overture in F minor	Hollins

Retrospection	Darke
Sonata in A Minor	Harris
Elegiac Romance	Ireland,
Impromptu, Op. 5	Jackson
Capriccietto	Butler
Introduction, Passacaglia and Fugue	Willan

Played by Andrew Bryden   **CD   CA**

2005. A Thing Most Wonderful

Lift up your heads	Mathias
Tantum ergo	De Séverac (edited Beaumont)
Ubi Caritas	Duruflé
It is a thing most wonderful	Moore
Civitas sancti tui	Byrd
O vos omnes	Casals
The Lamentation	Bairstow
Crucifixus	Lotti
Easter	Vaughan Williams
Blessed be the God and Father	Wesley
Now the green blade riseth	Arranged Andrew Bryden
An Easter Sequence	Leighton

Choir of Ripon Cathedral directed by Andrew Bryden.
Thomas Leech, Organ   **CD   CA**

<u>Ryemuse Records (Spot Records Ltd.), London</u>

1967. Organ Music at Ripon Cathedral

Two Trumpet Tunes and Air	Purcell
Chorale Prelude In Dir ist Freude	Bach
March Scherezetto	Walton
Fileuse	Perrin
Eco	Yon

Played by Ronald Perrin   **EP   NA**

Thompson-Beaumont, Ripon
(Robert Thompson)

2000. Inauguration of new Nave Console
Music by Sunderland, Gigout, Dupré, Cocker,
Bach, Handel and Soler (Ref. Page 172)

Kerry Beaumont and Andrew Bryden, Organ   **CD   NA**

Vista Recording Co., Leeds
(Michael Smythe)

1972. The Organ of Ripon Cathedral
Played by Ronald Perrin   **LP   NA**

1976. The Organ in Ripon Cathedral
Fantasia and Toccata in D minor	Stanford
Six Short Preludes	Stanford
Voluntary in E minor	Stanley
Chorale Preludes for organ	Peeters
Concerto for Organ and Piano	Peeters

Organ, Ronald Perrin, Piano, Mary Perrin

York Ambisonic, Lancaster
(Brendan Hearne)

1980. Ripon Cathedral Choir
On this day earth shall ring	Campbell Stewart
My soul there is a country	Parry
Litany to the Holy Spirit	Hurford
Hail gladdening light	Wood
O Lord, the maker of al thing	Joubert
Adoramus te, Christe	Joubert
Turn back of man	Holst
A Trumpet Minuet (R. Perrin, organ)	Hollins
Lo! star-led chiefs	Crotch
Beati quorum via	Stanford
An Evening Hymn	Purcell arranged Wilcocks

The heavens are telling   Haydn

Ripon Cathedral Choir
Director, Ronald Perrin, Organ, Marcus Huxley   **TC   NA**

1983. Ripon Cathedral Choir and Organ 2

Ascribe unto the Lord   Wesley
Trumpet Tune and Air
(R. Perrin, organ)   Purcell
Elves   Bonnet
Loving shepherd of they sheep   Cooke
War March of the Priests
(R. Perrin, organ)   Mendelssohn
The Lord is my shepherd   Stanford
Fiat lux   Dubois
It is a thing most wonderful   Ireland
Hallelujah Chorus   Handel edited Shaw

Ripon Cathedral Choir
Director, Marcus Huxley, Organ, Ronald Perrin   **TC   NA**

1987. Organ Favourites from Ripon Cathedral

Toccata and Fugue in D minor   Bach
Adagio   Albinoni
Allelujahs   Preston
Three Chorale Preludes (Nun danket alle Gott,
Ein feste burg, Lobe den Herren)   Reger
Voluntary in E minor   Stanley
Toccata from Symphony V   Widor
Radetzky March   Strauss
Lied to the sun   Peeters
Spanish Toccata   Perrin
Folk Tune   Whitlock
Carillon-Sortie   Mulet

Played by Ronald Perrin   **TC   NA**

2006. Christmas at Ripon Cathedral

O come all ye faithful   Wade/Bryden

Wassail Carol	Mathias
Jesus Christ the apple tree	Piccolo
People look east	Arr. Hemingway
I wonder as I wander	Arr. Carter
Vom Himmel hoch da komm ich her.	
Organ	Karg-Elert
The Angel Gabriel	Arr. Lloyd
Mater salutaris	Dalby
Joys Seven	Arr. Cleobury
Balulalow	Warlock
The Sycamore Tree	Warlock
Seek him out	Bryden
As I outrode this enderes night	Hendrie
La Nativité. Organ	Langlais
O magnum mysterium	Lauridsen
The Burning Babe	Jamieson
Candlelight Carol	Rutter
Hodie Christus natus est	Carter
Hark ! the herald angels sing	Mendelssohn/Bryden

The Choirs of Ripon Cathedral
Director, Andrew Bryden, Organ, Thomas Leech   **CD   CA**

KEY

CA	**=**	**Currently available (at the time of going to press)**
CD	**=**	**Compact disc**
EP	**=**	**Extended Play, 45rpm**
LP	**=**	**Long Playing Record**
NA	**=**	**Not available**
TC	**=**	**Tape Cassette**

L I S T S

DEANS & PRECENTORS OF
RIPON MINSTER – CATHEDRAL

DEANS OF THE MINSTER

1604 – 1607	Moses Fowler
1608 – 1624	Anthony Higgin
1624 – 1634	John Wilson
1635 – 1643	Thomas Dod
1642 – **The Civil War**	
1660 – 1668	John Wilkins
1668 – 1674	No Dean
1674 – 1675	John Neile

1675 – 1675	Thomas Tullie
1676 – 1686	Thomas Cartwright
1686 – 1710	Christopher Wyvill
1710 – 1750	Heneage Dering
1750 – 1791	Francis Wanley
1792 – 1828	Robert Waddilove
1828 –	James Webber

DEANS OF THE CATHEDRAL

– 1847	James Webber
1847 – 1859	Hon Henry Erskine
1859 – 1860	Thomas Garnier
1860 – 1868	William Goode
1868 – 1876	Hugh McNeile
1876 – 1876	Sydney Turner
1876 – 1895	William Fremantle
1895 – 1915	Hon William Fremantle

1915 – 1941	C. Mansfield Owen
1941 – 1951	Godwin Birchenough
1951 – 1968	F. Llewelyn Hughes
1968 – 1984	F. Edwin Le Grice
1984 – 1994	Christopher Campling
1995 – 2005	John Methuen
2004 – 2007	Michael Glanville-Smith (Acting Dean)
2007	Keith Jukes

PRECENTORS OF THE MINSTER

In 1230 Walter de Gray (Archbishop of York 1215-1255) decreed that the Prebendary of Stanwick (one of seven prebendaries at Ripon) should be the precentor and *Rector Chori*.

1230	Laurence de Toppeclive (appointed Prebendary of Stanwick 1226)
No date	Eadmund de Maundevill
1279	Antonius Beck

1285	Rogerus Sweyne
1311	Richard de Henney
1316	William de Seton
1320	Thomas de Cave
1322	Robert de Rypon
1333	Peter de Wetwang
1344	John de Crakhall
1378	John de Seggefeld
1384	John de Middleton
1397	John Dean
1435	Simon Alcock
1436	Richard Morton
1447	John Clere
1479	Robert Symson
1481	Thomas Bakhous
1535	Richard Dean
1537	Christopher Sale
1548	Dissolution of College of Canons
1604	James I grants Ripon a new charter reinstating the College of Canons. No statutory provision for a precentor, but thereafter the title and duties were given to vicars or minor canons.
1642	The Civil War commenced.
1662	John Wayt
1663	James Bardon
1735	John Wilson

PRECENTORS OF THE CATHEDRAL

1821 – 1840	Joseph Jameson
1875 – 1878	Samuel Joy
1879 – 1887	S. Herbert Lunn
1887 – 1908	Samuel Reed
1908 – 1917	Ernest Henry Swann
1917 – 1924	Ronald Macpherson
1924 – 1947	Hugh Robert Williams, known as 'Daddy Williams'
1947 – 1956	John Marshall
1956 – 1957	Duncan Thomson
1957 – 1960	Charles Kemp Buck

1960 – 1983	Duncan Thomson (Precentor & Headmaster of Choir School)
1983 – 1988	Paul Summers
1988 – 1993	Paul Greenwell
1993 – 1999	E. David Murfet (Precentor; thereafter Cathedral Chaplain)
1999 – 2008	No Precentor appointed – Dean John Methuen assumed this responsibility from 1999 to 2004
2008	Paul Greenwell (Canon Precentor)

SUCCENTORS OF THE CATHEDRAL

1880 – 1887	Samuel Reed (Succentor & Choir Chaplain)
1887 – 1907	Ernest Henry Swann
1907 – 1915	G.E. Alvis
1945 – 1953	S. H. Sharpe
1953 – 1955	Duncan Thomson
1955 – 1959	John Brunson
1959 – 1963	Michael Heckingbottom
1963 – 1965	Geoffrey N. R. Sowerby
1965 – 1968	Phillip Coulton
1968 – 1973	Michael J. Hardy
1973 – 1979	Robin P. Greenwood
1980 – 1983	Lawrence Bowser
1983 – 1985	Simon Gaunt (Lay Succentor)
1986 – 2004	Robert Thompson (Lay Succentor)
2004 – 2008	Simon Deller (Lay Succentor)

The records, particularly of the precentors and succentors of the nineteenth and twentieth centuries, are very sparse and consequently the above lists, particularly the precise years of the periods in office, may contain some inaccuracies.

ORGANISTS OF RIPON CATHEDRAL

1447	Thomas Litster
1478	Lawrence Lancaster
1511	John Watson
1513	William Swawe
1520	Adam Bakhouse

1540	William Solber

1548	Collegiate church dissolved and choral foundation disbanded by Edward VI
1604	Collegiate church reconstituted and choral foundation re-established by James I

1613	John Wanlass (maybe Wanless)

1642	The Civil War commenced
1643	Minster ransacked, collegiate church dissolved and choral foundation disbanded
1660	Restoration of the monarchy. Collegiate church reconstituted and choral foundation re-established

1662	Henry Wanlass
1670	Mr Wilson
1674	Alexander Shaw
1677	William Sorrell
1682	John Hawkins
1690	Thomas Preston, the Elder
1731	Thomas Preston, the Younger
1748	William Ayrton
1799	William Francis Morell Ayrton
1805	Nicholas Thomas Dall Ayrton
1823	John Henry Bond
1829	George Bates
1874	Edwin John Crow
1902	Charles Harry Moody, CBE
1954	Lionel Frederick Dakers, CBE
1957	Joseph Philip Marshall
1966	Ronald Edward Perrin
1994	Kerry Jason Beaumont
2002	Andrew John Bryden (Acting)
2003	Simon Morley
2003	Andrew John Bryden

ASSISTANT ORGANISTS

Dr Edwin Crow (1874 – 1901) and those before him had various articled pupils (some apprenticed to the organ loft) and they acted as deputies, but there was no formal appointment of, or payment to, a deputy organist.

Dr Charles Moody (1902-1954) also initially had articled pupils, but from 1928 official assistant organists were appointed:

1928 Dennis Cocks
1935 Alfred H. Allsop
      No assistant organist during the war
1947 Alex Forrest
1952 Paul Mace
1955 Keith Bond
1956 Peter Stephenson
1958 Lawrence Gibbon
1963 Alan Dance
1974 Marcus Huxley
1986 Robert Marsh
1998 Andrew Bryden
2003 Thomas Leech

CHOIR PHOTOGRAPHS; NAMES

12. **Dr Moody and the Choirboys, circa 1950.** Page 74
Back Row from Left to Right
Kenneth Dobbin, Colin (Chub) Reeve, Trevor Rhodes, Fred Swarbrick, Terence Walker,
Mr Alec Forrest (Assistant Organist), Unknown, Kelvin Gott, Kenneth Colbeck.
Middle Row from Left to Right
Kenneth Dobbin, Colin MacKay, Billy Wheldon, Dr Charles Moody, David Helmsley, Brian Atkinson, Roger Alder.
Front Row from Left to Right
Alan Atkinson, Harold Danby, Keith Kidd, John Milner,
Dr Charles Moody, Vicky Hainsworth, Tony Russell, Jimmy Taylor, Paul Radford.

18. **The Choir, circa 1937.** Page 88
Lay Clerks on Back Row from Left to Right
Frank Faulkner, Charles Beilby, C. Sproul, Frank Lowley, J. Leake.
Clergy Standing in front of Lay Clerks, from Left to Right
Rev J.H.L. Waterson, Rev Hugh R. (Daddy) Williams (Precentor), Rev W.S. McCutcheon.

Select Vestry (Holding Staves) Left, Front to Back
L. King, J. Mortimer, E. Corps, C. Hodgson.
Right Front to Back
Arthur Darnton, F. Wells *(right of verger)*, H. Booth, Mr Parkin.
Vergers (Holding Wands)
Left Harry Pearson.
Right A. Graham.
Boys from Left to Right
E. Corps, Richard Butler, Peter Casling, Fred Parnaby, Douglas Marston, Dennis Metcalfe, Raymond Wright, Peter Gill, Lawrence Coldbeck, David Burnet and Head Choristers Harry Stephenson & Peter Flockton.
Clergy on front row
Canon James Tuckey, Dean Godwin Birchenoff, Canon Cunningham, Canon Donald Bartlett.

19. **Choirboys with the tape recorder, circa 1955.**   Page 88
Boys clustered around Tape Recorder (Left to right)
Keith Anderson, Adrian Little, Chris Pearson, Trevor Dutton, Dave McKay, John Beilby.
Three older boys standing behind Tape Recorder (Left to Right)
Ralph Benson, Francis Jeffrey, Jimmy Taylor.
Adults:
Left Rev John Brunson (Succentor).
Right Lionel Dakers (Organist).

20. **The Choir, July 1957.**   Page 89
Back Row from Left to Right
Frank Smith, Tom Horner (Alto), Peter Stephenson (Assistant Organist), Lionel Dakers (Organist), Rev Duncan Thomson (Precentor), Rev John Brunson (Succentor), Charles Beilby, ** , Tom Paulden, Frank Faulkner.
*** On one copy of this photograph the head & shoulders of Don Corkish (the lay clerk missing on the original) has been inserted at this point.*
Middle Row from Left to Right
Chris Pearson, Francis Jeffreys, David Suddards, John Beilby (Head Boy), Peter Smith (Head Chorister), Anthony Cawood, David McKay, Keith Anderson, John Parker.

Front Row from Left to Right
Trevor Rhodes, Roy Waite, Trevor Hayton, Stephen Orton, Unknown,
Andrew Orton, Peter Anderson, John Metcalfe, John Dinsdale,
Adrian Little.

21. **The Choir, 1964.** Page 89
Back Row from Left to Right
Frank Faulkner, Peter Barnwell, Charles Beilby, Rev Geoffrey Sowerby
(Succentor), Rev Duncan Thomson (Precentor), Dr Philip Marshall
(Organist), Rev Philip Coulton (Succentor), Alan Dance (Assistant
Organist), Owen Kennedy, Robin Davidson, Don Corkish.
Middle Row from Left to Right
William Graham, Nicholas Carter, Roger Hemingway,
Christopher Shone, Robin Symonds, Christopher Wright,
Nigel Castledine, Martin Streeting, Julian Vardy, David Brooks.
Front Row from Left to Right
Jeremy Wedgwood, David Peek, Stephen Wilson, Mathew Smalley,
Phillip Duffy, Christopher Reid, Robert Lightowler, Richard Abbott,
John Postlethwaite.

22. **The Choir, circa 1968.** Page 90
Back Row, Lay Clerks, from Left to Right
Alan Dance (Assistant Organist), Robin Beaumont, Robin Davidson,
Simon Deller, Kelvin Gott, Charles Beilby, Charles Edmondson.
Second to Back Row from Left to Right
James Ferrington (Canons Verger), Rev. Duncan Thomson (Precentor),
Ronald Perrin (Organist), Rev Michael Hardy (Succentor).
Boys from Left to Right
Simon Murley, Matthew Stuttard, Kerry Beaumont, Nicholas Willis,
Richard Duffield, ?Jonathan Shires?, Michael Millar, Nicholas Wright,
Martin Roberts, Kim Jones, Michael Moorsom, Martin Pring,
Richard Pantcheff, Unknown, John Marshall, Timothy Tubbs.
Front Row Clergy from Left to Right
Canon Ralph Emmerson, Archdeacon John W. Turnbull,
Dean Edwin Le Grice, Canon James Ashworth.

23. **The Choir, 1972.**

Back Row from Left to Right
Michael Proctor, Simon Gaunt, Roger Hemingway, Robin Davidson,
Rev Michael Hardy (Succentor), Rev Duncan Thomson (Precentor),
Ronald Perrin (Organist), Alan Dance (Assistant Organist),
Charles Beilby, John Crimp, Malcolm Beer, Kelvin Gott.
Boys Middle Row from Left to Right
Simon Maguire, David Hall, Timothy Tubbs, Martin Pring,
Richard Pancheff, Anthony Eastland, Michael Moorsome,
Nicholas Willis, Matthew Stuttard, Simon Lee, Christopher l'Anson,
Harry Pearson (Dean's Verger).
Boys Front Row from Left to Right
Nicholas Tubbs, John Marshall, Simon Clay, Ian Clethero, Oliver Nelson,
Charles MacIntyre, Andrew Baxter, James Rawes.

24. **The Choir, 1974.**

Back Row from Left to Right
Archie Keighley (Dean's Verger), Charles Beilby, Simon Gaunt,
Alan Duffield, Malcolm Beer, Robin Davidson, John Crimp,
Unknown Canons' Verger.
Two Middle Rows of Boys from Left to Right
Miles Homer, Robin A. Jones, David Wroe, Andrew Lee, Andrew Baxter,
Nicholas Willis (Head Boy), Simon Lee, Simon Clay (Head Boy),
Simon Maguire, John Marshall (Head Boy), Oliver Nelson, David Hall
(Head Boy), Christopher I'Anson, Ian Cletheroe, James Rawes,
Rupert Ring, Christopher Eastland, Nicholas Tubbs.
Front Row from Left to Right
Rev Duncan Thomson (Precentor), Canon James Ashworth,
Dean Edwin Le Grice, Canon Walter Dillam, Ronald Perrin (Organist).

25. **The Choir, July 1981.**

Back Row from Left to Right
Ronald Perrin (Organist), Simon Gaunt, Richard Jackson,
Iain Ward-Campbell, Malcolm Beer, John Newton, Harry Colley,
Robert Thompson, Roger Taylor, Harry Winter, Marcus Huxley
(Assistant Organist).
Boys Middle Row from Left to Right
Paul Ibberson, Andrew Middenhall, Simon Beer, Robert Ward-Campbell,
Malcolm Tone, Tom Milligan, Richard Millward, James Ward-Campbell,

Jonathan Barrow.
Boys on Front Row from Left to Right
Geraint Price, Crispin Bailey, David Rout, Edward Clayson,
Simon Girling, Stephen West, Jonathan Blair, James Lancaster,
Phillip Belben, Richard Garbutt, Owen Leech.

26. **The Choir, May 1989.**   Page 92
Back Row from Left to Right
Robert Marsh (Assistant Organist), Paul Greenwell (Precentor),
Graham Hermon, Adrian Roberts, Tony Coates, Harry Winter,
Roger Taylor, Peter Williams, Kerry Beaumont, Chris Tunnard,
Kelvin Gott, Robert Thompson, Malcolm Beer, Ronald Perrin (Organist).
Boys, Both Rows, Left to Right
Matthew Standish, David Ashton-Cleary, Matthew Watts, James
Carter, Ralph Thomas, Edwin Stonestreet, Edward Monkhouse, Rupert
Derbyshire, Simon Palfreeman, Thomas Williams, David Glover,
Ben Drury, Hugh Thomas, Alexander Field, Jonathan Carberry, John
Swindells, William Gaunt, Andrew Coulton-Tordoff, Christopher Lusby.

27. **The Choir, 2006.**   Page 92
Back Row from Left to Right
Roger Taylor, Tom Cooke, Justin Martindale, Simon Deller,
Peter Condry, David Penn, Howard Crawshaw.
Middle Row from Left to Right
Thomas Leech (Assistant Organist), Benjamin Lenighan,
Edward McDonald, Alexander Peter, Tristram Cooke, Piers Dance,
Harry Brownlie, John Hewlett, Andrew Bryden (Organist).
Boys Front from Left to Right
Ben Nabarro, Liam Forster, Angus Smith, Edward Beese, Harry Hickey,
Tom Graham, Maximillian Wilson.

35. **The Girl Choristers, 2006.**   Page 112
Back Row from Left to Right
Aloise Hickey, Emily Gee, Claudine Wivell, Melisa Kenber,
Dilara Kenber, Gwen Wilks, Anna Smith, Milli Shaw, Lucinda Taylor,
Kate I'Anson.
Front Row from Left to Right
Jessica Bryden, Elizabeth Churchouse, Clara Holden, Imogen Pearson,
Olivia Hinchcliffe, Hannah Gee, Sonia Gray, Natalie Mounsey.

RIPON CATHEDRAL CHOIR SCHOOL

HEADMASTERS

Duncan Thomson, Stephana Thomson	1960 – 1983
Robert Horton, Ann Horton	1983 – 1987
Richard Moore, Sheila Moore	1988 – 2000
Richard Pepys, Jane Pepys	2001 – 2007
Patricia Burton	2008

MEMBERS OF STAFF
(Serving 5 years or more)

TEACHING, ADMINISTRATIVE STAFF AND MATRONS

Full-Time

Susan Ankorn (1996 to present)
Ian Atkinson (1996 to present)
Nancy Beecroft (1960 – 1968)
Irene Brown (1976 – 1998)
Joy Bull (1970 – 1977)
Edward Childs (1986 – 1996)
Alan Dance (1963 – 1974)
Robin Davidson (1963 – 1975)
Margaret Evans (1963 – 1970)
Rachael Evans   (1994 to present)
Tim La Trobe-Foster (1963 – 1980)
Simon Gaunt (1975 – 1985)
Joyce Johnson (Matron 1966 – 1972)
Douglas Mans (1960 – 1965)
Andrea Milsom (Matron 1989 – 1995)
John Mylcreest (1961 – 1977)
Iona Nicholson (Matron 1996 to present)
Bob Peek (1974 – 1989)
Simon Pickering (1999 to present)
Liz Reese (1987 – 2000)
Flora Scott (Matron 1963 – 1968)
Nicola Shillam (1998 to present)

Moira Smith   (1975 – 1999)
Judith Stewart (1965 – 1970)
Josie Suddards (1981 – 2005)
Steve Tait (1965 – 1973)
Roger Taylor (1975 to present)
Robert Thompson (1975 – 2005)
Helene White (1960 – 1965)
Jill Wood (1998 to present)
Susan Wordsworth (1968 – 1973)

Part-Time
Linda Allen (1998 to present)
Juliet Campling   (1986 – 1995)
Jackie Elsey (1987 – 1994)
Marcus Huxley (1974 – 1986)
Claire Ingledew (1987 – 1994)
Carol McIntyre (1982 – 2004)
Dorothy Maddocks (1962 – 1972)
Wilfred Parnaby (1960 – 1974)

MUSIC STAFF
Bernard Armour (1970 – 1995)
Andrew Bryden (1998 – 2003)
Donald Corkish (1960 – 1978)
Olive Corkish (1960 – 1978)
Diana Critchley (1990 to present)
Kelvin Gott (part-time 1963 – 2004)
Muriel Ingleby (1960 – 1967)
Robert Marsh (1986 – 1998)
Robina Morgan (1990 to present)
Karen Ounsley (1987 to present)
Ivan Routledge (1970 – 1993)
Claire Strafford (1994 to present)
Stephana Thomson (1960 – 2006)
Christina Thomson-Jones (1991 to present)
Cynthia Wood (1980 – 1991)

NON-TEACHING STAFF

Cooks

Anne Cawthra (1983 to present)
> Cooks boarders' breakfasts, teas and generally mothers them

Madge Harrison (1960 – 1975) } These ladies were renowned for their
Mabel Benson (1960 – 1966) } Yorkshire puddings and apple pies
Beattie Rogers (1972 – 1997)
Carol Gibson   (1975 – 1986)
Lynn Hart (1988 to present)   Her treacle sponge is legendary

Domestic, Maintenance and Groundsmen

Carl Abbott (1963 – 1976)
Cedric Caine (1985 – 1991)
Pam Cawthra (1989 to present)
Jim Chapleo (1974 – 1985)
Eileen Cox (1975 – 1985)
Barbara Dobbs (1976 – 1983)
Mrs Game (1970 – 1980)
Vera Jackson (1963 – 1981)
Gladys McKay (1968 – 1980)
Ivy Moore (1968 – 1980)
Jean Page (1970 – 1977)
Paul Quinn (1994 – 2001)
Sylvia Weighell (1963 – 1981)

The authors wish to express their thanks to the numerous people who have helped compile this list. Every effort has been made to ensure that it is as accurate and comprehensive as possible, but inevitably there may be some errors and omissions for which sincere apologies are offered.

SCHOLARSHIPS

JJD	Mullaly	Cheltenham	1961
JC	Horsfall	Dean Close	1962
NR	Jordan	Trent	1963
DJK	Halliday	Sedbergh	1964
CM	Thomson	Wycombe Abbey	
CF	Wright	Rydal	
R	Hemingway	Uppingham	1965
KA	Moules	Giggleswick	
CG	Johnson	St Peter's, York	
RCK	Symonds	Oundle	
SF	Cooper	Oundle	1966
WJ	Graham	Oakham	
GJ	Mason	Uppingham	
RH	Midgley	St Peter's, York	
NP	Carter	Repton	1967
GS	Courtney	Giggleswick	
TP	Hancock	Uppingham	
CP	Reid	Oakham	
CSM	Thomson	St Swithin's, Winchester	
JP	Wedgwood	Sedbergh	
RD	Abbott	Sedbergh	1968
MRJ	Smalley	Sedbergh	
WL	Conran	Bishop's Stortford	
P	Duffy	Worksop	
PA	Frazer	Stowe	
NH	Moll	King's Canterbury	
DG	Peek	King's Canterbury	
RAG	Duffield	Sedbergh	1969
MJ	Millar	Rossall	
CAR	Moorsom	Clifton	
SJM	Murley	Worksop	
RF	Peill	Bootham	
MG	Roberts	Ellesmere	
RF	Rowling	Worksop	
QD	Storrs-Fox	Christ's Hospital	
NC	Wright	Rydal	

KJ	Beaumont	Repton	1970
KS	Jones	Uppingham	
JR	Markland	Giggleswick	
JC	Shaw	Eton	
NM	Murray	Eton	1971
CJ	Bushby	Gordonstoun	1972
AHJ	Eastland	Malvern (2)	
MHF	Moorsom	Clifton	
RA	Pantcheff	Merchant Taylors'	
MS	Pring	Worksop	
RN	Storrs-Fox	Pangbourne	
IRH	McDonald	Oakham	1973
TJ	Tubbs	Eton	
PJ	Westwood	St Edward's	
SDJ	Clay	Repton	1974
MG	Entecott	Ellesmere	
AG	Henley	Worksop (2)	
S	Lee	Winchester	
SW	Maguire	Worksop	
JW	Marshall	Rossall	
OPL	Nelson	Malvern	
JM	Rawes	Giggleswick	
PM	Storrs-Fox	Bryanston	
NJ	Willis	Radley	
GA	Royle	Rossall	
MJ	Court	Oakham	
DA	Abbott	Rydal	1975
SF	Bardsley	Sedbergh	
AP	Baxter	Rossall	
RI	Clethero	Winchester	
NS	Royle	Rossall	
AJ	Carter	Ellesmere	
RB	Jackson	King's, Ely	
DAR	Wright	Sedbergh	
CCM	Eastland	Malvern (2)	1977
AJM	Gilfillan	Fettes	
RA	Jones	Oundle	
AM	Thomas	Rossall	
LH	Thomson	Oakham	

NP	Tubbs	Durham	
DE	Wroe	Lancing	
PM	Froggatt	Rugby	1978
LL	Nelson	Malvern	
RCM	Ring	Durham	
MJ	Bardsley	Sedbergh	
PJ	Conway	Ellesmere	1979
AP	Froggatt	Repton	
AJH	Ibbs	Bloxham (2)	
RM	Knowles	Sedbergh	
MJ	Maguire	Lancing	
AG	Slayter	Harrow	
JS	Tinning	Bootham	
SMF	Tweedie	Ellesmere (2)	
PM	Wragg	Oundle	
MKL	Young	Sedbergh	
NCR	Clay	Repton	1980
PL	Cree	Shrewsbury	
WR	Dawe	Malvern	
GP	Dean	King's, Worcester	
JPM	Latham	Charterhouse	
GC	Tweedie	Ellesmere	
CH	Barrow	Malvern	1981
JHB	Blair	Clifton	
EC	Clayson	Rossall	
SAJ	Girling	St John's, Leatherhead	
SAJ	Henley	Ashville	
DJK	Hobbs	Sedbergh	
RA	Hornsey	Durham	
HJ	Lesster	St Andrew's, Delaware	
BO	Smith	Radley	
JK	Walton	Ellesmere	
SR	West	Leeds Grammar School	
DN	Wilson	Worksop	
CCM	Bayley	Malvern	1982
JK	Lancaster	Rossall	
AJT	Milligan	Tonbridge	
SR	Smith	Uppingham	
JM	Willat	Worksop	

JP	Bailey	Woodhouse Grove	
CM	Alexander	Pocklington	
PM	Ibberson	Malvern	
DJ	Rout	Shrewsbury	
TA	Wilson	Worksop	
MJ	Belben	Repton	1983
RM	Garbutt	Silcoates	
DB	Hornsey	Durham	
OB	Leech	Bloxham	
RW	Millard	Clifton	
ADS	Ryding	Malvern	
AS	Watson	Oakham	
MJ	Wellman	Worksop	
GJ	Price	Uppingham	1985
AMN	Stanton	Malvern	
DJ	Bleiker	Sedbergh	1986
LC	Kealy	Queen Margaret's	
DM	Wesling	Chetham's	
GAB	Crawford	Malvern	1987
CJ	Durant	Ellesmere	
AMW	Green	Uppingham	
JS	Groundwater	Giggleswick	
NS	Lofthouse	Bootham	
RJS	Drury	Marlborough	1988
MF	Groundwater	Rossall	
OJB	Jackson	Harrow	
RJS	Kell	Barnard Castle	
EH	Price	Uppingham	
RJ	Walker	Bradfield	
AS	Coulton-Tordoff	Radley	1989
RH	Darbyshire	Eton	
EE	Stonestreet	Uppingham	
DL	Wrighton	Woodhouse Grove	
EA	Alm	Queen Ethelburga's	1990
JJ	Carter	Denstone	
CH	Lusby	Rossall	
SJM	Palfreeman	Repton	
BS	Price	Marlborough	
AP	Field	Radley	1991

DJ	Glover	Worksop	
KL	Grimsditch	Polam Hall	
TE	Jackson	Uppingham	
RG	Thomas	Sedbergh (2)	
TJ	Williams	Uppingham	
D	Ashton-Cleary	Shrewsbury	1992
VC	Bailey	Queen Margaret's	
JA	Carberry	Loretto	
DTS	Drury	Fettes	
CE	Sanderson	Giggleswick	
WJM	Swindells	Giggleswick	
HWC	Thomas	Sedbergh	
MG	Watts	Sedbergh	
WA	Armstrong	Rossall	1993
SM	Davis	Harrogate College	
TEF	Frankland	Uppingham	
WS	Gaunt	Uppingham	
MTS	Standish	Glenalmond	
AM	Steed	Repton	
DA	Tarter	Loretto	
JM	Beaumont	Eton	1994
RJG	Darby	Uppingham	
V	Fuller	Giggleswick	
EJ	Higson	Moreton Hall	
MK	Russell	Stowe	
OE	Saul	Uppingham	
AWdeL	Young	Shrewsbury	
OJC	Duckett	Uppingham	1995
EA	Forsythe	Ampleforth	
EK	Jenkins	St Peter's, York	
MTS	Jones	Stowe	
OC	Longbottom	Denstone	
PTJ	Mason	Uppingham (2)	
AW	Porter	Wycombe Abbey (2)	
OA	Sanderson	Giggleswick	
WSS	Standish	Glenalmond	
TFV	Thomas	Sedbergh	
RT	Austerberry	Uppingham	1996
GWA	Horton	Eton (2)	

TD	Rowlay	Ashville	
DNE	Carter	Uppingham	1997
OR	Cullingworth	Stowe	
ATA	Duckett	Uppingham	
AC	Forsythe	Queen Margaret's	
SC	Jarvis	Shrewsbury	
ML	Linstead	Pocklington	
DBH	Winpenny	Eton	
MW	Almack	Giggleswick	1998
PJ	Austerberry	Uppingham	
JPL	Eskell	Marlborough	
AJR	Higson	Shrewsbury	
DSJ	Hornby	Sedbergh	
AA	Merriam	Yarm	
RD	Merriam	Yarm	
AG	Apostoli	Worksop	1999
KE	Dallas	Queen Margaret's	
DCR	Munton	Eton	
HCA	Rawlinson	Harrogate Ladies'	
SEM	Wells-Cole	Uppingham	
MR	Forsythe	Ampleforth	
AJ	Rawlins	Leeds Grammar School	
LA	Whitton	The Mount	
EA	Jones	Stowe (2)	2001
N	Beeby	Sedbergh	
CC	Brackett	Giggleswick	
ETB	Nickell-Lean	Shrewsbury	
BH	Smeeden	Uppingham	
JC	Tunnard	Worksop	
J	Wilson	Sedbergh	
CC	Ash	Wycombe Abbey	2002
LMM	Iles	Sedbergh	
BD	Kirk	Monkton Combe	
HPG	Loveless	Shrewsbury	
CAA	Menage	Uppingham	
HDC	Munton	Shrewsbury	
AH	Smeeden	Uppingham	
RJA	Varley	Sedbergh	
CE	Williams (2)	Uppingham	

IC	Wood (2)	Sedbergh	
STL	Barnard	Stowe	2003
KE	Holden	Shrewsbury	
JP	Kilpatrick	Sedbergh	
GCL	Maud	Queen Mary's	
ES	Robinson	Queen Margaret's	
TR	Timothy	Uppingham	
JWR	Ash	Winchester	2004
AJW	Dance	Eton	
AL	Hope	Queen Margaret's	
PTH	Wood (2)	Cheltenham	
TW	Baker	Winchester	2005
DH	Byron-Chance	Shrewsbury	
LAE	Crowson	Sedbergh	
SEL	Hewlett	Chetham's	
HD	Smith	Worksop	
RCR	Timothy (2)	Uppingham	
JE	Bryden	Harrogate Ladies'	2006
TGF	Cooke	Stowe	
PSW	Dance	Uppingham	
SE	Hurst	Queen Mary's	
BTM	Kirk	Christ's Hospital	
DM	Lane	Tring Park	
BT	Lenighan	St Peter's	
AN	Peter	Uppingham	
LH	Taylor	Harrogate Ladies'	
HH	Ash	Uppingham	2007
SH	Duffield	Sedbergh	
EAM	Gee	St Peter's, York	
CJL	Hewlett	Eton	
ETD	McDonald	Stowe	
IFM	Schofield (2)	Sedbergh	

RIPON CATHEDRAL OLD CHORISTERS' ASSOCIATION

PAST CHAIRMEN

Medallion titled "Ripon Cathedral Choir Old Boys"
Presented by Mr & Mrs Geary 1951 (silver hall mark)

1951	M. Geary	1980	R.J. Sowley
1952	M. Geary	1981	
1953	C.J. Baines	1982	S.C. Gaunt
1954	P.F. Thorpe	1983	S.C. Gaunt
1955	A.T. Crossley	1984	G.S. Keers
1956	F.C. Lowley	1985	J.R. Parker
1957	H. Pearson	1986	J.M. Rawes
1958	G.H. Elsy	1987	G. Colley
1959	H.H. Benson	1988	A.H. Graham
1960	F. Orton	1989	D. Mackay
1961	C. Hall	1990	R. Appleton-Metcalfe
1962	L. Alexander	1991	C.T. Tunnard
1963	E.C. Robson	1992	D.G. Suddards
1964	H.I. Dunning	1993	P.G. Smith
1965	G.H. Mees	1994	K.H. Gott
1966	A.H. Graham	1995	K.J. Beaumont
1967	J. Hall	1996	E.M. Thompson
1968	D.H. Abbott	1997	R. Taylor
1969	P.P. Mortimer	1998	R.H. Moore
1970	M.G. Duffield	1999	M. S. Beer
1971	J.H. Adams	2000	A. Dance
1971	J.J. Watson (Chairman Elect)	2001	S. Deller
1972	D.W. Elsy	2002	S. Deller
1973	D.T. Burnett	2003	T. Russell
1974	Rev D. Thompson	2004	T. Russell
1975	P. Earwaker	2005	R. Metcalfe
1976	F. Proctor	2006	R. Metcalfe
1977	E. Witts	2007	M. S. Beer
1978	E. Witts	2008	M. S. Beer
1979			

MENDELSOHN'S 'HEAR MY PRAYER'

LIST OF SOLOISTS

1978	5th March	Marcus Maguire
1979	18th March	Marcus Maguire
1980	16th March	Stephen West
1981	22nd March	Stephen West
1982	14th March	David Rout
1983	6th March	Paul Ibberson
1984	25th March	Richard Garbutt
1985	10th March	Darcy Bleiker
1986	9th March	Charles Frank/Adam Green
1987	22nd March	Adam Green
1988	6th March	Marcus Groundwater
1989	26th February	Thomas Williams
1990	18th March	James Carter
1991	10th March	Thomas Williams
1992	22nd March	David Cleary
1993	14th March	William Gaunt
1994	6th March	Jesse Beaumont
1995	20th May	Oliver Longbottom
1995	14th October (Concert)	Sam Jarvis
1997	2nd March	Peter Wilcock
1998	15th March	Adam Apostoli
1999	7th March	James Spurgeon
2000	28th March	Joseph Nabarro
2001	25th March	Edmund Jones
2002	3rd March	Henry Loveless
2003	23rd March	Alexander Dance
2004	21st March	James Ash
2005	27th February	Tristram Cooke
2006	19th March	Piers Dance
2007	18th March	Henry Ash
2008	9th March	Liam Forster

BIBLIOGRAPHY

Title	Author	Publisher/Source	Year
A Biography of Vaughan Williams	Ursula Vaughan Williams	Oxford University Press	1964
A Few Words on Cathedral Music with a Plan of Reform	S.S.Wesley	Hinrichsen (Reprint 1965)	1849
A Guide to Ripon	John R. Walbran	Reprinted by Smiths, Easingwold	1862 Reprinted 1976
A History of English Cathedral Music 1549-1889	John S. Bumpus	T. Werner Laurie, London	1908
A History of the Church in England	John R. H. Moorman	Adam & Charles Black, London	1953
A Musical Pilgrimage in Yorkshire	J. Sutcliffe Smith	Richard Jackson, Leeds	1928
A Notebook	Sperling	Five Notebooks, RCO Library, London	Circa 1850
A Ripon Record 1887-1986	Edna Ellis, Mary Mauchline, Ted Pearson & John Whitehead	Phillimore & Co. Ltd., Chichester (Ripon Civic Society)	1986
A Short History of the Bells of Ripon Cathedral & the Bell Ringers	Geoffrey Johnson	Privately published and printed	1985
An Illustrated History of Ripon	Maurice Taylor	Stratus Books	2005
Anglican Chant & Chanting in England, Scotland & America 1660-1820	Ruth M. Wilson	Clarendon Press, Oxford	1996
Cathedral Organists	John E. West	Novello & Co., London	1899
Cathedral Music Links website	Ron Sherlock	www.cathedralmusiclinks.org.uk	2006
Chantry Foundations at Ripon	Paul Burbridge	Ripon Historical Society & Friends of Ripon Cathedral	2003 & 2005
Choral Responses & Litanies	Rev John Jebb	George Bell, London	1847

Title	Author	Publisher/Source	Year
Choral Services of the Church	Rev John Jebb	Harrison & Co., London	1843
English Church Music 1650-1750	Christopher Dearnley	Barrie & Jenkins Ltd.	1970
Harrogate	Malcolm Neesam	Smith Settle, Otley	1989
History of the English Church; 1714-1899	F. Warre Cornish	Macmillan, London	1910
In Quires & Places	Joy Dean	Dean & Chapter, Ripon Cathedral	1985
J Stor (Journal Storage)	Various	USA on-line access to accademic journals	1955
Memorials of Ripon. Vols I, II & III	The Surtees Society	Ripon Cathedral Library	1881 to 1886
Music & the Reformation in England 1549-1660	Peter Le Huray	Herbert Jenkins, London	1967
Notes on the Church Bells of the West Riding of Yorkshire	J. Eyre Poppleton	Yorkshire Archaelogical Journal	1904
Organs of Ripon Cathedral	Laurence Elvin	The Organ. Vol XLVI. No 184	1967
Panther Organ History Web Site	J.H. Cook	www.panther.bsc.edu/-jhcook/OrgHist	2008
Peel Web Site	Dr Marjorie Bloy	www.historyhome.co.uk/peel/religion	2007
Report of the Bells at Ripon Cathedral	Canon Garrod	Privately published and printed	Circa late 1920s
Restoration Cathedral Music 1660-1714	Ian Spink	Clarendon Press, Oxford	1995
Ripon Cathedral 1,300 years of Worship and History	Allan Barton & Mark Punshon	Ripon D.&C. and Maxiprint, York	2001
Ripon Cathedral Organ	Charles Moody	J.H.Taylor	1926
Ripon Cathedral; A Short History of the Organ	Robert Marsh	Dean & Chapter, Ripon Cathedral	1994

Title	Author	Publisher/Source	Year
Ripon Cathedral; History & Architecture	W. Forster; B. Robson, Jennifer Deadman	William Sessions, York	1993
Ripon Gazette; Ackrill Newspapers	Various	Local Weekly Newspaper	1830 to 2008
Ripon Millenary Record	Various	William Harrison, Ripon	1892
Ripon Minster/Cathedral Chapter Archives	Various	The Brotherton Library, University of Leeds	1399 to 1985
Ripon, The Cathedral & See	Cecil Hallett	George Bell & Sons, London	1901
The Age of Bede	J.F. Webb & D.H. Farmer	Penguin Classics	2004
The Antient and Modern History of the Loyal Town of Rippon	Thomas Gent	A, Bettesworth, London	1733
The Choral Revival in the Anglican Church 1839 -1872	Bernarr Rainbow	Oxford University Press	1970
The English Chorister	Alan Mould	Hambledon Continuum Books, London	2007
The History of the English Organ	Stephen Bicknell	Cambridge University Press	1996
The Music of the English Church	Kenneth R. Long	Hodder & Stoughton	1972
The Music of the English Parish Church	Nicolas Temperley	Cambridge University Press	1983
The Musical Times	Numerous	The Musical Times Publications Ltd.	1844 to 2008
The Reformation	Owen Chadwick	Pelican Books	1964
The Ringing World (formerly Bell News)	Various	Magazine of The Central Council of Church Bell Ringers	1911 to 2008
The Singing Church	C. Henry Phillips	Faber & Faber Ltd.	1945
The Story of Ripon Minster	Lucius Smith	Richard Jackson, Leeds	1914
Towers and Bells of Britain	Ernest Morris	Robert Hale	1955

ACKNOWLEDGEMENTS

The authors wish to express their sincere thanks to the following for help, information and the loan of documents, photographs and music:

Abbey Recording Company Ltd	Oxford
Keith Anderson	Ripon
Phillip Arundel	Diocese of Ripon & Leeds
Kerry Beaumont	Coventry Cathedral
John Beer	Cambridge
Susan Beer	Cambridge
Kathleen Benson	Ripon
Keith Bond	Saxmundham
Andrew Bryden	Ripon Cathedral
Paul Burbridge	Newtonairds, Dumfries
Marion Burnett	Ripon
Joy Calvert	Ripon
Cantoris Records (Paul Pinchbeck)	Lincoln
Edward Childs	Port Isaac, Cornwall
Humphrey Clucas	Cambridge
Anthony Cooke	Cookridge, Leeds
Alan Cunningham	Harrogate
Alan Dance	Driffield
Catherine Dance	Driffield
Robin Davidson	Worcester
Martin Davies	Ripon
Mike Deeming	Asenby, York
Simon Deller	Kirkby Malzeard, Ripon
Peter Dodson	Ripon
Alan Duffield	Highbury, London
Rachael Evans	Dishforth
Margaret Evans	Ripon
William Flynn	Leeds University
Bill Forster	Ripon
Foxglove Records (Don Atkinson)	Leeds
Toria Forsyth-Moser	Ripon
Janet Fraser	Harrogate
Lawrence Gibbon	Slingsby, York.
Michael Glanville-Smith	Ripon

Susan Goldsborough	Copt Hewick, Ripon
Karl Greenall	Organist, Wigan Parish Church
Nicholas Hancock	Ripon
Brendan Hearne	York Ambisonic, Lancaster
Herald AV	London
Roger Hemingway	Ripon
Graham Hermon	Ripon
Peter Horton	Royal College of Music, London
Ray Hutchinson	Wigan Parish Church
Hyperion Records (Simon Perry)	London
Francis Jackson	East Acklam, Malton
Alasdair Jamieson	Great Ouseburn, York
Helen Jones	Lambeth Palace Library, London
Gareth Jones	Ripon
Michael Jones	Ripon
Keith Jukes	Ripon
Brian Kealy	North Stainley, Ripon
Xenophon Kelsey	Ripon
Peter Kirk	Aldershot
David Knight	Council for the Care of Cathedrals, London
Tom Leech	Ripon Cathedral
Simon Lindley	Leeds Parish Church
Philip Manser	Scothern, Lincolnshire
Robert Marsh	Keighley
Margaret Marshall	Potterhanworth, Lincoln
Felicity McCormick	Bramhope, Leeds
David McKay	Ripon
Hilary McKay	Ripon
Ronnie Metcalfe	Ripon
Phillip Miles	Harrogate
Richard Moore	Exelby, Thirsk
Robbie Morgan	Ripon
John Newton	Ashton Keynes, Swindon
Andrew Palmer	Friends of Cathedral Music Magazine, Ripon
John Payne	Chaplain, Queen Mary's School, Topcliffe
Bob Peek	Holme-on-Swale
Oliver Pickering	Brotherton Library, Leeds University
Janet Pickering	Menston, Leeds
Sylvia Pinkney	East Keswick, Leeds
Priory Records (Neil Collier)	Leighton Buzzard

Keith Punshon	Ripon Cathedral
Mark Punshon	London
Eric Record	Ripon
Regent Records (Gary Cole)	Wolverhampton
Ryemuse Records Ltd	London
Tony Russell	Stockton on Tees
John Sayer	Ripon
Moira Smith	Grantley, Ripon
Mike Smith	Ripon
Claire Strafford	Kilburn, York
David Suddards	Ripon
Josie Suddards	Ripon
Guy Taylor	Ripon
Helen Taylor	Ripon
Maurice Taylor	Ripon
Roger Taylor	Ripon
Robert Thompson	Ulverston, Cumbria
Stephana Thomson	Bedale
Christina Thomson-Jones	Ripon
Christopher Tunnard	Ripon
Di Tunnard	Ripon
Mark Venning	Harrison & Harrison, Durham
Katherine Venning	Harrison & Harrison, Durham
Vista Recording Co. (Michael Smythe)	Leeds
Toby Wallis	Ripon
Richard Wilkinson	Aysgarth
Loretta Williams	Ripon
David Winpenny	Ripon
Eric Witts	Stockton on Tees
Jack Yarker	Ripon
York Ambisonics (Brenden Hearne)	York

LIST OF MAJOR SPONSORS

Michael Abrahams   Mickley, Ripon
Brewin Dolphin   Leeds
Dorothy Clegg   Linton, Wetherby
Jürgen Kaiser   Leathley, Pool
Andrew & Catherine Kitchingman   Burton Leonard
Harold North   Harrogate

PATRONS

Keith & Joan	Anderson	Ripon
George & Valerie	Armitage	Aldborough
Robert & Charlotte	Ash	Ripon
John & Dorothy	Avery	Ponteland
Malcolm & Joan	Beer	Harrogate
Michael & Jan	Beer	West Wittering
Jürg & Jane	Bleiker	Burton Leonard
John & Bronwen	Brindley	Galphay
Andrew & Margot	Budge	Birstwith, Harrogate
Iain & Chris	Budge	Burnt Yates
Rex & Jean	Clark	Morpeth
Andrew & Arlene	Coulson	Sharow, Ripon
Howard & Susan	Crawshaw	Ripon
Robin & Janet	Davidson	Worcester
Peter & Elsie	Dean	Menston
Simon & Mollie	Deller	Kirkby Malzeard
Jane	Donald	Harrogate
Roger & Janet	Dowling	Ripon
Paul & Christine	Drury	High Stittenham, York
Alan	Duffield	London
Brian & Karen	Duffield	Ripon
Howard & Alison	Duffield	Ripon
Bill	Forster	Ripon
Robert & Pamela	Goring	Ilkley
John & Christine	Groundwater	Ripon
Peter & Pat	Harris	Frant.
Colin & Nina	Harrison	Bishopton, Ripon

Karen & David	Harrison	Eldwick, Bingley
Phillip & Jane	Ingham	York
Trevor	Ingham	Ripon
Elizabeth	Ingham	Ripon
Margaret & Peter	Jackson	Wickhambrook
Richard & Judith	Jackson	Glasshouses
Brian & Scilla	Kealy	Ripon
Terry & Una	Knowles	Harrogate
John & Margaret	Lindley	Studley Royal, Ripon
John & Anne	Mace	Barkestone-le-Vale, Nottingham
Nicolas & Jennifer	Mason	Headley Down
Ronnie & Heather	McFadden	Ripon
David & Hilary	McKay	Ripon
Ronnie & Margaret	Metcalfe	Ripon
Richard & Sheila	Moore	Exelby, Bedale
John & Jean	Newton	Ashton Keynes
David & Di	Owen	Eldwick
John	Packer	Bishop of Ripon & Leeds
Sylvia	Pinkney	East Keswick
Tom & Jane	Ramsden	Slenningford, Mickley
Carl & Val	Rehor	Newton Kyme
Bill & Frances	Richardson	Littlethorpe, Ripon
Stein	Rogstad	Hexham
Peter & Cathy	Russell	Sevenoaks
John	Sayer	Ripon
Peter	Scott	Linton, Wetherby
Simon & Anna	Scott-Beer	Harrogate
Paul & Margaret	Shepherd	Birstwith, Harrogate
Rodney & Moira	Smith	Grantley
David & Josie	Suddards	Ripon
Dennis & Anne-Marie	Tarter	Ripon
Eric & Barbara	Thompson	Harrogate
Michael & Lorraine	Tomlinson	Birkenshaw
Chris & Di	Tunnard	Ripon
Patrick & Anna	Turner	Harrogate
Iain & Chris	Ward-Campbell	Harrogate
John & Diane	Whelan	Ripon
Eric & Mavis	Whitehead	Harrogate
Mike & Joan	Williams	Ripon

LIST OF SUBSCRIBERS

Brian	Best	Harrogate
Dicky	Black	Green Hammerton
Peter	Blayney	Harrogate
Donald	Braidwood	Gauldry, Dundee
Andrew	Bryden	Ripon
Donald	Bunce	Leeds
Andrew	Calvert	Birstwith
Simon	Chalton	High Kilburn
Anthony	Cooke	Leeds
Martin	Davies	Walton, Wetherby
David	Elsey	Ripon
Margaret	Evans	Ripon
Eric	Forster	Harrogate
George	Fowler	Harrogate
Susan	Goldsborough	Copt Hewick
Nicola	Harding	North Stainley
Roger	Higson	Mickley
Oliver	Jackson	Radlett, Herts
Simon	Lindley	Fulneck
Barry	McQuire	Harrogate
Chris	Pearson	Ripon
David	Penn	Dacre Banks
James	Rawes	Carlisle
Eric	Record`	Ripon
Margaret	Richardson	Harrogate
Tony	Russell	Stockton
Ann	Scott	Ripon
Robert	Sowley	Abergele, Wales
Gill	Steer	Ripon
Ian	Stewart	Newark
Guy	Taylor	Ripon
Michael	Taylor	Corsley, Warminster
Roger	Taylor	Ripon
Stephana	Thomson	Bedale
Christina	Thomson-Jones	Ripon
Toby	Wallis	Ripon
Joan	Webster	Askham Bryan
Peter	Williams	Repton

RIPON CATHEDRAL MUSIC CUSTODIANS

Richard & Susie	Abott	Ropley, Hampshire
David & Vimy	Aykroyd	Boroughbridge
Malcolm & Joan	Beer	Harrogate
John & Bronwen	Brindley	Galphay, Ripon
Esmond & Susie	Bulmer	Alton Pancras, Dorchester
Joy	Calvert	Ripon
Dorothy	Clegg	Linton, Wetherby
Andrew & Arlene	Coulson	Sharow, Ripon
Roger & Janet	Dowling	Ripon
Howard & Alison	Duffield	Ripon
John & Gillian	Elvidge	Ripon
David	Eyles	Masham
Molly	Forster	Ripon
Anthony & Susannah	Frieze	London
John & Carol	Hainsworth	Burton Leonard
Colin & Nina	Harrison	Bishopton, Ripon
Jolyon & Carol	Harrison	York
Lykle & Elizabeth	Hogerzeil	Ripon
Pippa	Hudson	Bramham
Margaret	I'Anson	Littlethorpe, Ripon
Andrew & Catherine	Kitchingman	Burton Leonard
Adrian & Suzanne	Lamb	Otley
John & Margaret	Lindley	Studley Royal, Ripon
John	Lowry	Bedale
William & Anna	Nabarro	Ripon
Christopher & Wendy	Orme	Littlethorpe, Ripon
David & Rosemary	Page	Sharow, Ripon
John & Carol	Parker	Burton Leonard
Richard	Pepys	Well, Bedale
Jane	Pepys	Well, Bedale
David & Jean	Rayner	Wetherby
Michael & Hilary	Ring	Sand Hutton, Thirsk
John	Sayer	Ripon
Ann	Scott	Ripon
Rodney & Moira	Smith	Grantley, Ripon
Nicolas & Mary	Younger	Great Thirkleby, Thirsk

ABOUT THE AUTHORS

Malcolm S. Beer

Malcolm was born in Leeds in 1940. At the age of eight he joined the choir of St Edmund's Anglican Church, Roundhay, Leeds where, with the encouragement of the vicar, Rev Richard H. Talbot and the organist Raymond G. Sunderland his long-standing love of English church music began. He later became an organ pupil of Raymond Sunderland and continued to sing at St Edmund's as an alto.

In the mid 1960s through his friendship with the Reverend Duncan Thomson, Malcolm became a supernumerary lay clerk at Ripon Cathedral and sang in the choir for over 22 years. During this period he studied with Duncan and obtained his Licentiateship of Trinity College of Music, London.

After leaving school aged 16, Malcolm went into insurance and for over forty five years worked as a Chartered Loss Adjuster in Bradford and Leeds. He was elected president of the Insurance Institute of Leeds in its centenary year and became a main board director of McLarens, a large national firm of Loss Adjusters, from which he retired in 2000

Malcolm is married to Joan and they have two children: Their daughter, Jane, was for a time an assistant in the pre-prep department at Ripon Choir School and their son, Simon, was a chorister at the cathedral. For many years Malcolm was a governor of the Cathedral Choir School and he continues to take a keen interest in the music at Ripon Cathedral.

Howard M. Crawshaw

Howard was born in Dewsbury, West Yorkshire, in 1947, and at the age of four moved to Devon.

He was a chorister at Exeter Cathedral under Reginald Moore and Lionel Dakers before moving on to Malvern College.

Howard studied medicine at Edinburgh, and while an undergraduate sang with the Exon Singers. He became a Fellow of the Royal College of Surgeons of Edinburgh in 1976, and subsequently spent a year working in Boston, Massachusetts. Later he was appointed Consultant Surgeon to the Edinburgh Hospitals and Honorary Senior Lecturer in the University Department of Clinical Surgery.

Howard moved to Ripon in 1998, and for a number of years combined the posts of lay clerk and chapter clerk at the cathedral.

Married to Susan, he has four children and one grandchild and is now retired.

INDEX

Fremantle, William 46-48

George I 39
girls' choir *see* choir, girls'
Goldsborough, Susan 240
Goode, William 50
Gott, Jim 105
Gott, Kelvin 105-07, 128, 238, 242, 247
Graham, Harry 75, 79, 80, 93
grammar school *see* Ripon grammar school
Gray, Archbishop of York 20
Greenfield, Archbishop of York 18

Hackett, Maria 43, 120
Hadley, Patrick 206
Harrison & Harrison, organ builders 104, 160-64, 166-68, 170, 207
Hawkins, John 118-19
Hayward Mills of Nottingham, bell hangers 220
head chorister's badge 233-34
Hemingway, Roger 206
Henry V 17
Henry VIII 25
Higgin, Anthony 29, 80
Hill & Son, organ builders 127,160
Holgate, Archbishop of York 26
Horton, Ann 100
Horton, Robert 100, 101
Hughes, F. Llewelyn 42, 75, 77
Huxley, Marcus 202, 209, 240
hymns, for Ripon 208

Jacob, Samuel 48, 49
Jackson, Francis 95,132,135,193
James I 22, 25, 28, 29, 148, 241
Jameson, Joseph 198
Jamieson, Alasdair 202
Jebb, Revd Dr John 44
Jepson's Hospital Bluecoat school 43, 63-65
Joy, Samuel 51-52, 123, 186

Rogationtide Procession 41-42
Romanus, John, Archbishop of York 15, 17
Royal College of Organists 70, 71
Royal Commission 52-54
Royal Maundy Service 100-01, 193

'Sacred Spinnaker' 96
Schmidt, Gerhard 36, 150:
        Schmidt organ 150-52, 153, 156, 169
Scott, Sir George Gilbert 46, 157, 163
Scott, J. Oldrid 49, 55
secular music, for Ripon 211
services 14, 21, 26, 27, 40, 46, 53, 62, 65, 69-73, 95, 175-77, 182, 184-96, 234
service settings, for Ripon 180, 199-203
Shaw J. & Co, bells 215
Shaw, Alexander 118, 180, 203
singing men (*see also* lay clerks) 22-23, 29, 36:
        behaviour 37
        pay 32, 36, 50
        rules 29-31, 32-34
Solber, William 116, 148
Sorrell, William 36, 118, 149-50
spire, collapse of the 36, 149, 176
St Cecilia Orchestra 107, 210, 237, 247-48
St Olave's school 81, 82, 86
Suart, Richard 239
Swann, Ernest H. 61, 127, 197, 198, 233
Swawe, William 115, 116

Taylor, John (& Co), Bell Foundry 215-16, 220, 221
Taylors, Eayre & Smith, Bell Foundry 220-21
Thompson, Robert 101, 188, 194
Thomson, Duncan 75, **77-87**, 93, 95, **98-100**, 194, 239
Thomson, Stephana 77-78, 81, 85, 100
Thomson-Jones, Christina 242, 247
tower, central, collapse of the 176
Tuckey, Canon James 65

undercroft 93-95
university, projected at Ripon 28

Vann, Stanley 202, 207
Vaughan Williams, Ralph 70
vicars choral 15-16, 22, 25, 29, 32
      behaviour 16-20
      duties and rules 16, 33-34
      housing 16-17
      pay 16, 32
Vikings 14, 176
virginals 104

Wakeman Singers 238-39
Walbran, John Richard 150-51, 153
Wanlass, Henry 32, 117, 149
Wanlass, John 31-32, 116, 148
Watson, John 115, 116
Webber, James 41, 42, 45
Wesley, S.S. 44
Whitechapel Bell Foundry 229
White Doe, The 101
Whythorne, Thomas 27
Wicks, Alan 101
Wilby, Philip 202, 203, 207
Wilfrid, St 13, 108, 175
Wilkins, John 36
William IV 45
Williams, Hugh 71
Willibrord 14
Willoughby-Meade, Angela 239
Wilson, Mr 117-18
wooden hand 151-52

TIMELINE : MUSIC AT RIPON CATHEDRAL

657	Monastery established in heathen village of Rhypum. The abbot was Eata and Cuthbert was guestmaster, both monks being from the Celtic monastery of Melrose.
661	Wilfrid (born 634 in Northumbria) appointed Abbot of Ripon by Alchfrid (son of King Oswiu of Northumbria). Eata and his Celtic monks returned to Scotland and Cuthbert went to Lindisfarne. Ripon was one of the first monasteries in England to adopt the Benedictine (Roman) rule.
663	Song school founded at York by Archbishop Chad.
664	Synod of Whitby: Celtic versus Roman rites. Wilfrid and the latter prevailed.
669	Bishop Benedict Biscop, Abbot of Wearmouth & Jarrow (where Bede was a young monk and spent most of his life) returned from Rome and established schools for the oblates (young boys) at both these monasteries.
672	First stone church (crypt remains) built at Ripon by Wilfrid, then Bishop of York, and dedicated *with a great concourse of priests and nobles and much feasting.*
680	Benedict Biscop set up choral workshop in Wearmouth *bringing John, Archcantor of the Apostolic See, to teach the monks chant for the liturgical year as it was sung at St Peter's, Rome.*
687	John of Beverley, Bishop of Hexham, kept a school for oblates in the north. Also monastic schools established about this time at York & Ripon. Oblates were taught Latin, chant & liturgy. They had to memorise (words & plainsong) all the psalms.
691	Wilfrid banished by Alchfrid, King of Northumbria, and went to Mercia (Midlands). Wilfrid later became Bishop of Leicester.
703	Wilfrid returned to the north with Aeona & Aedde (Eddi - probably Eddius Stephanus) to teach singing to monks & oblates at the monasteries at Ripon & Hexham.
709	Wilfrid died at Oundle aged 75 years.
860	Ripon sacked by the Danish Vikings and all the monks and oblates were dispersed. Second wave of attacks occurred in 950. Most monasteries did not revive until the reign of King Edgar (959 - 975).
1066	Norman Conquest: soon after this Ripon Monastery became a collegiate church.
1132	Fountains Abbey founded by Cistercian Monks (dissidents from St Mary's, York) who were supported by Archbishop Thurston. They tramped up Skelldale on 26th December after singing mass at Ripon Minster.
1180	New Ripon Minster completed (built of sandstone in the Transitional Norman style) by Roger de Pont L'Evêque, Archbishop of York 1154-1181. Choir, chapter house (undercroft), transepts and central nave remain.
1220	West end, including the west towers and their spires completed by Walter de Gray, Archbishop of York 1216-1255.
1230	Archbishop Walter de Gray decreed that the Prebendary of Stanwick (one of seven prebendaries at Ripon) should be the Precentor and *Rector Chori* in charge of the music.
1230	By this time the foundation at Ripon comprised 7 prebendaries, 6 vicars choral, 6 deacons, 3 sub-deacons, 5 choristers, 6 thuriblers & 1 sub-thuribler.

1280	East end of the choir collapsed - three bays and east window rebuilt circa 1300. High altar in second bay from east end.
1293	Archbishop John Romanus of York (1286-1298) visited Ripon *to improve the singing which was universally considered disgraceful.* He directed the canons *to remove their inefficient chanters and supply their place with properly qualified singers.*
1303	Each of the six vicars choral had a salary of £4 per year.
1304	Nicholas of Bondgate provided the six vicars choral with a bedern (Anglo-Saxon word for *home of prayer*) where they all lived together. Its location was thought to be outside the west end of the minster - hence Bedern Bank.
1312	Archbishop Greenfield complained about the behaviour of the vicars choral. They attended dances and public shows and went out on the town at night and *sought favours of women of doubtful reputation.*
1318	Ripon Minster raided by the Scots. Some years later a protective wall was built around the east end.
1348	First mention of a dedicated grammar schoolmaster.
1354	Earliest reference to bells at Ripon Minster - *Lawrence Wright mended the clappers.*
1379	The 'Mary Bell' from Fountains Abbey given to Ripon Minster, and, after re-casting, was installed in the NW tower.
1380	It is thought that about this date the original pulpitum screen between the choir and the nave was installed. The ancient stone pulpit (now standing at the north end of the west side of the screen) was mounted thereon - hence its name.
1391	New bell cast; *A new hearth was made in the hall of the Prebend of Thorpe in compensation for one that had been broken up for the purposes of casting a bell in the said hall.*
1396	Three bells at least in west towers – records state *William Wright hung two bells and repaired others.*
1399	First reference to an organ in the Fabric Rolls. *Bellows organorum de novo faciendis - 2s. 8d.*
1408	Mention in minster accounts of an organ on top of pulpitum screen (though probably not the present screen which was thought to have been brought in from elsewhere and installed about 1480 following the collapse of the central tower).
1415	Charter granted to vicars choral by Henry V. The seal survives – kept at the Brotherton Library, Leeds University.
1415	New bedern built for the vicars choral on the site of what later became The Old Deanery.
1418	The Ripon Psalter - see entry for 1874.
1439	Archbishop Kemp of York (1426-1452) established a commission to enquire into complaints concerning the musical arrangements at Ripon minster. *Choir books not all noted alike and inadequate supply of Graduales and Processionals.*
1447	First known organist: Thomas Lister. He was a priest; records state he was paid 10 shillings per annum.
1450	Central tower (SE section) collapsed causing major disruption. Rebuilt, circa 1465-1485 when the two damaged east and south Norman (round) arches were rebuilt in the Perpendicular (pointed) style.
1453	Will the Organ Maker *paid 20 shillings for mending the organ* (damaged by the collapse of SE corner of the central tower).
1475	Chamberlain's Rolls state choristers' livery was *coloris blodii* – coloured blue.
1478	Organist appointed: Lawrence Lancaster. He was paid 10 shillings per annum plus 3s.4d. for playing at the daily Lady Mass.
1480	The original choir screen, damaged by the collapse of the tower in 1450, was replaced with the present screen, thought to be fourteenth century.

1494	Bromflet carvers completed the choir stalls, misericords & canopies and the woodwork on the east side of the pulpitum screen, including the oriel gallery for the organ console. Work started 1489 & three separate teams of carvers were involved.
1502	Chapter resolution passed that funds set aside for copes & vestments be used instead for books for the choir.
1511	Organist appointed: John Watson.
1513	Organist appointed: William Swawe.
1520	Organist appointed: Adam Bakhouse.
1531	New organ: James Dempsey was paid £4 8s. 4d. *for making an organ*. It is thought that the console was in the purpose-made oriel gallery which had been built some forty years earlier.
1535	It is recorded that the six vicars choral were each paid £4 per annum plus a pension (see 1303).
1537	Archbishop Edward Lee of York (1531-1544) issued various injunctions against the vicars choral at Ripon.
1538	Nave aisles completed; south aisle in about 1515 and north aisle about 1538 – both built in magnesium limestone. It was intended to finish the rebuilding of the central tower arches in the crossing, but the King's Commissioners confiscated the minster revenues and the work was never completed.
1539	Dissolution of Fountains Abbey. Abbot Farnley bought himself a Ripon Minster appointment.
1540	Organist appointed: William Solber.
1540	The third bell was recast by George Heathcott of Chesterfield.
1546	Minster records refer to *rent of 13s. 4d. payd yerlie to the organ player*.
1547	Edward VI (10 yrs old and under the Protectorate of Somerset, a friend of Cranmer and a supporter of Protestant reform) came to the throne and issued the Chantries Act Certificates.
1548	The Chantries Act was finally implemented at Ripon on Easter Day. The collegiate church including the music foundation was dissolved. All the nine chantry chapels and the chantry priests were also swept away.
1549	Act of Uniformity; First English Prayer Book issued. A later Second English Prayer Book issued in 1552.
1555	Re-foundation of Ripon Grammar School (original, circa 1348): Over the next 400 years many of the choirboys were educated here. There had been a grammar school attached to the church for several centuries prior to this. There was reference to a song school, which was possibly a room within the grammar school where the minster choristers were trained.
1562	Thomas Sternhold & John Hopkins issued the first complete English language Metrical Psalter (with tunes). Published by John Day, London. This remained the standard version in England for almost 200 years.
1571	Candlemas (2nd February): Ripon tradition of a procession in the candlelit minster was banned.
1596	University at Ripon proposed. Detailed prospectus published, but this idea did not find favour with Elizabeth I, probably due to lack of funds. The scheme was resurrected soon after James I came to the throne in 1603, but this too was rejected.
1604	James I Charter; re-established the collegiate church and choral foundation of Ripon Minster, comprising a dean, Moses Fowler (1604-1607), sub-dean, 6 prebendaries, 2 vicars choral, an organist, 6 singing men and 6 choristers.

1608	Dean appointed; Anthony Higgin (1608-1624). He later bequeathed to Ripon Minster his large library of books, including the 15th century Caxtons which were later sold to help establish the new choir school.
1608	*Statutes to be perfourmed by the syngingmen* issued by Dean Higgin on 20th Sept.
1613	Organist appointed: John Wanlass (maybe Wanless). Dates uncertain; he probably went to Lincoln in 1616.
1624	Dean appointed: John Wilson (1624-1634).
1635	Dean appointed: Thomas Dod (1635-1645).
1635	13th June; annual salaries fixed by Dean & Chapter. Organist & master of the boys £16, six choristers £2 each, four singing men £8 each & two other singing men £4 each. The Chapter also issued orders for the vicars choral, organist, singers and choristers.
1641	John Barnard's First Book of Selected Church Music. Printed by Edward Griffin, London.
1642	Civil War started. In 1643 Parliamentary troops (Roundheads) under Sir Thomas Mauleverer, raided Ripon Minster and despoiled contents, carvings, organ and stained glass.
1649- 1659	) THE COMMONWEALTH) Oliver Cromwell, Lord Protector) PERIOD) Puritans banned organs and choirs and purged *all unseemly music.*
1660	The Restoration: Charles II crowned and a new Dean of Ripon appointed; John Wilkins (1660-1668), a very gifted man, who was the brother-in-law of Oliver Cromwell.
1660	Ripon Minster's choral foundation restored.
1660	The spire of the central tower collapsed during a storm causing extensive damage to the SE transept and choir, including the organ and Bromflet choir stalls. In 1667 the two western spires were taken down because of fear of collapse, but the dean had to go to London to obtain special permission before this could be done.
1662	Book of Common Prayer issued.
1662	Organist appointed: Henry Wanlass (1662-1674). Possibly the son of John Wanlass.
1663	Dean & Chapter records set out the amounts paid to the organist and choir for weddings and funerals.
1663	Minster bells; by this date the number of bells had increased to 6.
1670	Acting Organist: Mr Wilson (May 1670-1674). He overlapped with Henry Wanlass due to the latter's deafness.
1672	Jepson's Hospital Bluecoat School established and endowed by Zacarias Jepson in Water Skellgate (on the site of present Ripon Club). This school was *for the education of orphan boys or sons of poor tradesmen of Ripon.* Over the ensuing 250 years many of the choirboys were recruited from, and educated at, this school.
1674	Organist appointed: Alexander Shaw (circa 1674-1677).
1674	Dean appointed: John Neile (1674-1675).
1675	Dean appointed: Thomas Tullie (1675-1675).
1676	Dean appointed: Thomas Cartwright (1676-1686).

1677	Chapter minutes; *To give unto William Preston the sum of Tenne pounds for making an organ to have five stops such as shall be approved by Mr Brownhill and Mr Sorrell.* It is thought that Preston probably undertook a rebuild of the organ.
1677	Organist appointed: William Sorrell (circa 1677-1682).
1681	Sub-dean Gresswold bequeathed money to augment the stipends of the choir.
1682	Organist appointed: John Hawkins (May 1682-1689).
1686	Dean appointed: Christopher Wyvill (1686-1710).
1690	Organist appointed: Thomas Preston, the Elder (May 1690-1730).
1695	Organ by Gerhard Schmidt (son of 'Father' Schmidt). Two manuals and 18 stops. It is believed that it was about this time that the carved wooden hand (attached to a foot pedal to enable the organist to beat time) was installed in the oriel gallery.
1708	Chapter minutes 29th May *Ordered that for ye better encouragement of Thomas Benson to continue his diligence as a chorister; he shall have twenty shillings paid unto him by Mr Deane.*
1710	Dean appointed: Heneage Dering (1710-1750).
1731	Organist appointed: Thomas Preston, the Younger (1731-1748).
1733	Thomas Gent recorded *7 bells at the minster; 1 in the SW tower; 5 in the NW tower and 1 in a turret on the central tower.*
1748	Organist appointed: William Ayrton (1748-1799). His brother was Dr Edmund Ayrton, Master of the Children at the Chapel Royal.
1750	Dean appointed: Francis Wanley (1750-1791).
1760	The Dean & Chapter of Ripon were listed as subscribers to Volume 1 of Dr Boyce's Collection of Cathedral Music.
1762	The 5 bells in the SW tower and the 'Mary Bell' in the NW tower were sold and a brand new ring of 8 bells, cast by Lester & Pack of London, was installed.
1789	Repairs to organ by Donaldsons of York, including new stop given by Dr Edmund Ayrton, brother of William.
1790	A visitor to Ripon Minster on the Sunday before Candlemas recorded in his journal that *the collegiate church was one continual blaze of light all the afternoon from an immense number of candles.*
1790	On Christmas Day, *the singing boys come into the church with large baskets full of red apples with a sprig of Rosemary stuck in each. They presented them to members of congregation who gave them 2d, 4d or 6d according to the quality of the lady or gentleman.* This tradition was discontinued in 1838.
1792	Dean appointed: Robert Waddilove (1792-1828).
1792	Hon John Byng (Lord Torrington) wrote in his travel journal for 8th June; *At 10 o'clock I repaired to the Minster where the service was going to begin, but there was no chaunting today.* Clearly not all services were choral.
1799	Organist appointed: William Francis Morell Ayrton (1799-1805) succeeded his father William.
1805	Organist appointed:. Nicholas T.D. Ayrton (1805-1822) succeeded his brother William.
1820	Dr Thomas Frogmore Dibdin (a literary-historian who left an account of the incident in his book 'Decameron') was, with Dean Waddilove's permission, *rummaging amongst the dusty books in the Lady Loft Library one hot summer's day,* when he discovered the Caxtons.

1823	Organist appointed: John Henry Bond (1823-1829).
1824	Dean Robert Darley Waddilove (1792-1828) finally replied (six years late!) to a letter from Maria Hackett (The Choristers' Friend) who campaigned for cathedral choir boys to be better housed, clothed and educated.
1828	Dean appointed: James Webber (1828-1847). He was to become the first Dean of Ripon Cathedral.
1829	Organist appointed: George Bates from Harrogate (1829-1873). He later became the first organist of Ripon Cathedral.
1830	Sir Edward Blore carried out major restoration work to the fabric of the minster between 1830 and 1834. Total cost £6,265.
1830	Rogationtide Procession & Candlemas discontinued by Dean Webber.
1833	Organ said to have been remodelled by Booths of Leeds, but this is very doubtful.
1833	Start of the 'Oxford Movement' which led to widespread and beneficial church reform.
1835	New organ (but retaining two and a half ranks of pipes from the 1695 Schmidt organ) built by Renn & Boston of Manchester. Great 13 stops, Swell 7, Choir 5 and Pedal 1. Also a new organ case was made by Booth of Wakefield, designed by Sir Edward Blore. Work completed in 1837.
1835	Ecclesiastical Commissioners (later to become the Church Commissioners) established. Led to major reforms in the Church of England. Redistribution of income and resources. Also cessation of plurality (i.e. clergy holding several appointments).
1836	CATHEDRAL: new Diocese of Ripon established. First Bishop was Charles Longley (Headmaster of Harrow School) consecrated at Ripon Cathedral on 11th November.
1847	Dean appointed: Hon. Henry Erskine (1847-1859).
1857	List of music sung at Ripon each Sunday in May of this year published in 'The Monthly Remembrancer', a magazine for clergymen and church musicians.
1859	Dean appointed: Thomas Garnier (1859-1860).
1860	Dean appointed: William Goode (1860-1868).
1862	Sir George Gilbert Scott commenced major restoration work which was completed in 1871 at a total cost of £40,000.
1862	Regular services were held during 1862-1865 in the nave, which was filled with oak pews from the choir which was being refurbished. Mr Jardine of Manchester and Mr Joy of Leeds were asked by the Dean & Chapter to provide an estimate for constructing a console on the west side of the organ, but this came to naught.
1865	Second and fifth bells cracked during cathedral restoration work. They were recast in 1866 by John Warner & Sons, London.
1866	Dean's traditional Christmas Concert given by cathedral choir (6 men 6 boys - all named) reported in Ripon Gazette 3rd Jan. 1867.
1868	Dean appointed: Hugh McNeile (1868-1876).
1872	The floor of the nave, which had hitherto been empty since its construction in 1180, was filled with permanent wooden chairs. Also rudimentary nave choir and clergy stalls were provided on a raised platform at the east end of the nave (see pages 47 and 94).
1874	Organist appointed: Edwin J. Crow (1874-1901).
1874	Ripon Psalter (1418) presented to the cathedral by the Marquess of Ripon. Contains the lectionaries for the three festivals of St Wilfrid in an appendix.

1875	The regular singing of daily choral matins and evensong was established.
1876	Dean appointed: Sydney Turner (only three month in office due to ill health).
1876	Dean appointed: William Fremantle (1876-1895).
1876	Arrangements made for providing a school for choristers. Premises in St. Agnesgate bought and Rev James Cornford appointed headmaster and choir chaplain, with a second master to assist with the teaching.
1878	1st June. Letter in The Musical Times from Samuel Joy (Ripon Precentor) giving credit to Dr Crow for the marked improvement in the music at the cathedral.
1878	Bluecoat School rebuilt on same site. Over the years many choristers were educated at, and recruited from, here.
1878	Major organ rebuild by T.C. Lewis. Cost £4,000. Great 13 stops, Swell 14, Choir 9 and Pedal 7. Sir George Gilbert Scott designed the case. The old 1837 organ went to a church in South Wales.
1878	24th April: Special service for the opening of the new organ, when the Ripon choir was augmented by choirs from York and Durham Cathedrals and Leeds and Wakefield Parish Churches. Crow wrote his Te Deum & Jubilate in C for this occasion.
1883	Festival of The North Eastern Cathedral Choirs' Association held for the first time at Ripon. Magnificat & Nunc Dimittis in A specially composed for the occasion by Dr Edwin Crow.
1884	Parliamentary Commission Report on 'Condition of Cathedral Churches in England & Wales' published. This included submissions made in 1880 by the organist, Dr Crow, and the lay clerks, pleading for better remuneration and for pensions.
1884	Dr Edwin Crow founded the Ripon Choral Society which flourishes to this day.
1886	The Ripon Millennium was held to celebrate the 886 Charter, which was thought to have been granted to the city by King Alfred.
1891	Bells: the ring of 8 augmented to 10 and re-hung by J. Shaw & Co., Bradford.
1894	The choir school in St Agnesgate closed. Last headmaster was Dr Jacob, father of novelist Naomi Jacob (b. Ripon 1884).
1895	Dean appointed: Hon William Fremantle (1895-1915). Nephew of previous Dean.
1899	New purpose-built carved oak choir and clergy stalls, designed by J. Oldrid Scott (son of Sir Gilbert Scott), installed in the nave.
1902	Organist appointed: Charles H. Moody (1902-1953).
1904	Dean and Chapter agreed that in future they would pay the fees for all the choristers, including the probationers, at Jepson's School or other approved day schools, plus a cash payment to the boys.
1905	Ripon Operatic Society formed by Charles Moody. It had its ups and downs, being revived in 1921 with more problems in 1930, but is now thriving.
1907	The Ripon Chant Book, compiled by Moody, published by Novello, London.
1908	Ripon Psalter; compiled by Ernest Henry Swann, precentor. Published by William Harrison, Ripon.
1909	Choir cassocks changed from blue to red. This turned out to be Royal Scarlet which 77 yrs later caused a furore.
1910	Dean and Chapter organised a re-union for old choir boys and provided a meal for them and the precentor, succentor and organist.

1911	Founding of the Ripon Cathedral Choir Old Boys' Association on the initiative of the organist, Charles Moody, and the precentor, Ernest Henry Swann.
1912-1914	Major organ restoration and enlargement by Harrison & Harrison. Phase I: New blowing apparatus in chamber outside cathedral and specification upgraded to Great 13 stops, Swell 14, Choir (Enc) 10, Solo 6 and Pedal 8. Total cost £3,000. The work was interupted by the war and not completed until Phase II, see 1926 below.
1915	Dean appointed: C. Mansfield Owen (1915-1941).
1922	18th May. Rules & regulations issued for choir boy boarders at Jepson's School.
1922	Federation of Cathedral Old Choristers' Associations annual festival held in Ripon for the first time.
1923	Royal visit to cathedral on Monday 23rd August by Queen Mary - see illustration page 63.
1925	Ripon Gazette 9th April reported *the combined Cathedral & Oratorio Choirs, conducted by Dr Moody, performed the Mozart Requiem. The article said of the collection at the end of the performance, looking at the collection plate the wonder was aroused as to where all the copper had come from compared to the small amount of silver:*
1925	26th November. Ripon Gazette reported on a Haydn Concert given by choir to raise money to increase lay clerks' salaries.
1926	Phase II of the organ restoration by Harrison & Harrison completed at a cost of £1,500. Dr Moody gave the opening recital. The side wings of the west organ case were removed and used to front the pipes on either side of the choir.
1927	Jepson's Hospital Bluecoat School (which supplied some of the choristers over many years) closed and the teachers and pupils were merged into the grammar school.
1932	Entire ring of 10 bells recast by John Taylor Bell Foundry of Loughborough, and the whole belfry restored.
1932	18th Sept. The first ever BBC radio broadcast from Ripon Cathedral; 'A Religious Service for Cyclists & Wayfarers'.
1934	20th May. The first broadcast from an English cathedral to America, in co-operation with Columbia Broadcast Corporation.
1934	Federation of Cathedral Old Choristers' Associations annual festival held in Ripon (Second time) on 7th-9th September.
1940	First broadcasts of choral evensong by the Ripon Cathedral choir on Tuesday 6th August and a week later on 13th August. Note; the first ever BBC broadcast of choral evensong was from Westminster Abbey in Oct. 1926.
1941	Dean appointed: Godwin Birchenough (1941-1951).
1943	A letter, dated 4th June, sent to the Dean and Chapter by the Ripon PCC with a resolution, proposed by the Mayor, Alderman Nettleton, asking them to consider *making the Sunday services at the cathedral more congregational.*
1943	On 15th June the Dean and Chapter decided that canticles at both morning and evening services on Sundays would in future be sung to chants instead of settings. Special meeting with Dr Moody on 6th July, but despite his plea the decision was upheld.
1943	Ralph Vaughan Williams wrote a spirited letter to Dr Moody in support of his fight against the Dean & Chapter's decision to replace settings of the canticles sung by the choir on Sundays with chants.
1943	Letters received by Chapter from Royal College of Organists and Ripon Cathedral Choir Old Boys' Association protesting at the changes and asking them to reconsider, but they declined; chapter meeting 28th October.

1945	Court case concerning Sunday services brought by RCO against Dean & Chapter. Case dismissed, being deemed to be a matter for an Ecclesiastical Court. The Dean & Chapter later agreed a compromise.
1945	Grammar school fees for choristers no longer payable, but Dean & Chapter resolved to pay each chorister three guineas per term into a post office savings account.
1946	Tuesday 18th June; after this date the boys, and hence the full choir no longer sang daily matins.
1947	Carved figures inserted into the niches of the choir screen. The Princess Royal attended the service of unveiling and dedication on Saturday 28th June. The figures were coloured and gilded in 1958.
1950	Organ; cleaning, restoration, and installation of electric action by Compton of London. Cost £4,900.
1950-1952	Mrs Jean Mortimer of Leeds University examined and catalogued all the books in the cathedral library, and verified the existence of the Caxtons and other ancient books, which were transferred to the Brotherton Library, Leeds University in 1986.
1951	Dean appointed: F. Llewelyn Hughes (1951-1968).
1951	A fine silver and enamel chairman's badge and chain of office was presented by Maurice Geary to the Ripon Cathedral Choir Old Boys' Association.
1952	Dr Moody's article 'The Glorious Tradition of English Church Music' published in The Church Times, proposing that cathedral authorities should sell their valuable unused assets, such as books in their libraries, to fund choral foundations.
1953	Duncan Thomson appointed succentor.
1954	Henry (Harry) Burrans Graham (who was to play a major part in raising money for the 'Repair Ripon' campaign and in establishing the new choir school) arrived as a minor canon and was soon appointed Archdeacon of Richmond. He resigned in 1961 and died tragically in 1963.
1954	Organist appointed: Lionel Dakers, previously assistant at St George's Chapel Windsor. He left Ripon in 1957 to be organist of Exeter Cathedral.
1955	Ripon Choral Society re-founded (after 60 years) by Harry Graham, Lionel Dakers (whose wife Elizabeth was the accompanist), Frank Orton, Jim Hall and Elvet English.
1956	Duncan Thomson appointed precentor.
1957	Organist appointed: Philip Marshall. He left Ripon in 1966 to become organist of Lincoln Cathedral.
1957	Federation of Cathedral Old Choristers' Associations annual festival held in Ripon (Third time). Friday-Sunday 6-8th September. Dr Moody wrote in an article for this event in which he stated *There is now no Choral Eucharist at Ripon, even on the Great Festivals.*
1957	Duncan Thomson (precentor) resigned and moved to Aysgarth School as chaplain.
1960	31st May; two Caxtons and other ancient books sold by the Dean and Chapter at Sothebys. They fetched a total of £45,000 that helped to fund the purchase of St Olave's, which became the choir school.
1960	New choir school founded, with Duncan Thomson as headmaster.
1961	The vaults in the west end of the undercroft beneath the chapter house were dismantled, and the coffins reburied in the graveyard east of the cathedral.
1961	September; the twelve choristers from the new choir school commenced singing in the cathedral.

1962	West undercroft finally cleared, foundations strengthend and fitted out as the choir practice room, vestry and music library.
1963	Organ: major rebuild by Harrison & Harrison, costing £12,000.
1963	Bell ringing stopped because of lack of ringers.
1964	Candlemas revived by Dean Llewelyn Hughes.
1964	The old bell turret (on top of the central tower from the early eighteenth century until it was removed in 1939) was reconstructed and a 'service bell' installed by John Taylor Ltd of Loughborough.
1966	Organist appointed: Ronald Perrin, previously assistant to Francis Jackson at York Minster. He resigned in 1995 due to ill health, and was appointed Organist Titulaire.
1968	Dean appointed: F. Edwin le Grice (1968-1984).
1969	Christmas: 'A Ceremony of Carols' by Benjamin Britten first introduced by Ronald Perrin. Sung every year since.
1971	Choral Eucharist at 9.15 am on Sundays once a month introduced by Dean le Grice. Matins sung at 11 am.
1972	Organ alterations by Harrison & Harrison in consultation with Ronald Perrin.
1975	The 'Sacred Spinnaker' curtain hung over the choir screen arch. This was not successful and was taken down in about 1978.
1976	Monthly Choral Eucharist on Sundays increased to weekly. This meant that the choir sang three services every Sunday.
1977	Peal of bells and fittings overhauled.
1978	Choir school: the governors decided that the school should be co-educational and girls were admitted.
1978	New bell ringers recruited and trained. On Sunday 1st Oct. the first ringing of the bells by a local band since 1963 took place.
1979	12th March. Duncan Thomson was interviewed by music historian Peter Phillips on the Ripon Cathedral Choir School.
1983	Choir School; Duncan Thomson died on 12th April. A new headmaster, Robert Horton was appointed, taking up his duties in September.
1984	Dean appointed: Christopher Campling (1984-1994).
1985	Royal Maundy Service held at Ripon on 4th April. Ripon choir joined by The Gentlemen & Children of Her Majesty's Chapel Royal. For this occasion the choir and clergy cassocks were replaced with a new red colour (not Royal Scarlet).
1985	The Choir school started to take girl boarders; new dormitory facilities installed.
1986	City of Ripon 1,100 years Anniversary Charter Day Service attended by the Queen Mother on 1st June. First performance of 'Let God be Gracious', an anthem composed for the occasion by Ronald Perrin.
1986	3rd December; premier of 'The White Doe', an opera for children by Alan Ridout, performed in the cathedral by the choir school pupils and staff. An LP record was later made.
1987	Robert Horton, the choir school headmaster, resigned unexpectedly in May. Edward Childs stepped into the breech pending the arrival of Iain McDougall, a retired housemaster from Sedbergh School.
1987	ITV Yorkshire Television's Christmas programme 'Rejoice', broadcast from Ripon Cathedral.
1988	Richard Moore commenced his duties as new headmaster of the choir school in January.

1988	Organ: major overhaul undertaken by Harrison & Harrison, which included an up-dating of the console and the addition of a new Orchestral Trumpet stop.
1990	New movable stalls and matching nave altar installed replacing the old (1899) carved oak stalls. The service of dedication was held on Sunday 4th March.
1990	July; Federation of Cathedral Old Choristers' Associations annual festival held in Ripon (Fourth time).
1991	From this year onwards the old Christmas traditions (see 1790) were partially revived and the Dean now gives a £1 coin to each of the choristers who in turn give apples to the children in the congregation.
1994	Organist appointed: Kerry Beaumont, who had been a chorister at Ripon 1965-70, appointed in October. Previously organist at St David's Cathedral, he served at Ripon from January 1995 to 2002.
1996	Dean appointed: John Methuen (he was suspended by the Bishop in September 2004 and resigned in December 2005).
1996	Girls' choir founded by the Dean & Chapter.
2000	Richard Moore retired as headmaster of the choir school in July. Canon Robert Western (previously at Sedbergh School & Lincoln Cathedral Choir School) was appointed for the interregnum.
2000	New mobile organ console installed in the nave. Built by Harrison & Harrison and first used at the Services of Nine Lessons and Carols.
2001	General improvements to bells and complete repainting of frames and fittings.
2001	Final closure of the College of Ripon & York St John. In the 1970s to the 1990s some of the male students became choral scholars in the cathedral choir under a joint scholarship scheme.
2001	Richard Pepys appointed as the new headmaster of the choir school, taking up his duties in September.
2002	Kerry Beaumont resigned as organist in July and left in August. Andrew Bryden became acting organist in September 2002 and continued until April 2003.
2002	Organist appointed November: Simon Morley, previously assistant at Truro and Lincoln, took up his duties in April 2003, but resigned in October 2003.
2003	Organist appointed: Andrew Bryden, previously organ scholar at Canterbury Cathedral, assistant organist at Ripon Cathedral 1988-2002 and acting organist Sept 2002 to April 2003, was appointed Director of Music in November.
2003	October; boy choristers sang in the chapel at The House of Lords by invitation of Lady Brittan.
2004	Acting Dean appointed: Michael Glanville-Smith, following the suspension of Dean John Methuen in September.
2005	31st December; Dean Methuen resigned and left Ripon.
2006	December; Benjamin Britten's 'A Ceremony of Carols' performed jointly by the boy and girl choristers for the first time.
2007	Dean appointed: Keith Jukes (previously at Selby Abbey).
2008	April; Cathedral bells augmented to a peal of twelve. The three new treble bells were cast at Taylor Eyre & Smith Bell Foundry, Loughborough.
2008	Ripon Cathedral choir sang at the Festival of the Sons of the Clergy (First held in 1655) at St Paul's Cathedral on 13th May.

2008	Federation of Cathedral Old Choristers' Associations annual festival held in Ripon (Fifth time). July 4th - 6th.
2009	Major overhaul and cleaning of organ. The Choir division re-enclosed.
2009	Celebrations for the 1,300th anniversary of the death of St Wilfrid in 709.

NOTES